voicing concepts

jazz piano

Philipp Moehrke

jazz workbooks

All Rights Reserved
Copyright © 2007
AMA Verlag GmbH
P.O. Box 1168
D-50301 Bruehl
E-mail: mail@ama-verlag.de
http://www.ama-verlag.de

Jacket Design: au gratin graphics

Photos:
P. 26 "Duke" Ellington: © Tom Hanley/Redferns/MUSICPICTURES.COM
P. 47 Dave Brubeck: © Peter Pakvis/Redferns/MUSICPICTURES.COM
P. 79 Earl Hines: © Gai Terrell/Redferns/MUSICPICTURES.COM
P. 86 Ray Charles: © David Redfern/Redferns/MUSICPICTURES.COM
P. 115 Joe Zawinul: © Eamonn McCabe/Redferns/MUSICPICTURES.COM
P. 147 Tommy Flanagan: © Andrew Lepley/Redferns/MUSICPICTURES.COM
Portrait Photo: Markus Reck

Notation and Layout: Nico Schliemann
Philipp Moehrke notates exclusively with Sibelius and uses Apple computers,
Steinberg Plug-Ins and Yamaha Keyboards
Overall Production: Detlef Kessler

Printed in Germany

AMA 610375E
ISBN 3-89922-097-8
ISBN 978-3-89922-097-1
ISMN M-50155-044-9

Learn – Practice – Apply

Learn new voicings
Practice them in all variations and keys
Use your knowledge creatively on standards and in your own compositions

Table of Contents

Preface · 6

Chapter 1: Basics · 7

Chord Symbols · 8

Voice Leading · 11

Spread Voicings · 16

Chapter 2: Major Diatonic · 28

Diatonic Chords in Major · 28

II-V-I Cadence in Major · 35

Chapter 3: Minor Diatonic · 50

Diatonic Chords in Minor · 50

II-V-I Cadence in Minor · 57

Chapter 4: Left Hand Voicings · 74

Bud Powell Voicings · 74

3 Note Spread Voicings for the Left Hand · 80

Guide Tone Voicings · 86

3 Note Voicings (3 Note Left Hand Voicings) · · · · · · · · · · · · · · · · · · · 92

4 Note Voicings (4 Note Left Hand Voicings) · · · · · · · · · · · · · · · · · · · 98

Chapter 5: Two Hand Voicings · 104

Drop 2 Voicings · 105

Upper Structure Voicings · 114

Chapter 6: Reharmonization · 122

Dominant Substitution (SubV) · 123

IIm7 Extension · 128

Chromatic Approach · 130

Chord Substitution · 134

Changing Chord Extensions · 137

Changing Chord Type · 137

Pedal Point · 138

Contrary Motion · 140

Chapter 7: Grooves **142**

Rhythm Patterns for Jazz Accompaniment 142

Jazz Waltz 146

Easy Stride 148

Stride Piano 151

Walking Bass 154

Bossa Nova 160

Kapitel 8: Arrangement **166**

Spread Voicings with Melody 166

Appendix **172**

CD Contents 172

Voicings, Voicings, Voicings 174

II-V-I Circle of Fifths 176

Repertoire Checklist (Master Copy) 177

Reference Books 178

Preface

The famous jazz trumpet player Dizzy Gillespie often said: "You have to know the piano". If you listen to and analyze his numerous compositions, it quickly becomes clear that this outstanding musician knew his harmony and voice leading and thus knew his way around the piano as well.

Jazz Piano – Voicing Concepts is primarily directed at "non-pianists" (saxophonists, guitarists, singers etc.) who would like to expand their knowledge of Jazz piano. The only prerequisite for working with this book is the ability to read notation in the treble and bass clefs. You should also be familiar with the layout of the piano and possess basic theoretical knowledge about keys, intervals and the major scale. As the book is designed for self-study, you can find proposed solutions for all the exercises in the separate accompanying Solution Key. It is recommended to start working with the book at the beginning so that the contents can be retained in an effective manner. Even advanced pianists should work through the first *Basics* chapter to be assured they don't have any knowledge gaps when it comes to constructing chords. In contrast to classical piano methods, you won't find any technical finger exercises in this book. What will primarily be shown is voicings (chord structures). Additionally study with a qualified teacher is highly recommended so you can learn other aspects of piano playing such as flexibility, notation, repertoire, interpretation, improvisation etc. *Voicing Concepts* is conceived to complement traditional piano instruction when it comes to the topic of creating and playing chords.

Almost all of the practical examples have been derived from well-known Jazz standards and thus allow direct application to your playing. But a book can never be an equivalent substitute for the musical experiences you make when playing with other people. Put what you have learned into practice as soon as possible by playing with other musicians.

The accompanying CD contains the most important exercises. Many exercises are repeated several times. At first, the piano should play the exercises as notated. The rhythms and voicings that a piano player would use with a rhythm section can then be played on the repeats. Using the balance knob on your stereo, you can fade out the recorded piano part.

The "Jazz Piano Concepts" series also includes the following titles: *Jazz Piano – Solo Concepts* (Solo Jazz Piano) and *Jazz Piano – Improvisation Concepts* (Jazz Improvisation). It is recommended to work with all 3 books simultaneously.

Special thanks again to Nico Schliemann for his excellent and patient layout work in this book and to Jan Reinelt for his critical and constructive reading of the manuscript. Very special thanks also goes to my excellent editor Brigitte Windolph who manages to find (almost) every mistake as well as to Detlef Kessler and the team at AMA Publishing for their confidence in me.

I dedicate this book to my wife Claudia because, as a singer, she not only appreciates her pianist but good piano voicings as well.

Finally, I would like to wish much fun and success working with this book!

Philipp Moehrke

Bad Krozingen, Dezember 2006

Chapter 1: Basics

One reason for this new edition of Voicing Concepts was that many students lacked the basic understanding of chord structures. However, these basics are necessary for understanding more complex harmonic concepts employing different voicings.

To minimize the contents of this book I will assume knowledge of the following basics:

- intervals and their names
- the major scale
- keys and accidentals

The enclosed bibliography provides a list of books that you should read to ensure that you have no major gaps of knowledge in these mentioned areas.

Continue with the following chapters when you are able to put the contents of the *Basics* chapter into action:

- **chord symbols**
- **3 and 4 note chords and their inversions**
- **classical cadence in major and minor**
- **rules of voice leading**
- **low interval limits**
- **3, 4 and 5 note spread voicings**

Chord Symbols

Triads

Chord symbols represent an abbreviated collection of notes. The chord symbol letter symbolizes the basic major triad. The suffixes "m", "min" or "-" change the basic triad from major to minor. The symbol "+" means augmented, an "o" means diminished.

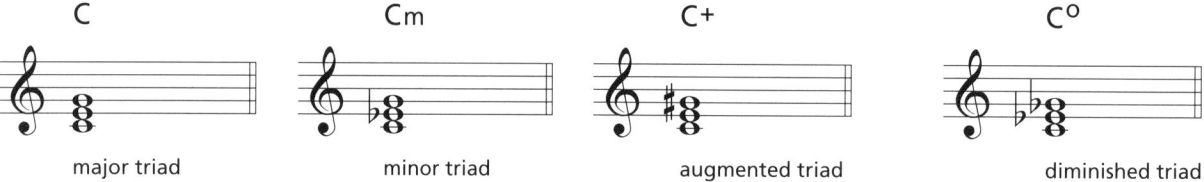

4 Note Chords

A number that follows a chord symbol indicates an added fourth chord tone. If it is a major seventh (counted from the root), the chord will be a "major seven chord" and will be labelled Xmaj7.
If a minor seventh is added, the chord will be a "dominant seven chord" and is labelled X7.
If the sixth is added to the chord instead of the seventh this will be indicated by the symbol X6.

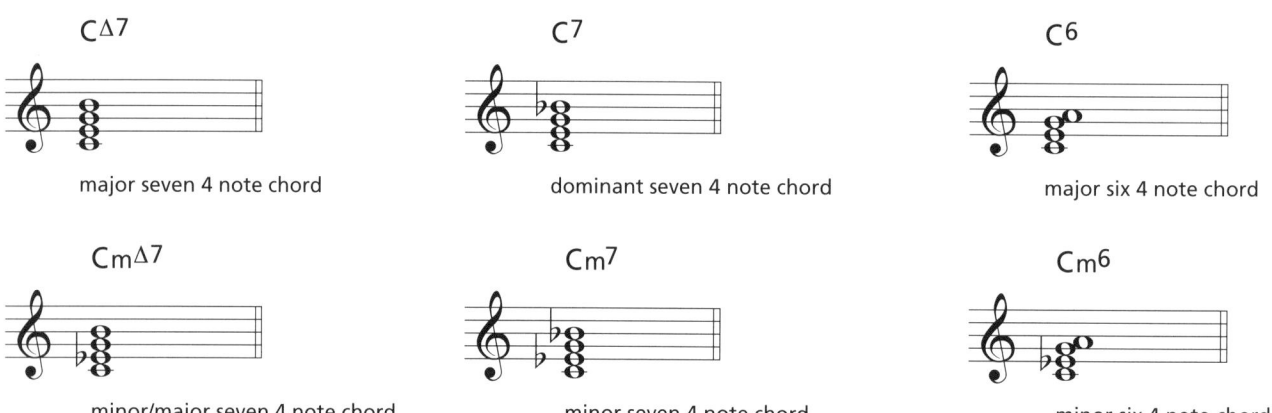

Chord Extensions

It is possible to indicate even more chord notes within the chord symbol. If a chord extension, e.g. a ninth, is to be played, it is written in parentheses following the letter and number of the chord symbol. For example: C7(9). The chord symbol C7(9) refers to a 5-note-chord with the notes C, E, G, B♭ and D.

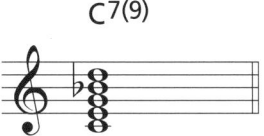

Jazz Chord Symbols

Unfortunately there is no standardized method for writing chord symbols. Here are the chord symbols that are most commonly used in real life and in this book:

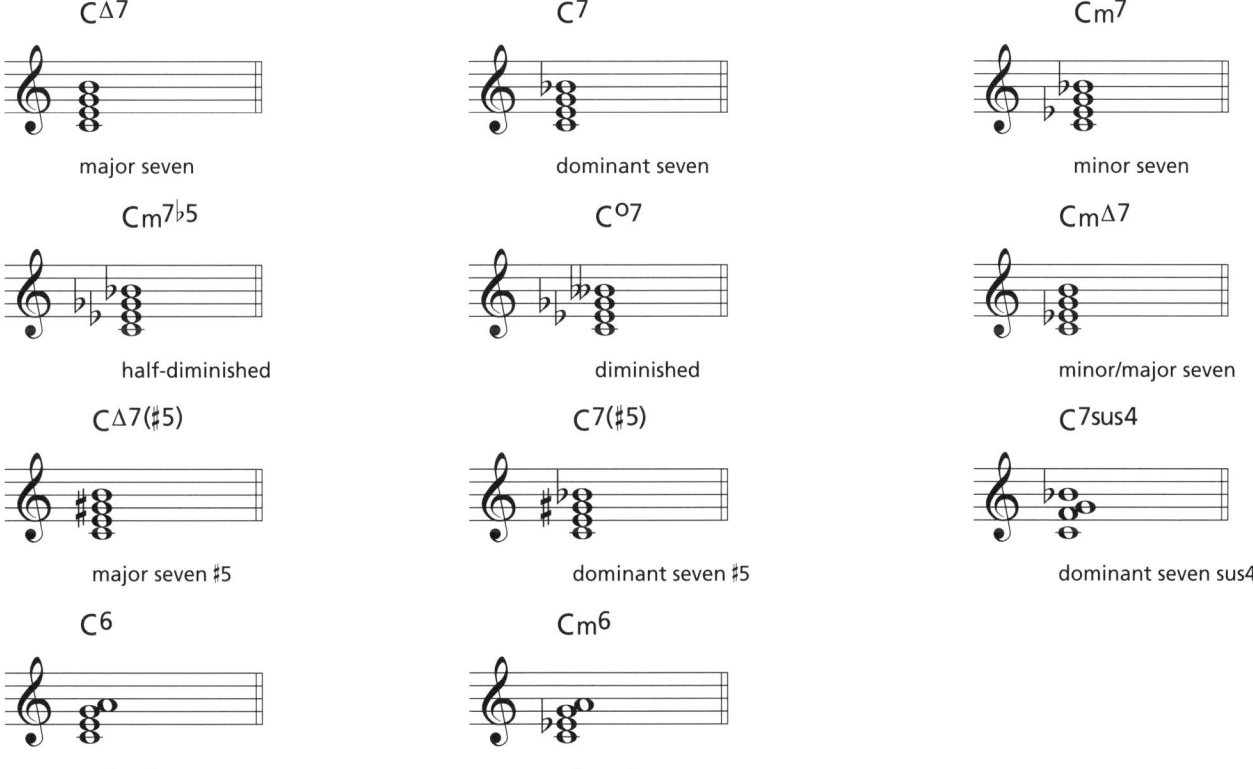

Exercise:

- Play the notated triads and seventh chords at a very slow tempo in their basic root position.
- Say the name of the chord out loud before playing the chord. Verbalizing it helps you to understand the chord structure better than if you only went through the physical motions. In practice: say "C major"; put your fingers on the C major triad; play the C major triad; listen to the sound of the chord for a few seconds (Have all notes been struck at once? Is one note louder than the others?). Then go on to the next chord.
- To keep track, you can check off every correct performance of an exercise in the following chart.

Check Boxes:

Major Triad

Minor Triad

Diminished Triad

Augmented Triad

∆7

Dom7

Minor7

Minor7♭5

Major6

Minor6

Voice Leading

When changing chords, you should try to play the new chord by changing as few notes as possible. Notes present in both chords should be repeated. Well performed voice leading lets chord changes sound smooth and well connected.

Inversions of Triads

The classical cadence with triads shows the movement of the single voices very clearly. Based on the voice leading, the triads will be played in different inversions.

Tip: Classical cadences (using the chords built on the first, fourth and fifth degrees of the major scale) avoid parallel movement of the individual voices. You could use the same hand position for F and G major but that would result in notorious "parallel fifths" which should be avoided.

Exercise:

- Play the classical major and minor cadence at a slow tempo in all keys. Use the same pattern you used for the triads and 4 note chords.
- Sing the individual parts (i.e. G–A–G–G; E–F–D–E; C–C–B–C). This will help you to grasp and comprehend the voice leading better.
- Keep track of your progress using the check boxes.

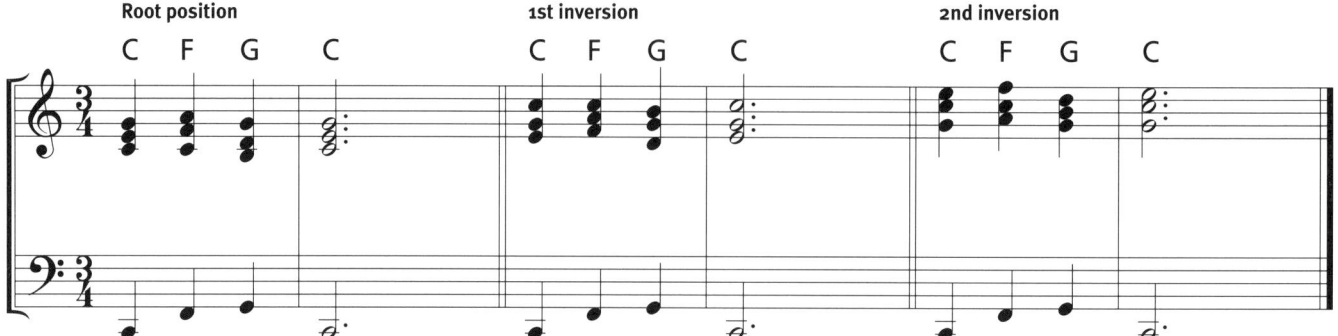

Check Boxes:

C Major

B♭ Major

A♭ Major

G♭ Major

E Major

D Major

F Major

E♭ Major

D♭ Major

B Major

A Major

G Major

Exercise:

- Play the classical major and minor cadence at a slow tempo in all keys. Use the same pattern you used for the triads and 4 note chords.
- Sing the individual parts (i.e. G–Ab–G–G; Eb-F-D-Eb; C–C–B–C). This will help you to grasp and comprehend the voice leading better.
- Keep track of your progress using the check boxes.

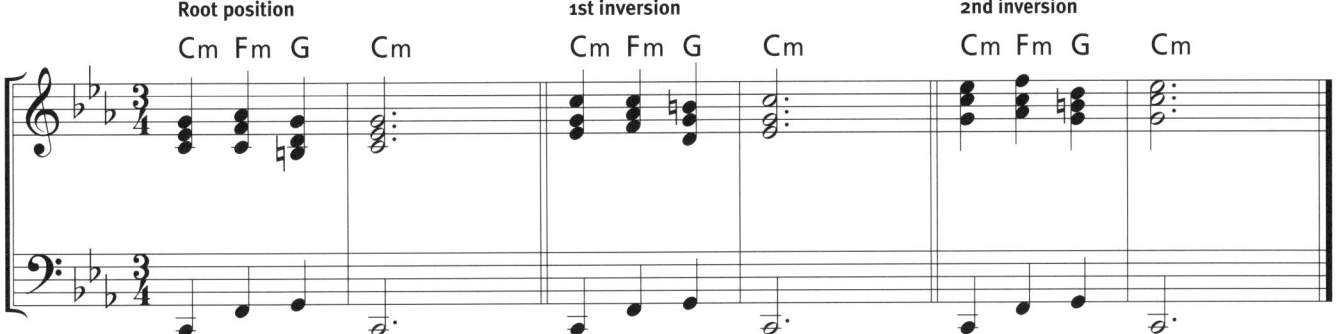

Check Boxes:

C Minor

F Minor

Bb Minor

Eb Minor

G# Minor

C# Minor

F# Minor

B Minor

E Minor

A Minor

D Minor

G Minor

Exercise:

A further, excellent exercise for practicing major triads with correct voice leading in all keys goes as follows:

Starting with root position:

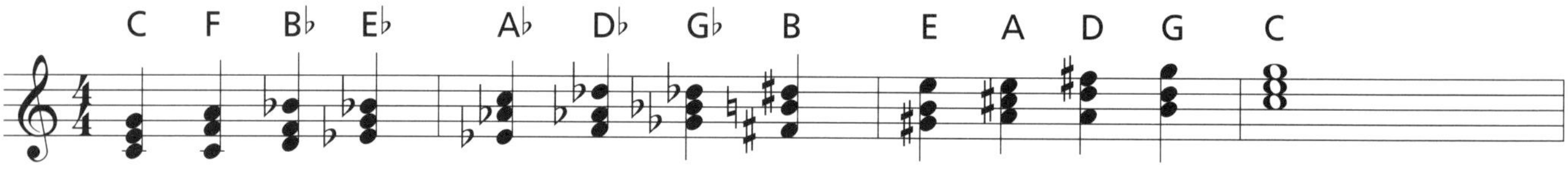

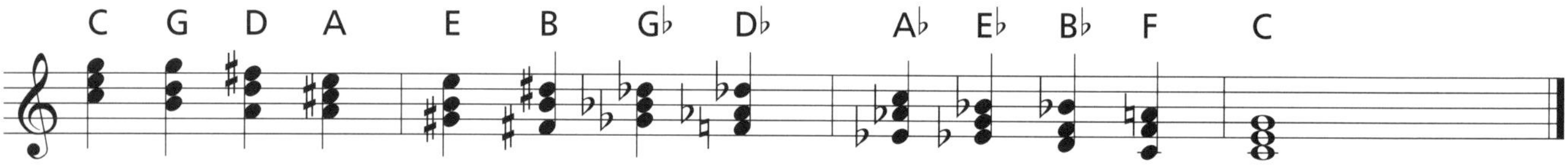

Check Box: Root Position

Starting with first inversion:

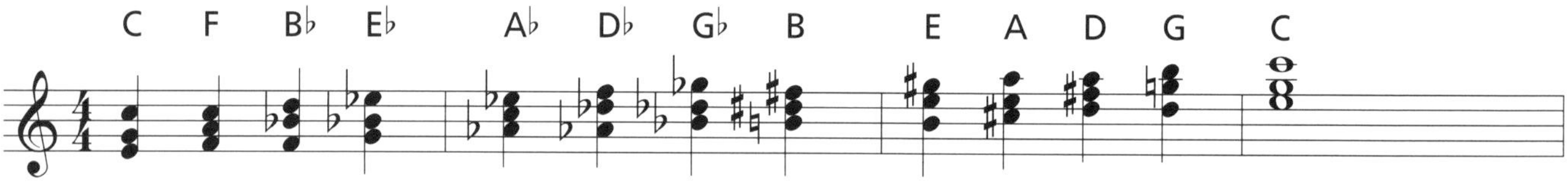

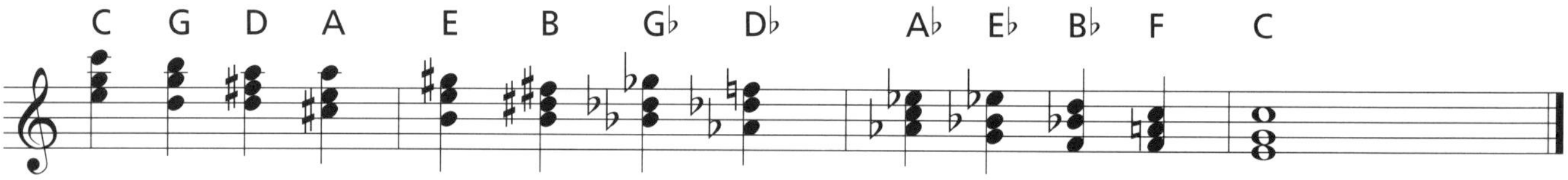

Check Box: First Inversion

Starting with second inversion:

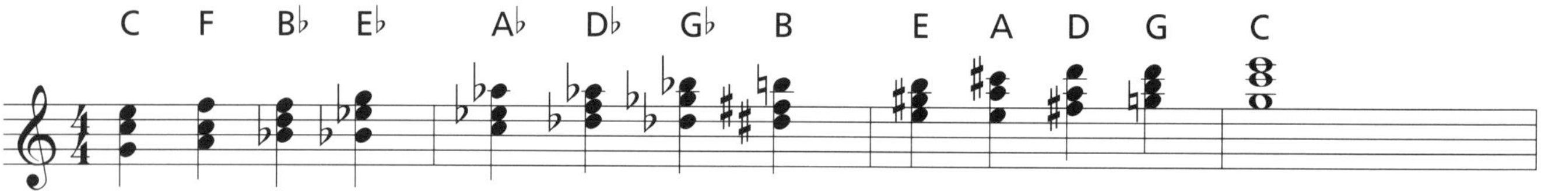

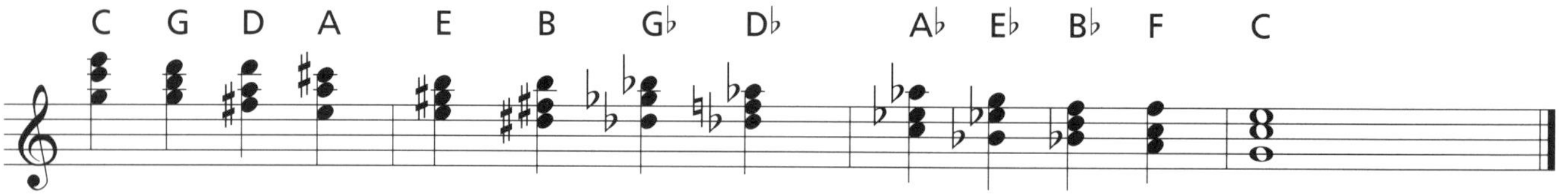

Check Box: Second Inversion

Tip: Also play this exercise with your left hand.

BASICS

Inversions of 4 Note Chords

4 note chords have three inversions plus their basic root position. The classical names of these three inversions (1st inv.: five-six chord, 2nd inv.: three-four chord, 3rd inv.: two chord) are rarely used in jazz music.

Example: C△7

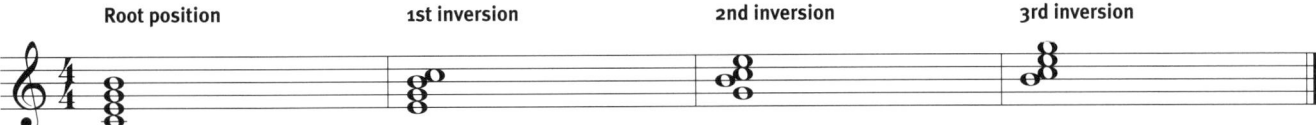

Exercise:

- Play the 4 note chords (see p. 8) and their inversions in all keys for the following chord types. Use the same practice pattern you used for the triads, 4 note chords and the classical cadence.

Check Boxes:

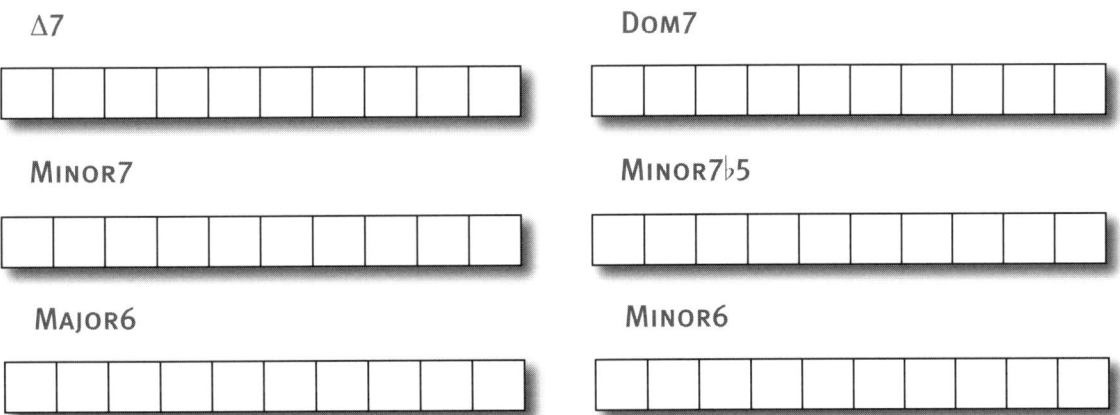

Exercise:

- Notate more chords analogous to the given chord symbols without using an instrument. Pay attention to correct voice leading (as little finger shifting as possible) and compare your version to the version in the Solution Key.

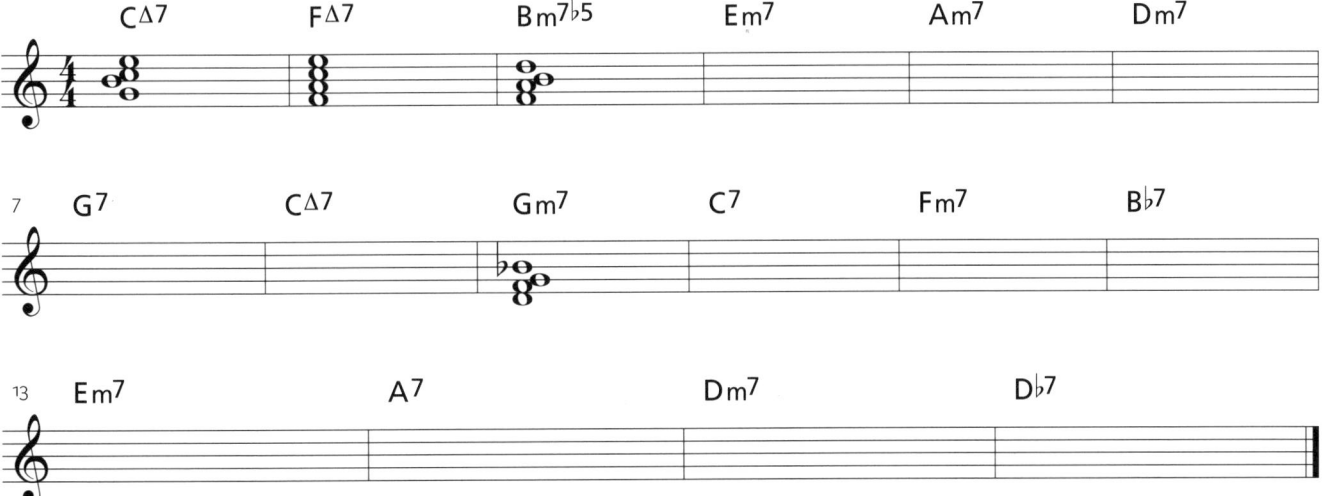

© 2007 by AMA Musikverlag

Spread Voicings

Voicing Pyramid

It is important to know the exact structure of jazz voicings. The voicing pyramid helps us to illustrate this structure. Depicting the exact sound characteristics of a chord symbol, every voicing is built as follows:

- The lowest note is the root.
- On top of the root note follow the so-called guide tones: the third and seventh.
- Now the chord extensions (optional notes) follow on top of the chord frame (root, third, seventh).
- The fifth can be played either above the root or the guide tones.

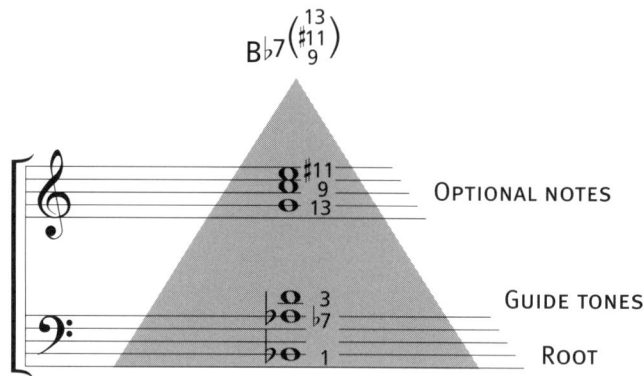

This logical voicing structure also represents the basis of jazz voicing notation:

- Jazz voicings should always be notated from the root up.
- The root is notated first.
- Then the guide tones.
- Finally, the chord extensions are added.

One feature of a well-constructed voicing is that it avoids doubled notes, i.e. every note only appears once in the voicing.
For the beginning pianist it is necessary to learn how to construct voicings without doubled notes. Doubled notes can be encountered in the real world, though.

An overview of the most common voicings used in Jazz follows. As you can see, the voicings are always constructed according to the rules of the voicing pyramid. All the voicings shown here will be discussed in this book.

All the Voicings for C7

Root Voicings

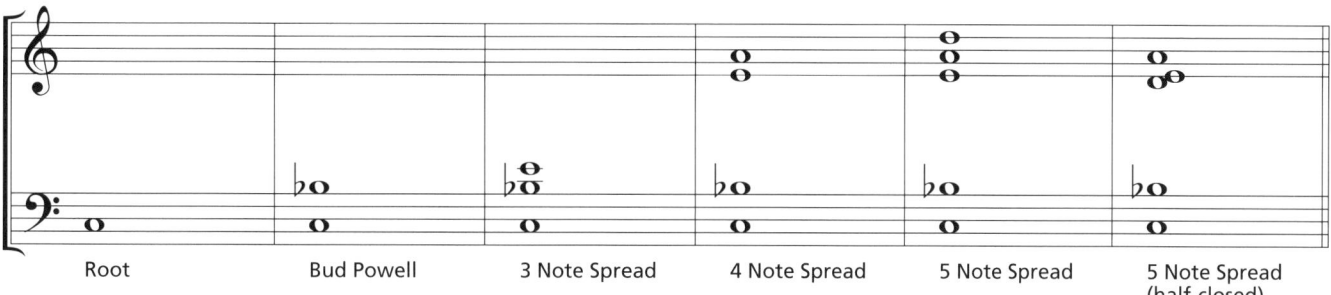

Rootless Voicings

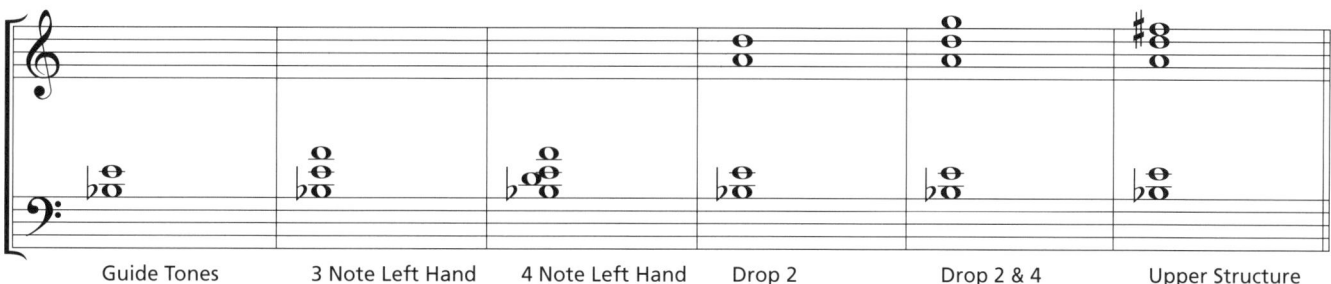

Root Voicings

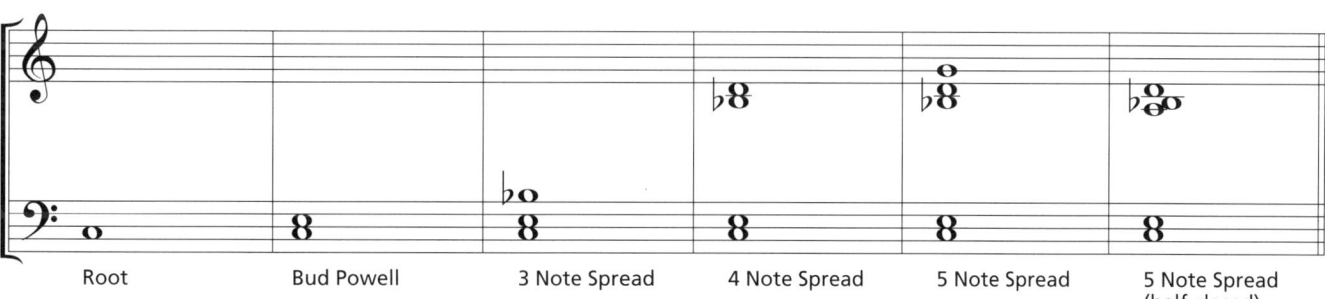

Rootless Voicings

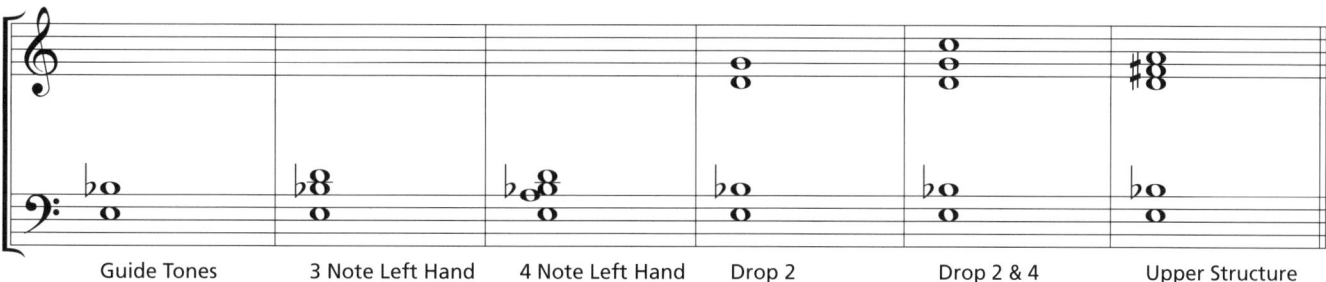

© 2007 by AMA Musikverlag

Spread voicings spread the chord notes over a wide range. These voicings are also called **open chord voicings**. Seventh chords in root position and inversions are called **closed position chords**. Spread voicings can have different shapes:

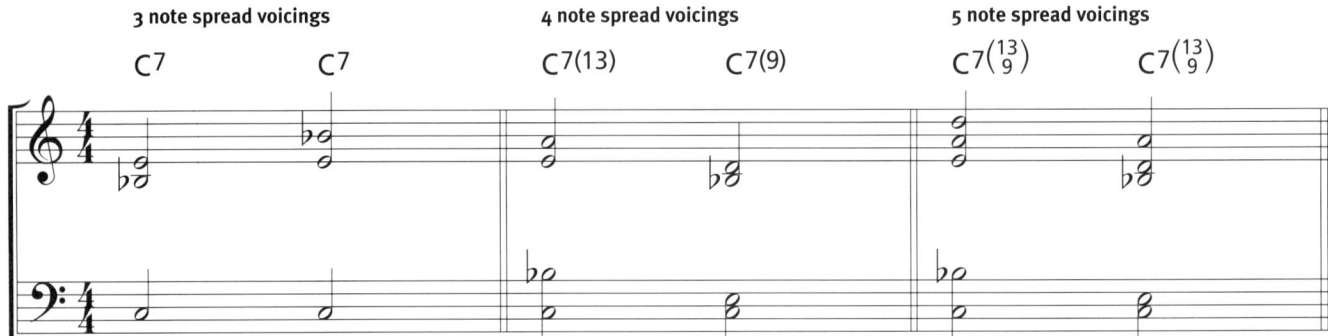

Low Interval Limits

It is important to play a chord at just the right spot on the keyboard to make it sound right. The "low interval limits" limit the range within which a chord should be played; they mark the lower limits of chord ranges.

The following example gives an overview of the low interval limits for the corresponding chord note. The notes in parentheses mark the root. However, it is not important to include these root notes in the voicing (see the chapter *Two Hand Voicings*).

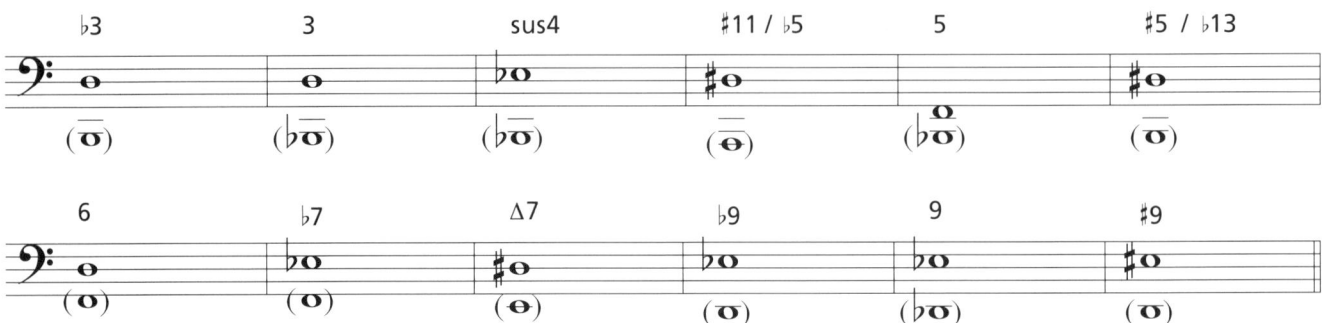

Examples of voicings notated too low:

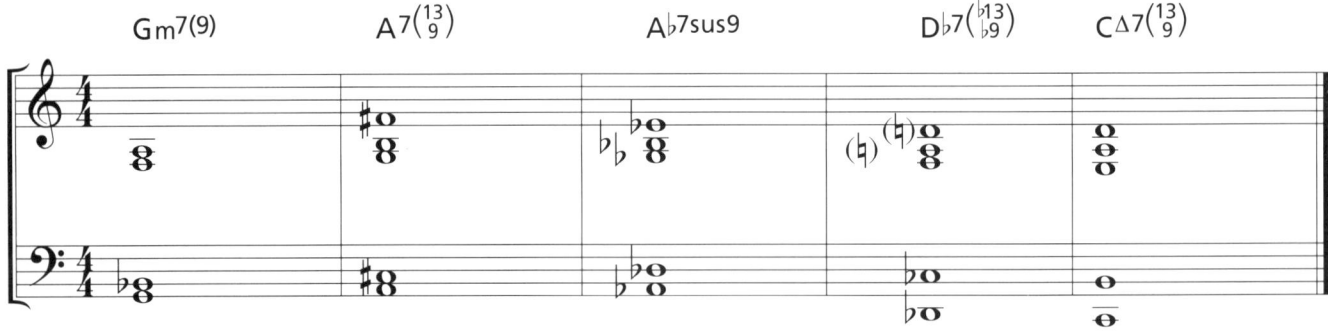

Enharmonic Notation

The use of double ♯ and double ♭ cannot always be avoided in the academically correct notation of music. They are hard to read – not only for beginners. For the sake of better readability we will avoid these double accidentals wherever possible.

Example

(from *Jazz Piano – Solo Concepts*, "Shana" p. 56)

3 Note Spread Voicings

This voicing is played with both hands and employs the root and both guide tones. It can have two shapes and is named according to the order of the chord notes from the root up.

a) 137 voicing and b) 173 voicing

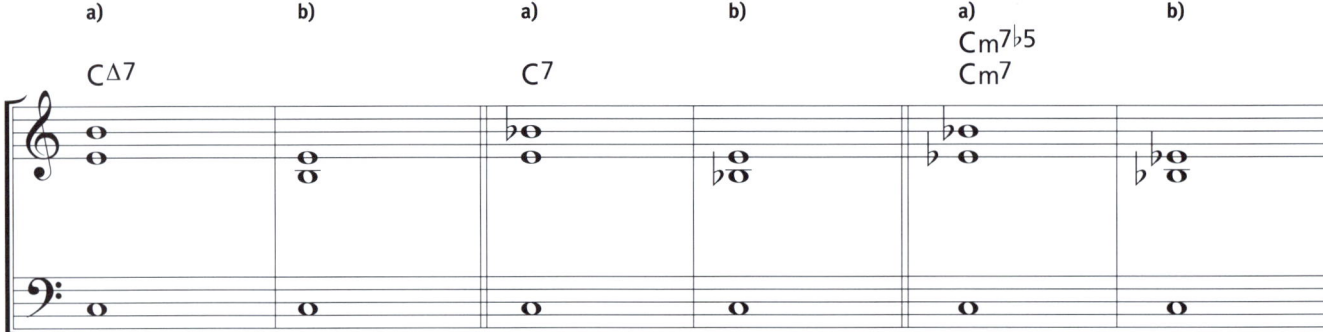

Exercise:

- Study the order of the notes and the shapes of the 3 note spread voicings. The voicings should be played in all keys.
- Practice with both hands right from the start.
- Play the chords as chords. Do not play the notes successively.
- Take your time for the individual chords (even practice without a constant tempo).
- Again, it helps the memorization process to say the chord name out loud before playing it.
- Consistently practice one chord type for 20 minutes every day (i.e. 137 type maj7) until you are able to play it correctly in all keys. Only then go on to the next chord type.

Tip: This exercise takes some patience and cannot be mastered in a day!
The challenge here is the thinking preparation involved – not playing the chords on the piano. It is imperative to take your time so that you can **see the chord on the keyboard** before playing it.

Practice Tracks on the CD

- As soon as you can play the chords fluently at a medium tempo, try to play the voicings along with the practice tracks on the CD.
- All practice tracks run through the circle of fifths as shown in following example for major7:
- Further practice tracks for these voicings can be found on tracks 7–11 on the CD.

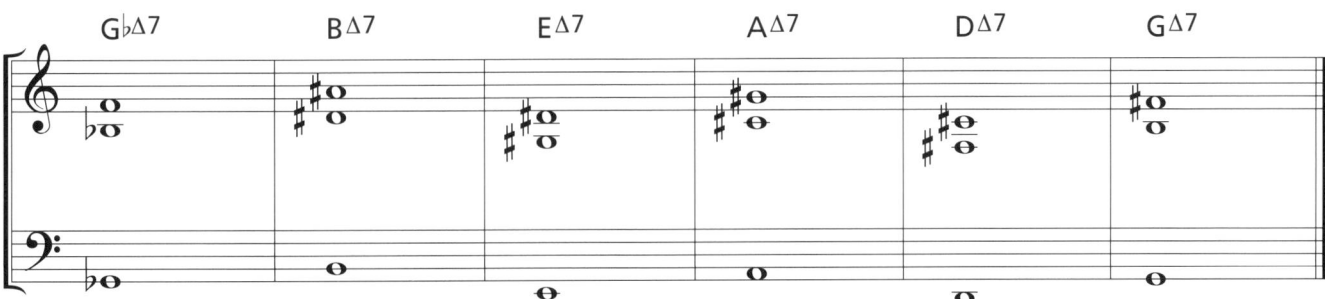

Check Boxes:

Tracks 1 & 2 ▸ Major 137 Voicing

Tracks 3 & 4 ▸ Minor 137 Voicing

Tracks 1 & 2 ▸ Major 173 Voicing

Tracks 3 & 4 ▸ Minor 173 Voicing

Tracks 1 – 4 ▸ Dominant 137 Voicing

Tracks 5 & 6 ▸ Half-diminished 137 Voicing

Tracks 1 – 4 ▸ Dominant 173 Voicing

Tracks 5 & 6 ▸ Half-diminished 173 Voicing

Tip: Press the sustain pedal after playing the first chord and move your fingers to the next chord.
In practice: beat 1: play the chord, beat 2: press the sustain pedal, beat 3: move your fingers to the next chord, beat 4: check your placement, beat 1: play the chord, etc.
This way you will be able to reduce the stress that might occur during this exercise.

© 2007 by AMA Musikverlag

4 Note Spread Voicings

There are two variations of 4 note spread voicings:

a) 1735 Voicing and b) 1379 Voicing

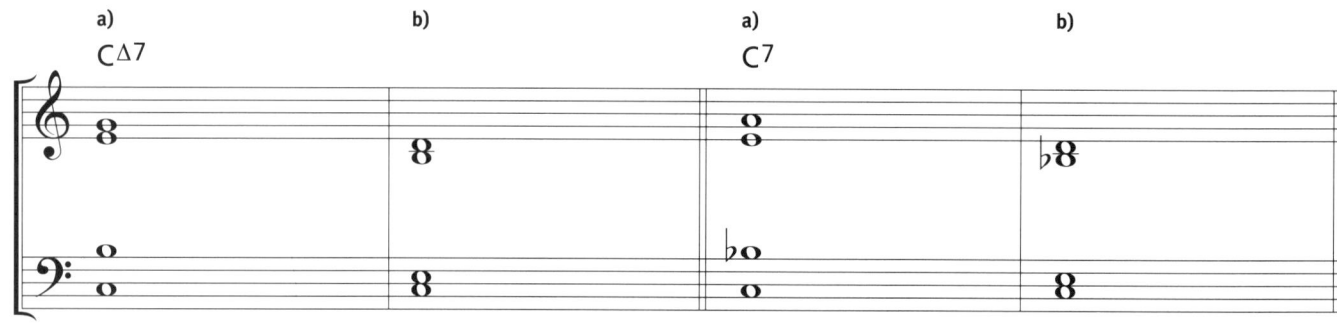

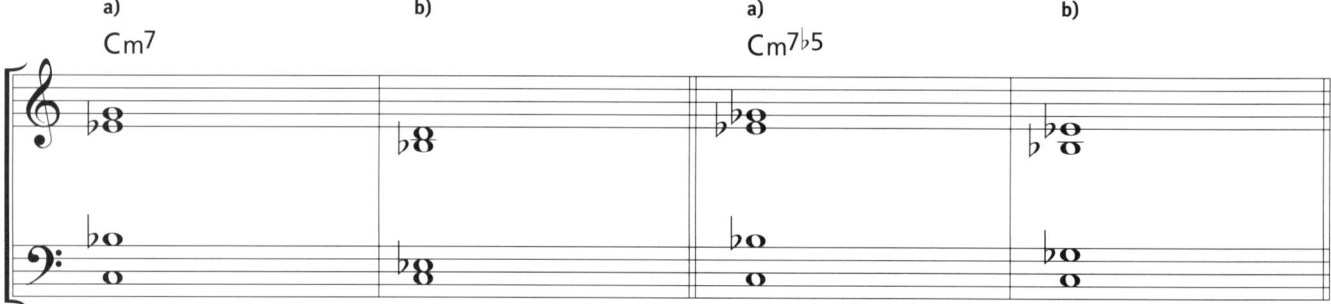

With dominant seventh chords, the sixth (13) is played instead of the fifth. With half-diminished seventh chords, the 1379 type is replaced by the 1573 type.

Fingerings

You should get accustomed to following these fingerings when practicing 3 note spread voicings. These fingerings will help you with voice leading.

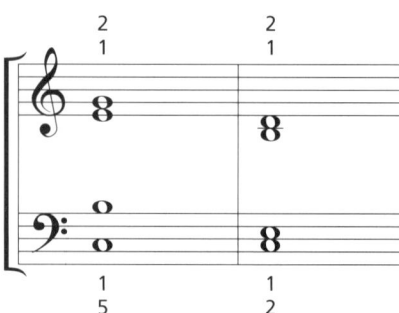

CD Practice Tracks

Exercise:

- Practice the 4 note spread voicings along with the practice tracks on the CD as you did with the 3 note spread voicings.

4 Note Spread Voicings

Check Boxes:

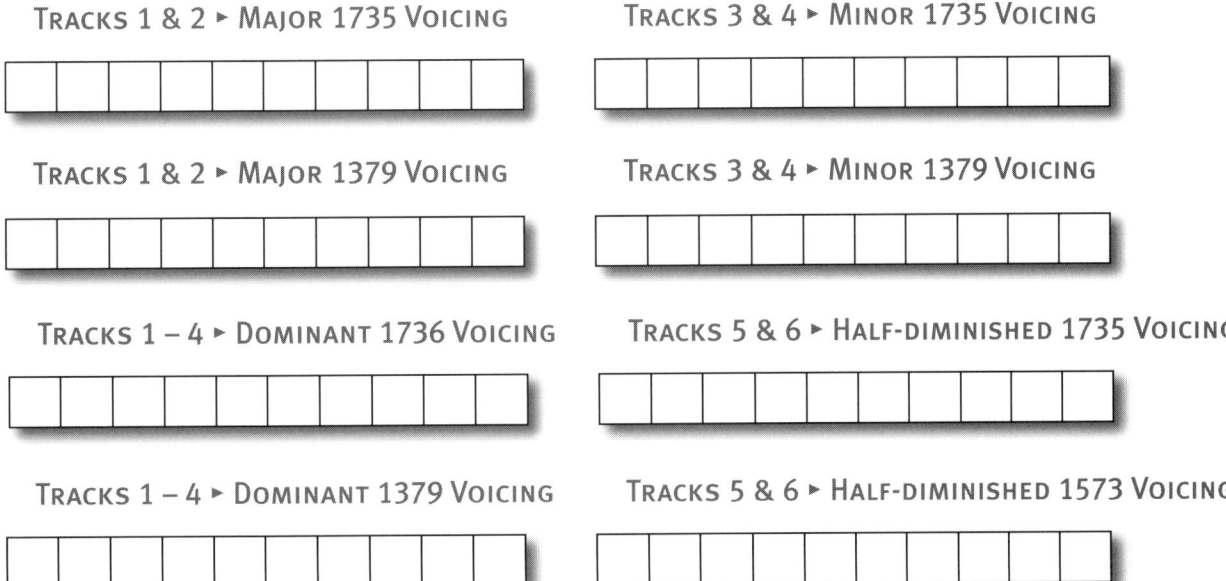

Tracks 1 & 2 ▸ Major 1735 Voicing

Tracks 3 & 4 ▸ Minor 1735 Voicing

Tracks 1 & 2 ▸ Major 1379 Voicing

Tracks 3 & 4 ▸ Minor 1379 Voicing

Tracks 1 – 4 ▸ Dominant 1736 Voicing

Tracks 5 & 6 ▸ Half-diminished 1735 Voicing

Tracks 1 – 4 ▸ Dominant 1379 Voicing

Tracks 5 & 6 ▸ Half-diminished 1573 Voicing

think – speak – finger – play

5 Note Spread Voicings

5 note spread voicings are the logical successor of 4 note spread voicings. Obeying the voicing pyramid, a note is added on top of the highest note, usually a chord extension.

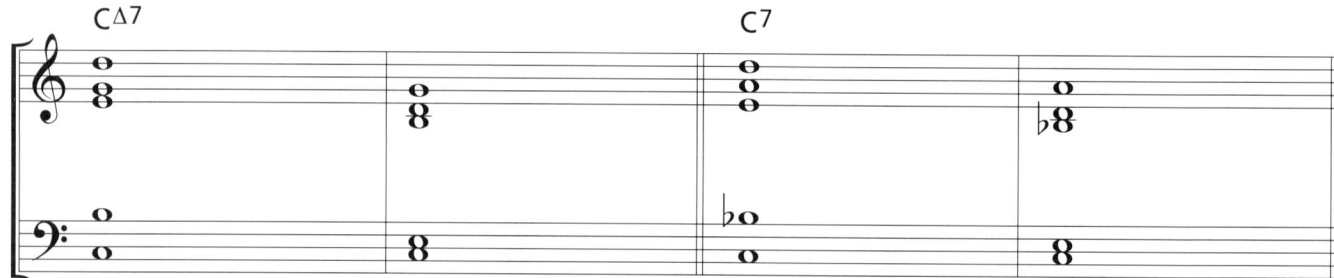

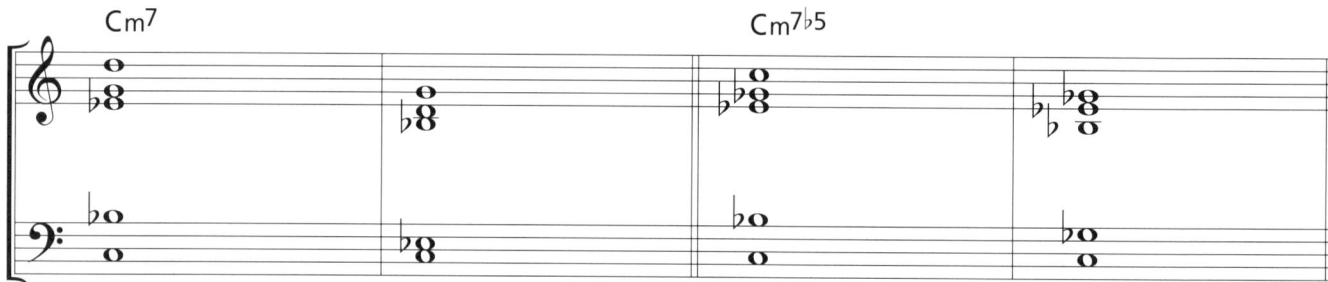

Chord Extensions

5 note spread voicings bring you a big step closer to the chord extensions that can be found in jazz as you now play up to two chord extensions (optional notes) on top of the chord notes. These extensions can be altered in accordance with the chord symbol. Examples:

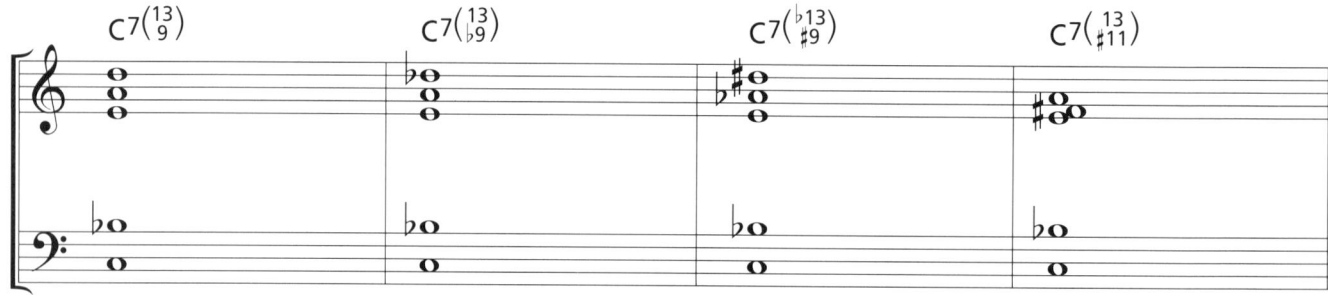

CD Practice Tracks

Exercise:
- Practice the 5 note spread voicings along with the practice tracks on the CD as you did with the other spread voicings before.

5 Note Spread Voicings

Check Boxes:

Tracks 1 & 2 ▸ Major 17359 Voicing

Tracks 3 & 4 ▸ Minor 17359 Voicing

Tracks 1 & 2 ▸ Major 13795 Voicing

Tracks 3 & 4 ▸ Minor 13795 Voicing

Tracks 1 – 4 ▸ Dominant 17369 Voicing

Tracks 5 & 6 ▸ Half-Diminished 17351 Voicing

Tracks 1 – 4 ▸ Dominant 13795 Voicing

Tracks 5 & 6 ▸ Half-Diminished 15735 Voicing

Example

(from *Jazz Piano – Solo Concepts*, "Cuban Jazz", p. 81)

Edward Kennedy "Duke" Ellington (* April 29, 1899, † May 24, 1974) was a remarkable jazz giant between the 1920s and 1960s and has had an influence on other musicians up to this day that cannot be overestimated. He is regarded as one of the greatest American composers. His numerous hits include *Take the A Train, Satin Doll, Rockin' in Rhythm, Mood Indigo, Caravan* and *Sophisticated Lady*. His mother gave him his first piano lessons at the age of seven. Already at a young age his aristocratic airs caused his schoolmates to give him the nickname "Duke". He started his professional career at the age of seventeen. After moving to New York he co-founded the band "The Washingtonians" at age twenty-four with a group of musicians from Washington. At this time Ellington had the chance to compose in a vast variety of styles for dancing night club acts and other special endeavours of the band. He was known as a musical experimenter his entire life and recorded numerous titles with John Coltrane, Charles Mingus and his orchestra.

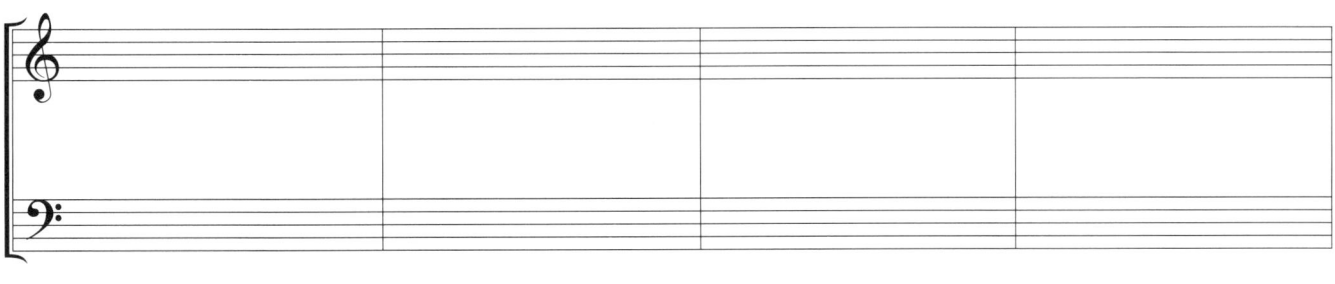

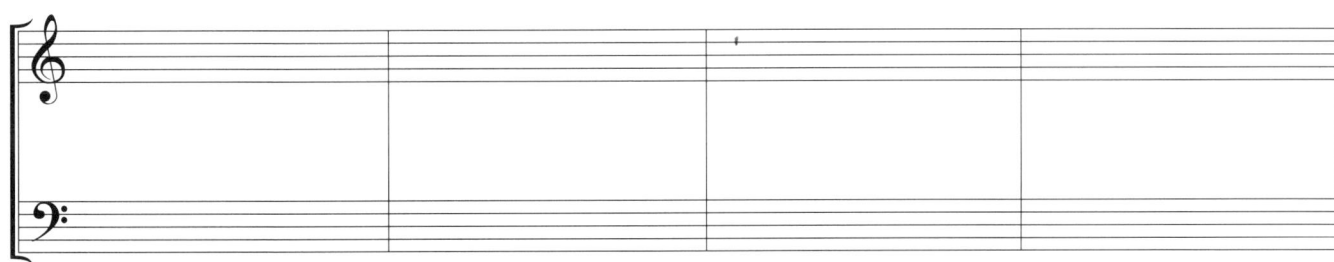

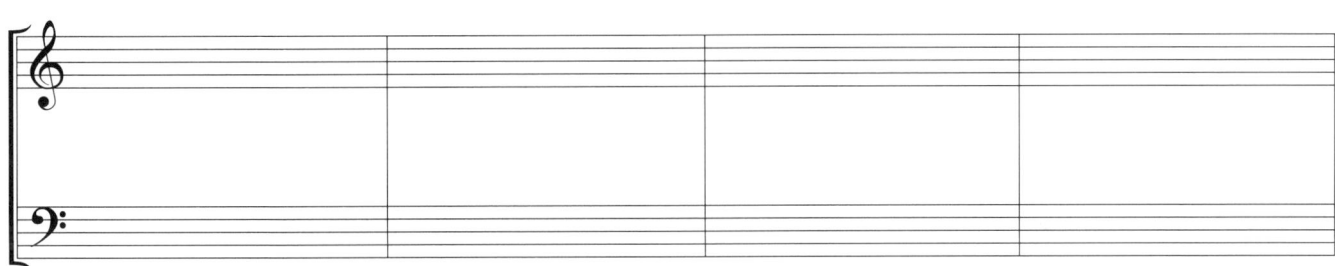

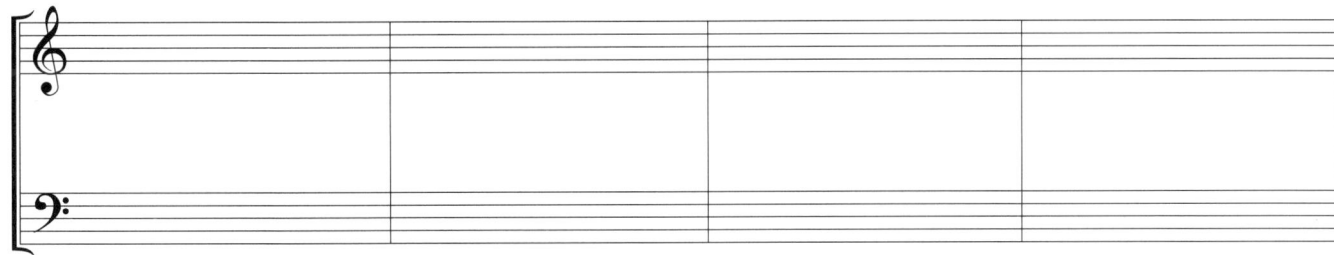

Summary: By now you should have learned the following:

- chord symbols
- 3 and 4 note chords with all inversions
- classical cadence in major and minor
- rules of voice leading
- low interval limits
- 3, 4 and 5 note spread voicings

Chapter 2: Major Diatonic

Diatonic Chords in Major

Chords are built by stacking thirds on top of each other using the notes of a scale. Since most jazz standards employ the chords of the diatonic system in major, it is useful to memorize the ionic system for the chord structures you already know. The knowledge of diatonic chords built on the degrees of the scale is essential for understanding how harmony works and how chords relate to each other.

Exercise:

- Play the diatonic seventh chords on all degrees of the scale using the following voicings, ascending and descending and in all keys.
- Again, take your time and if necessary, practice out of tempo.
- Speak the degree and the chord name out loud before playing it as is demonstrated on track 7.
- Measure your progress using the check boxes.

Root position

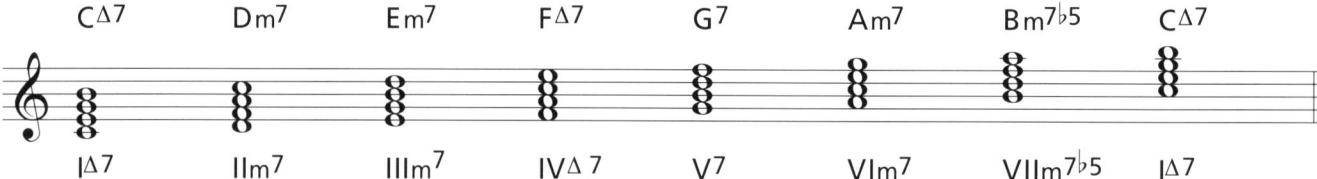

> **Tip:** Talk to other pianists, watch other pianists and do not hesitate to ask them questions!

CHECK BOXES:

C MAJOR

F MAJOR

B♭ MAJOR

E♭ MAJOR

A♭ MAJOR

D♭ MAJOR

G♭ MAJOR

B MAJOR

E MAJOR

A MAJOR

D MAJOR

G MAJOR

Tip: Play these seventh chords with the left hand, too!

173 Voicing

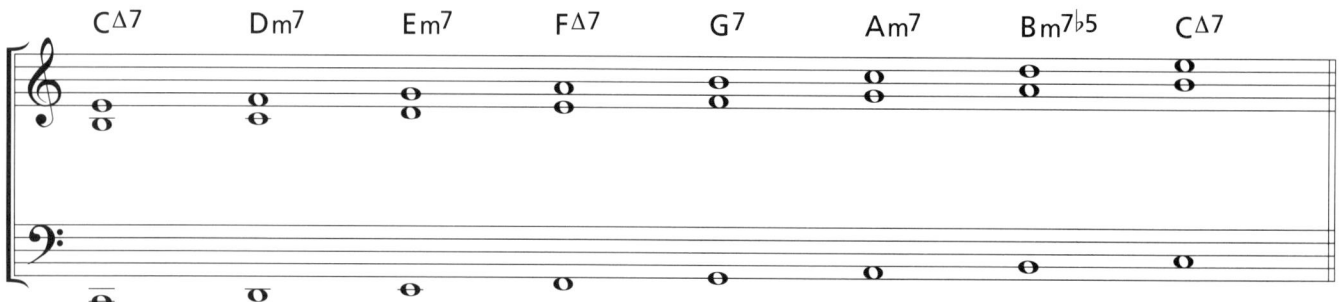

Check Boxes:

C Major

B♭ Major

A♭ Major

G♭ Major

E Major

D Major

F Major

E♭ Major

D♭ Major

B Major

A Major

G Major

137 Voicing

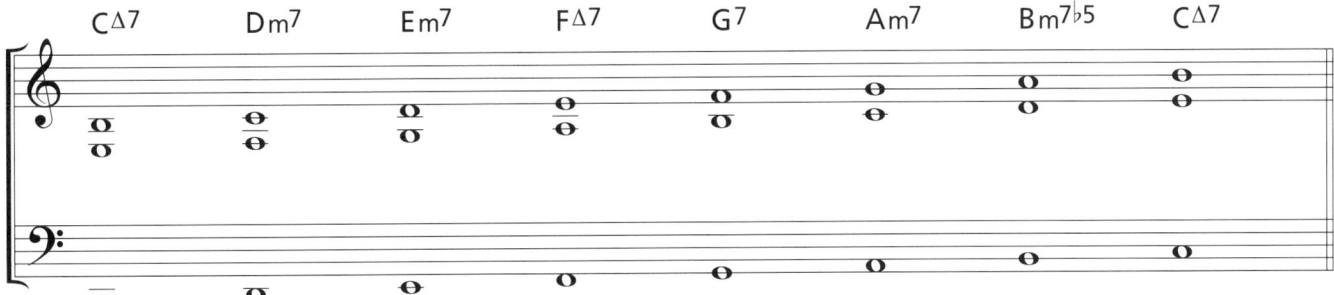

Check Boxes:

C Major

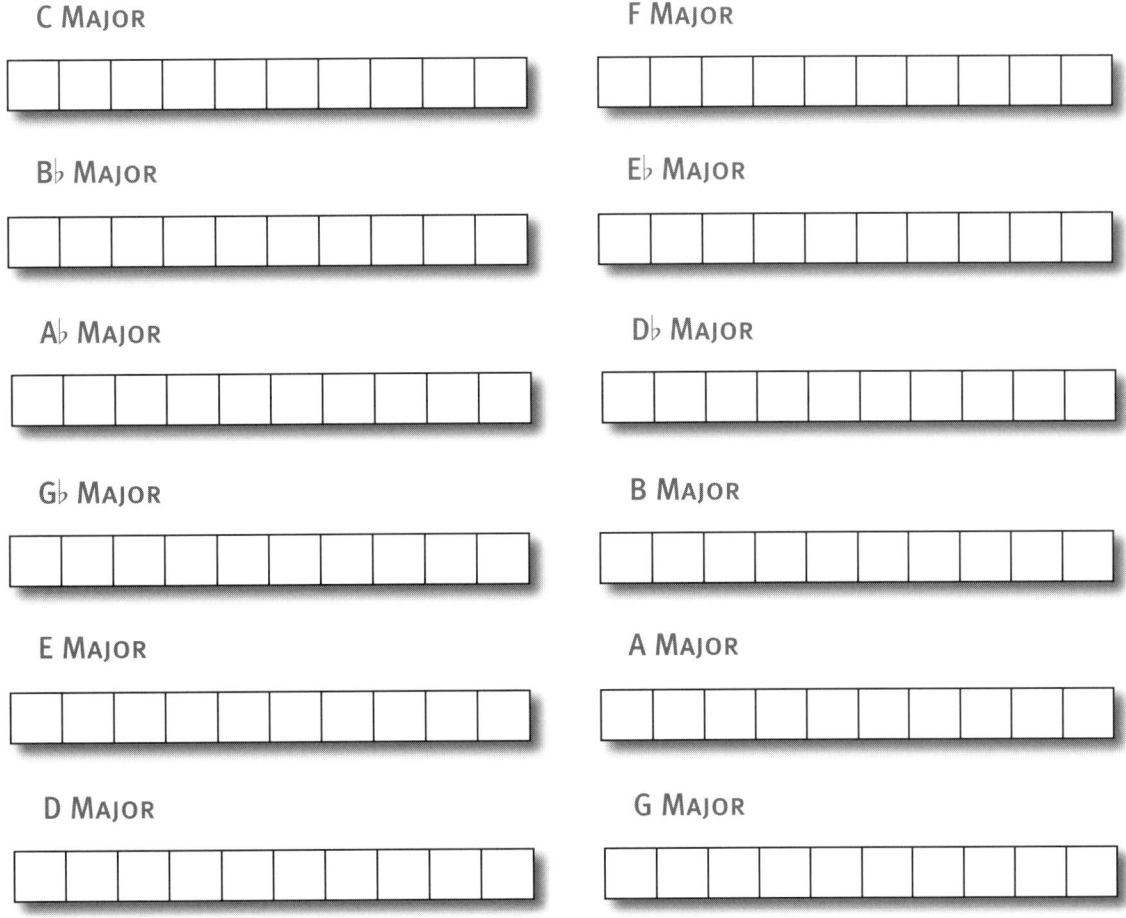

B♭ Major

A♭ Major

G♭ Major

E Major

D Major

F Major

E♭ Major

D♭ Major

B Major

A Major

G Major

1735 Voicing

Check Boxes:

C Major

B♭ Major

A♭ Major

G♭ Major

E Major

D Major

F Major

E♭ Major

D♭ Major

B Major

A Major

G Major

1573 Voicing

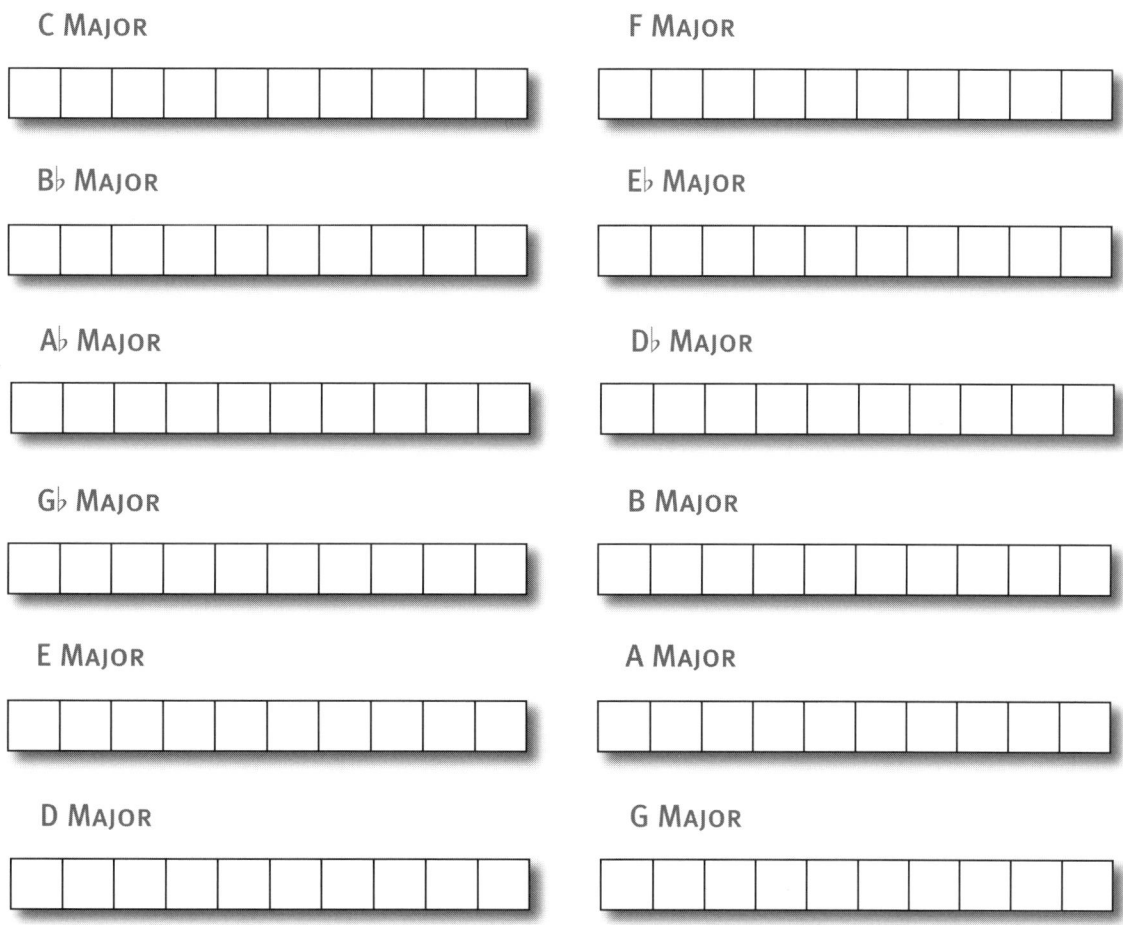

Check Boxes:

C Major

Bb Major

Ab Major

Gb Major

E Major

D Major

F Major

Eb Major

Db Major

B Major

A Major

G Major

Tip: We did not discuss the 1573 voicing so far. It is not commonly used in jazz. However, it is used in a drop 2 voicing (see the chapter *Two Hand Voicings*).

Example

(from *Jazz Piano – Solo Concepts*, "Waltz For Dario", p. 32)

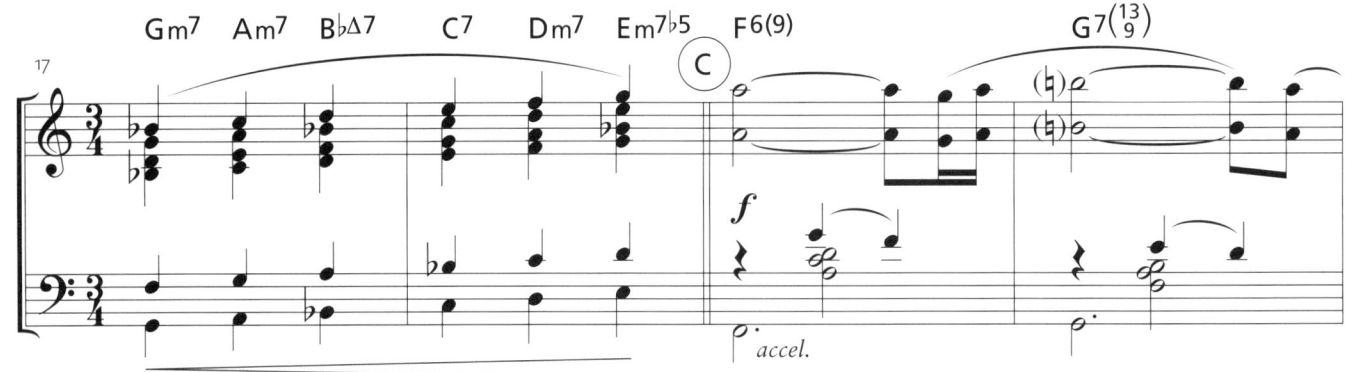

Exercise Tip:

Another way of memorizing the diatonic chords built on the degrees of the scale is to play the seventh chords melodically. Play the following example with the right hand slowly and in all keys. The fingering is always 1–2–3–5. Slowly increase the tempo.

Other variations that can also be used when soloing:

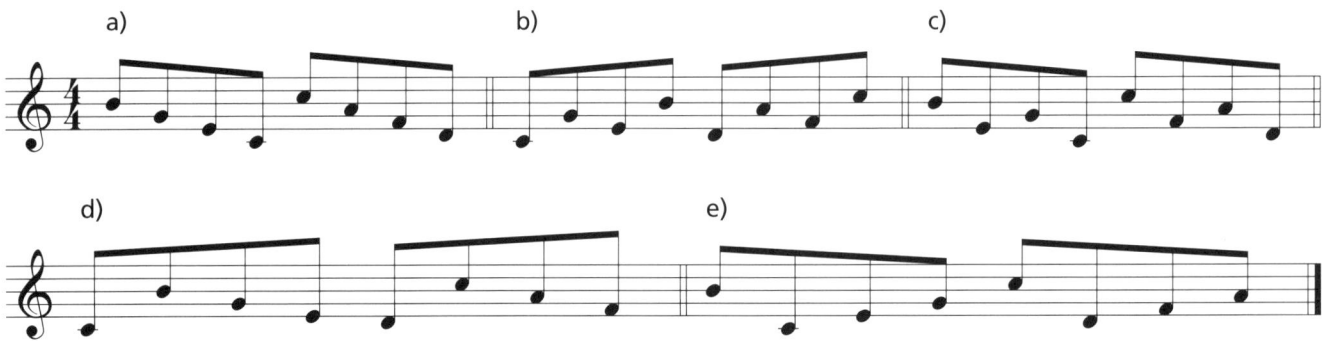

II-V-I Cadence in Major

The second, fifth and first degree of the diatonic chord system form the so-called II-V-I cadence which is used in almost every jazz standard. Therefore, the II-V-I cadence is also called the "jazz cadence".

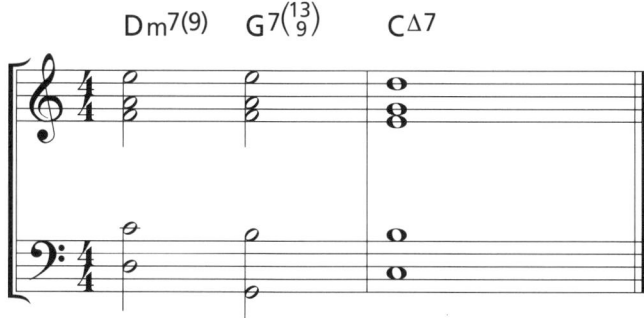

It is very important that you are able to play the II-V-I cadence literally forwards and backwards in every key and at any given time of the night or day. In other words: when you see a II-V-I cadence (found in almost every jazz standard), you should not have to think about voicings and voice leading. The studied patterns have to be automatically at hand. This results in many variations for spontaneous accompaniment which is a basic requirement for good jazz music.

Example

(from *Jazz Piano – Solo Concepts*, "Jazz Flowers", p. 61)

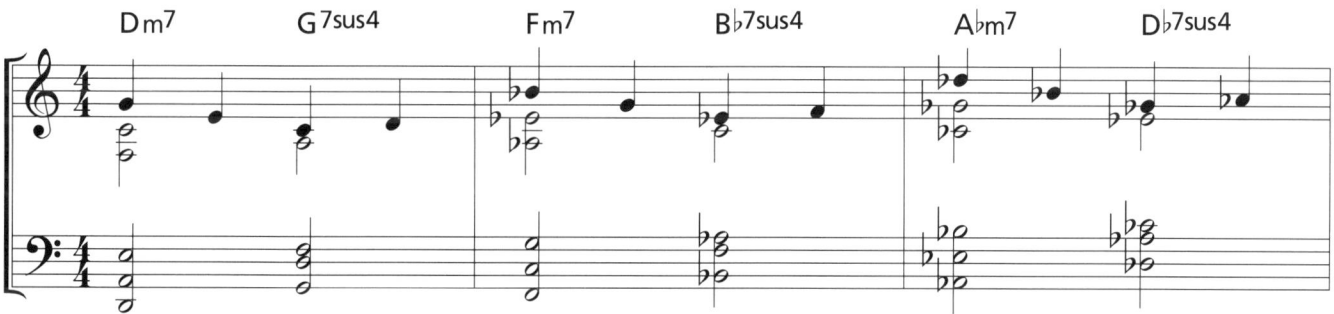

> **Learn everything – and forget it.**
> Charlie Parker

© 2007 by AMA Musikverlag

II-V-I Cadence in Major with 3 Note Spread Voicings

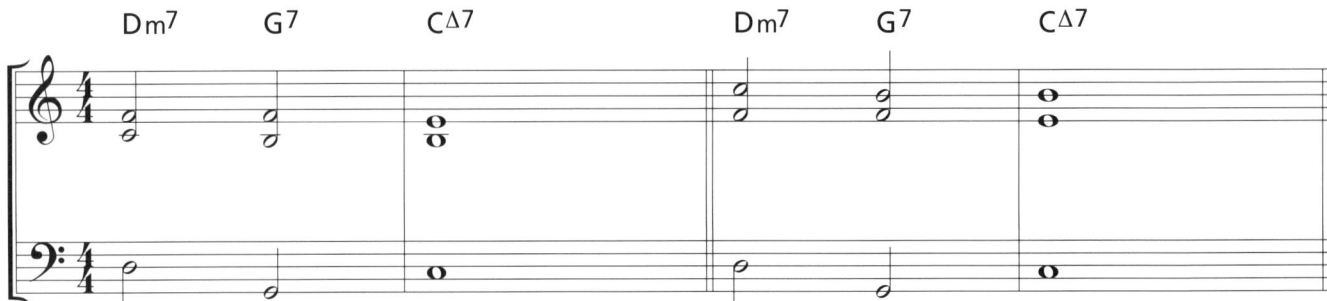

Exercise:

- Play both variations of the II-V-I cadence very slowly in all keys using 3 note spread voicings.
- Again, say the chord name aloud before playing it.
- Now, try to play the voicings along to the following CD tracks.

Track 12 & 13 ▸ II-V-I in Major – Circle of Fifths

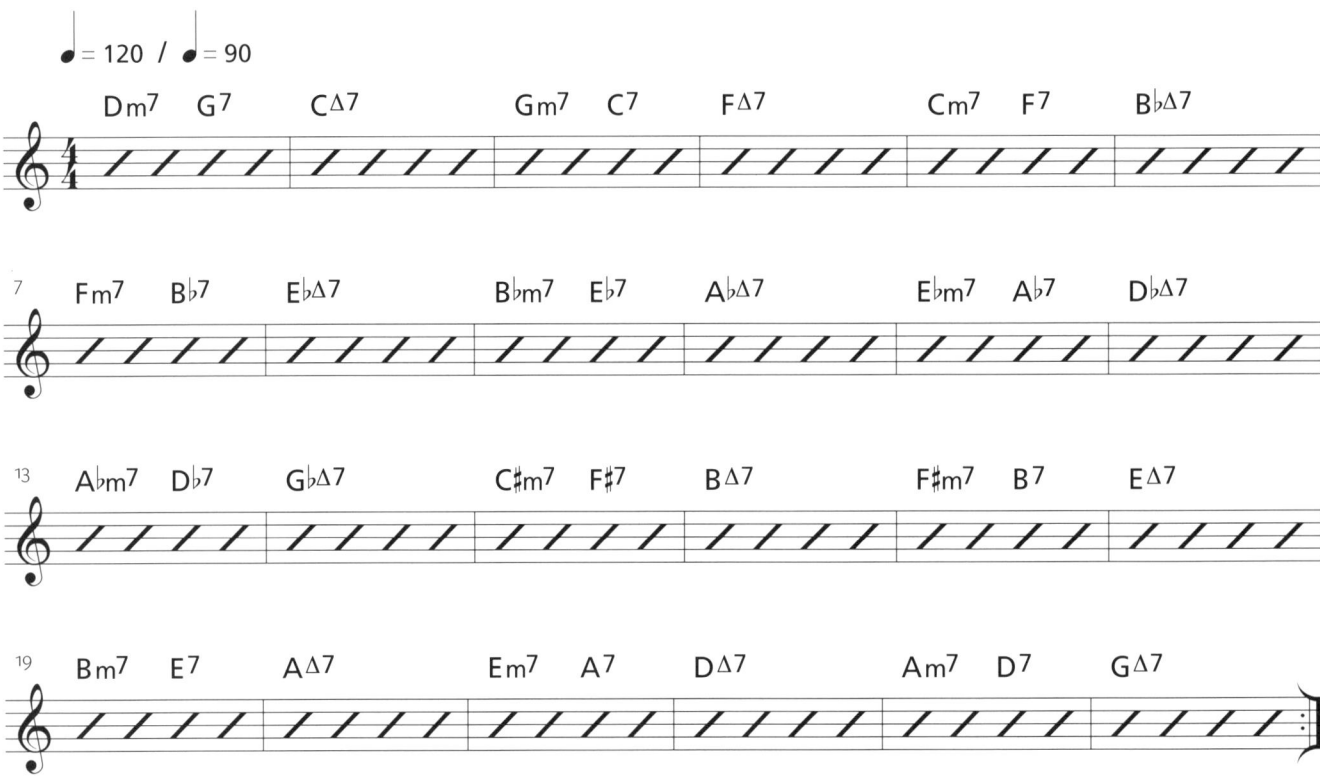

Note: On track 12, the three chords of the II-V-I cadence occur over the span of 8 bars. On track 13 the chords occur over the span of 4 bars!

Tip: By now you should know the circle of fifths without having to think twice. In the appendix you will find a diagram of the circle of fifths (p. 176) that will help you memorize the notated II-V-I sequence. Learn the II-V-I sequences in the circle of fifths by heart as soon as possible as many jazz standards use this harmonic progression.

Track 14 ▸ II-V-I in Major – Whole Tone Descending

Jazz Piano – Voicing Concepts

Track 15 ▶ II-V-I in Major – Chromatically Descending

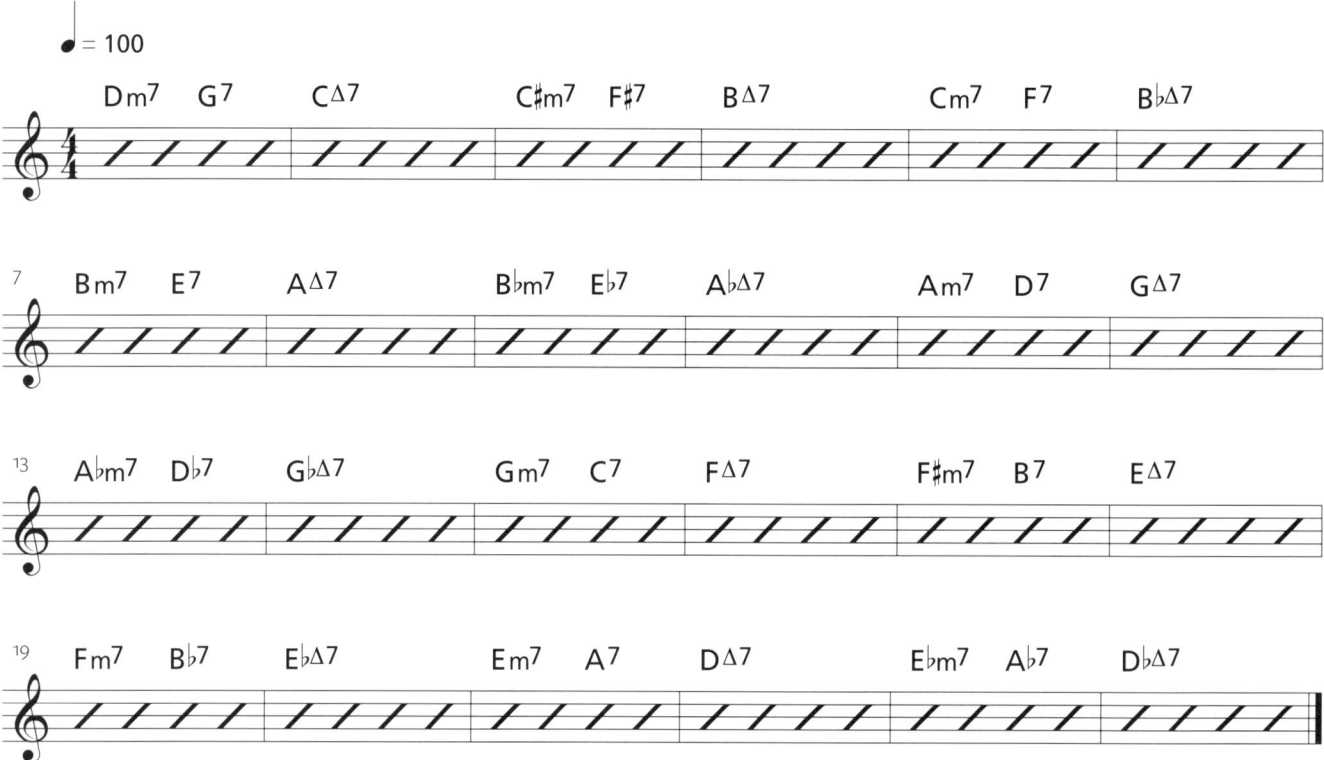

Track 16 ▶ II-V-I in Major – Chromatically Ascending

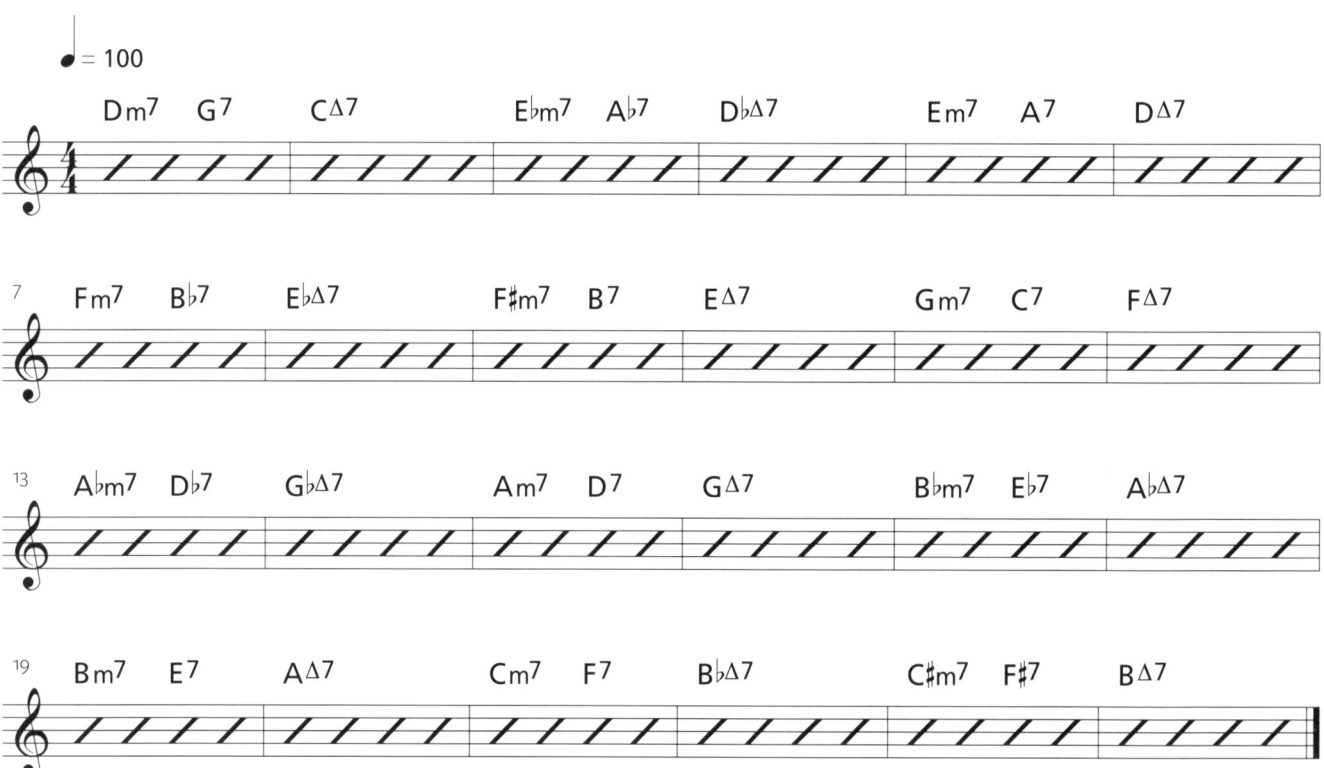

II-V-I Cadence in Major with 3 Note Spread Voicings

Check Boxes:

Tracks 12 & 13 ▸ II-V-I in Major – Circle of Fifths

Track 14 ▸ II-V-I in Major – Whole Tone Descending

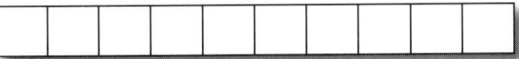

Track 15 ▸ II-V-I in Major – Chromatically Descending

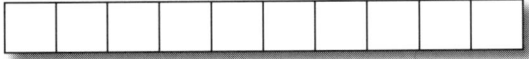

Track 16 ▸ II-V-I in Major – Chromatically Ascending

Exercise:

- Notate the 3 note spread voicings for the given chord progressions.
- Pay attention to smooth voice leading between the chords.
- Compare your version with the version in the Solution Key.
- Learn the chord sequence by heart and play it along to the CD.

Track 17 ▸ Progression 1

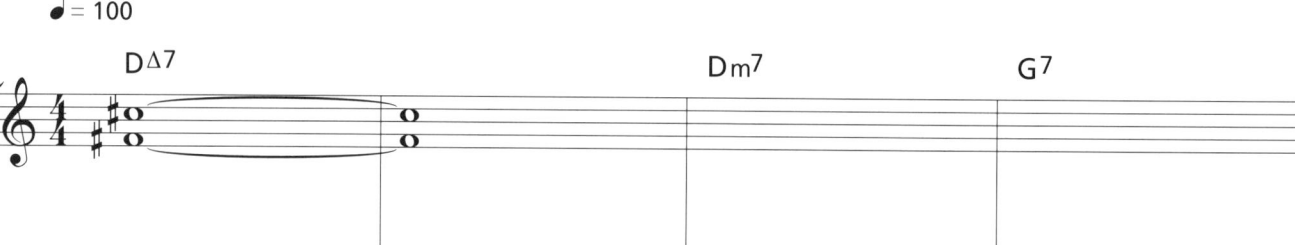

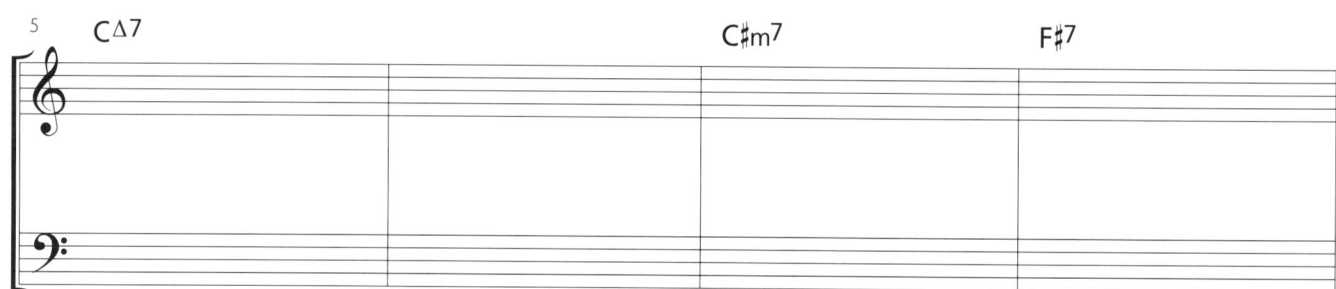

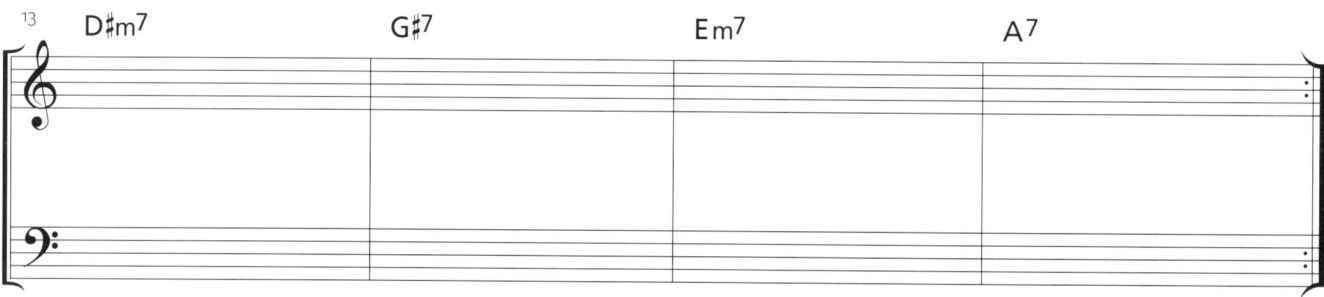

Tip: Harmonic progressions are easy to remember when you know the harmonic relationships. Watch out for material you already know like II-V-I sequences or diatonic movement. After recognizing these you do not have to memorize each chord individually but you can start to put chords into groups. The Solution Key proposes an analysis for the progression above.

Exercise:

- Notate the 3 note spread voicings for the given chord progressions.
- Pay attention to smooth voice leading between the chords.
- Compare your version with the version in the Solution Key.
- Learn the chord sequence by heart and play it along to the CD.

Track 18 ▸ Progression 2

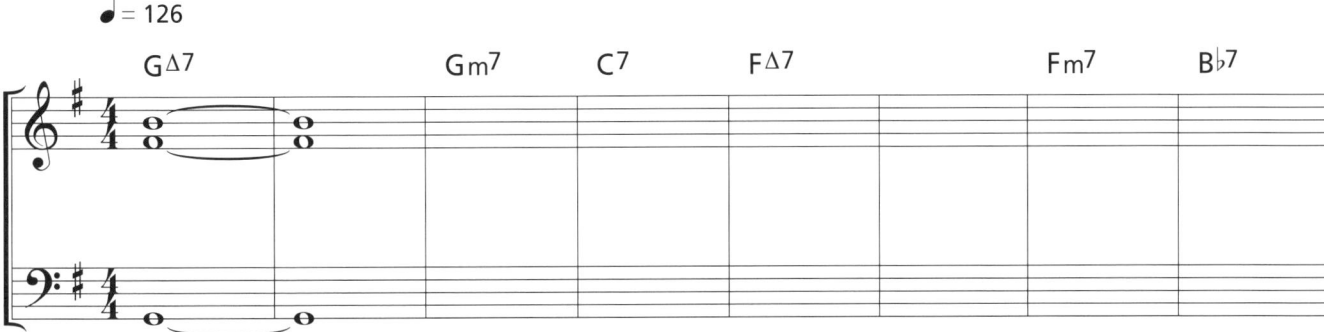

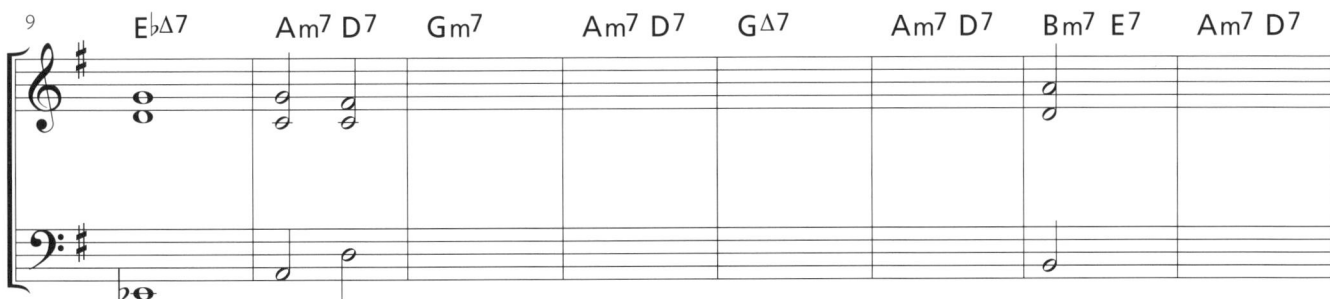

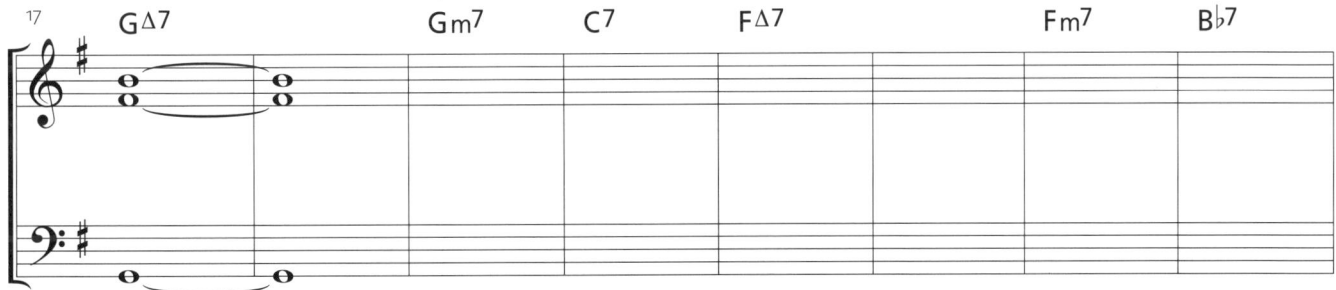

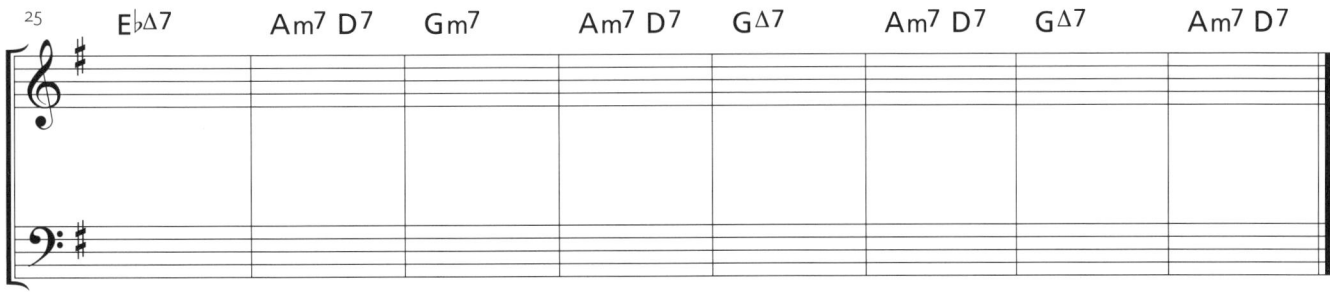

Tip: Chord progressions of jazz standards can also be memorized quite easily. Many jazz standards are written in an AABA form. Here, one only has to memorize one A part and one B part. The other parts are merely repetitions with minor changes. The example above uses an AB form with the B part (bars 17–32) being almost identical to the A part (bars 1–16) except for the second to last bar.

© 2007 by AMA Musikverlag

II-V-I Cadence in Major with 4 Note Spread Voicings

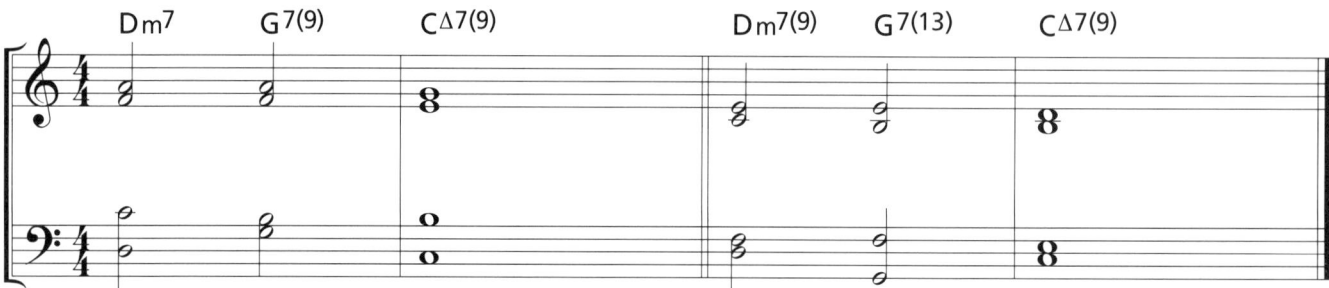

Exercise:

- Play both versions of the II-V-I cadence slowly in all keys using 4 note spread voicings.
- Then, try to play the voicings along with the following CD tracks.

Check Boxes:

Tracks 12 & 13 ▸ II-V-I in Major – Circle of Fifths

Track 14 ▸ II-V-I in Major – Whole Tone Descending

Track 15 ▸ II-V-I in Major – Chromatically Descending

Track 16 ▸ II-V-I in Major – Chromatically Ascending

Exercise:

- Notate the 4 note spread voicings for the given chord sequences.
- Pay attention to smooth voice leading between the chords.
- Compare your version with the version in the Solution Key.
- Learn the chord sequence by heart and play it along to the CD.

Track 19 ▸ Progression 3

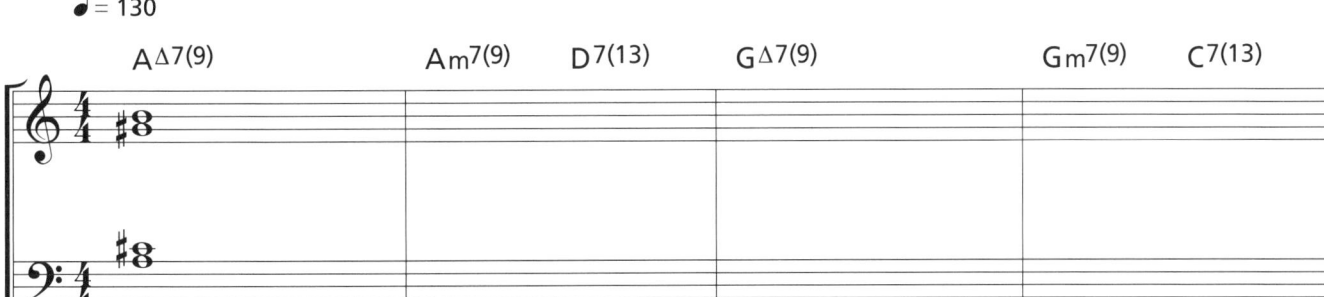

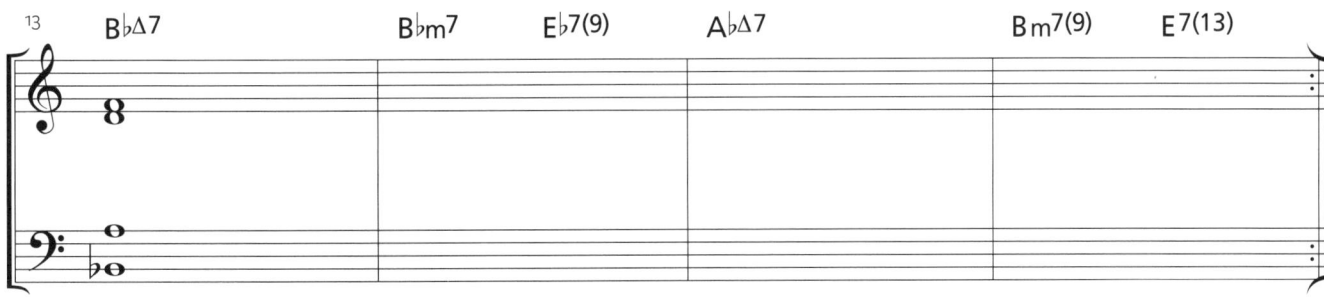

Tip: As most chord sequences in jazz standards move in descending fifths (the interval between two chords) the voicings move down, too. Therefore it is allowed to break with proper voice leading when it becomes necessary to move the voicings into a higher position. However, position changes within II-V-I cadences should be avoided.

Jazz Piano – Voicing Concepts

Exercise:

- Notate the 4 note spread voicings for the given chord sequences.
- Pay attention to proper voice leading between the chords.
- Compare your version with the version in the Solution Key.
- Learn the chord sequence by heart and play it along to the CD.

Track 20 ▸ Progression 4

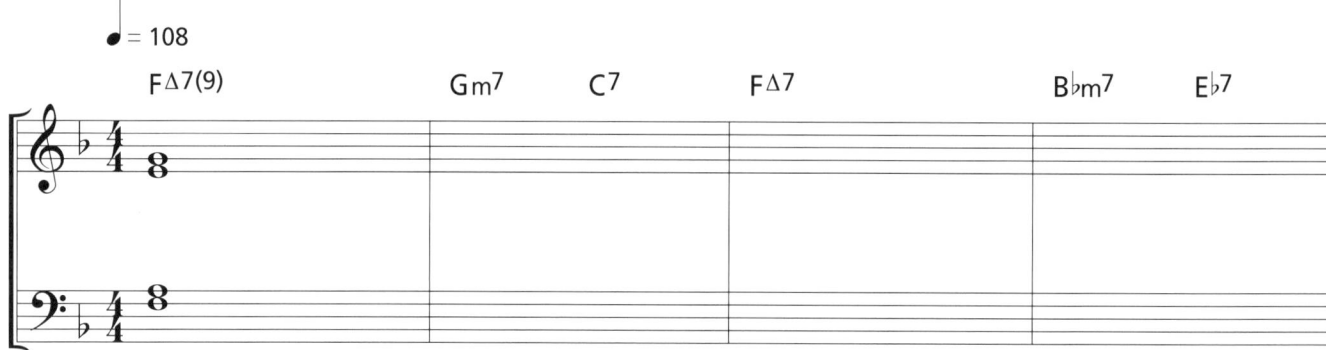

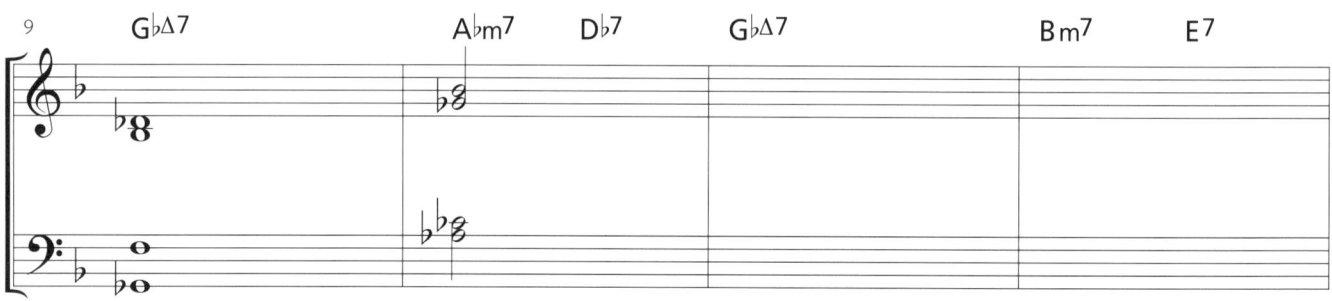

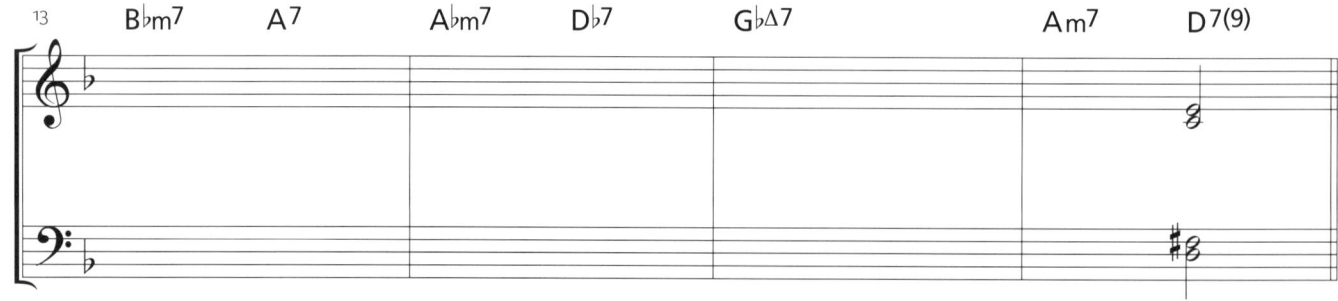

MAJOR DIATONIC

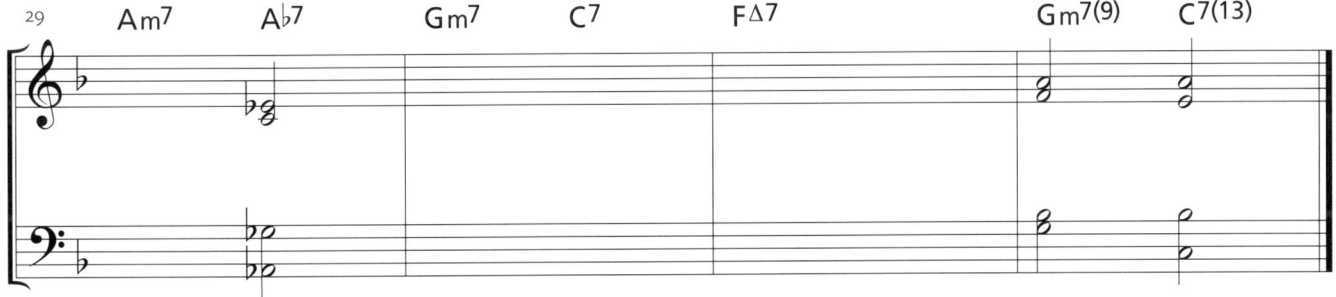

Tip: You can find more harmonic progressions to practice the new voicings with in the Solution Key to *Jazz Piano – Improvisation Concepts* (including CD).

II-V-I Cadence in Major with 5 Note Spread Voicings

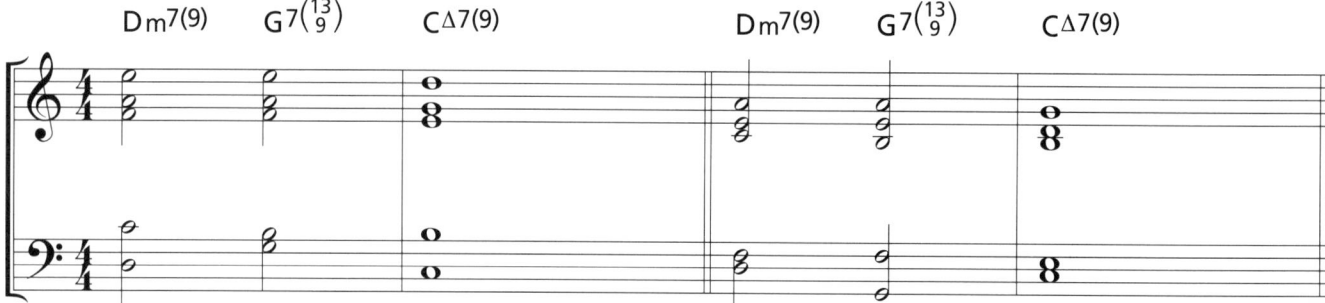

Exercise:

- Play both versions of the II-V-I cadence slowly in all keys using 5 note spread voicings.
- Then try to play these voicings along to the following CD tracks.

Check Boxes:

Tracks 12 & 13 ▸ II-V-I in Major – Circle of Fifths

Track 14 ▸ II-V-I in Major – Whole Tone Descending

Track 15 ▸ II-V-I in Major – Chromatically Descending

Track 16 ▸ II-V-I in Major – Chromatically Ascending

Exercise:

- Notate the 5 note spread voicings for the given chord sequences (the top note is given).
- Compare your version with the version in the Solution Key.
- Learn the chord sequence by heart and play it along to the CD.

Track 21 ▸ Progression 5

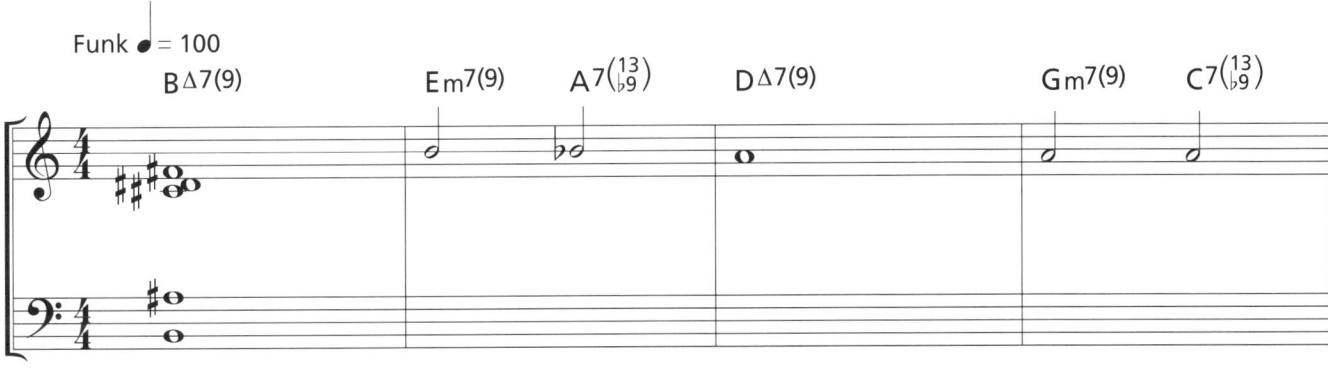

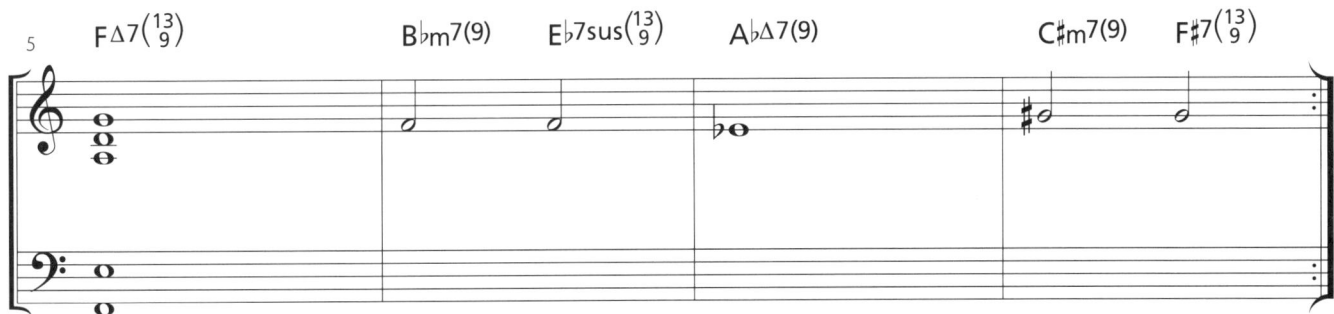

The American jazz pianist **Dave Brubeck** (born December 6th, 1920 in Concord/California) is one of the outstanding figures of Cool Jazz. He composed such standards as *In Your Own Sweet Way*. His style spans from "sophisticated" and "subtle" to "bombastic" and reveals both his classical training, which he received from his mother, as well as his improvisational skills. Brubeck never wanted to study by one method but wanted to create his own method – which led to never learning how to sight-read. When one of his professors found out that he could not read music he was almost expelled from college. Many of his tunes are written in odd meters. His long musical partner Paul Desmond (alto sax) wrote the tune that the Dave Brubeck Quartet is probably best known for – *Take Five* – in 5/4 time. Brubeck spent the bulk of his carrier experimenting with odd meters – *Pick Up Sticks* in 6/4, *Unsquare Dance* in 7/4, and *Blue Rondo a la Turk* in 9/8. These experiments started early at his parents' farm in a little town in the western part of the United States where he tried to play music in the odd meters that were generated by the different pieces of farm machinery.

© 2007 by AMA Musikverlag

Exercise:

- Notate the 5 note spread voicings for the given chord sequences.
- Compare your version with the version in the Solution Key.
- Learn the chord sequence by heart and play it along to the CD.

Track 22 ▸ Progression 6

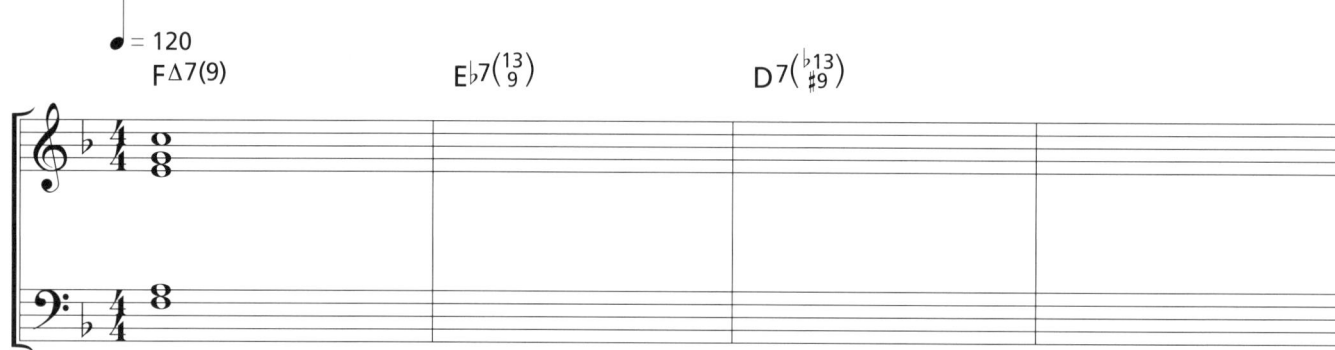
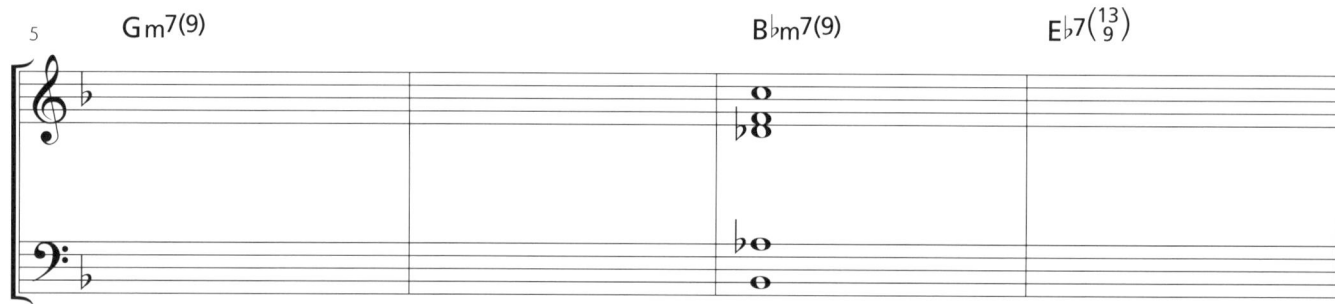
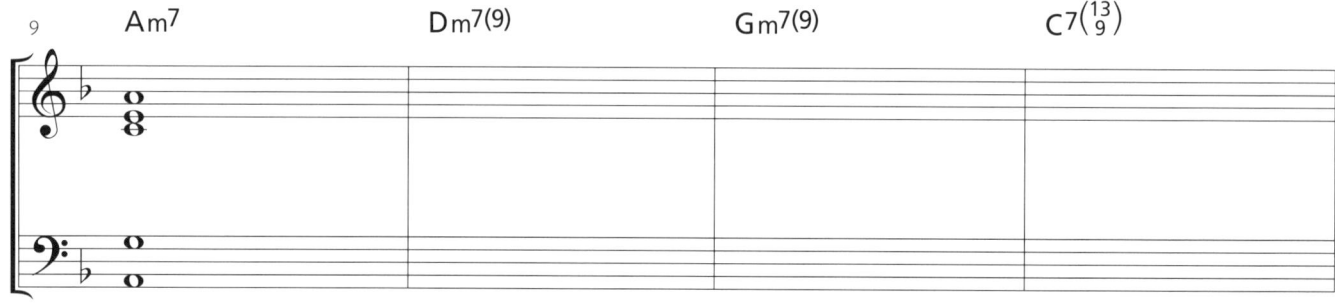
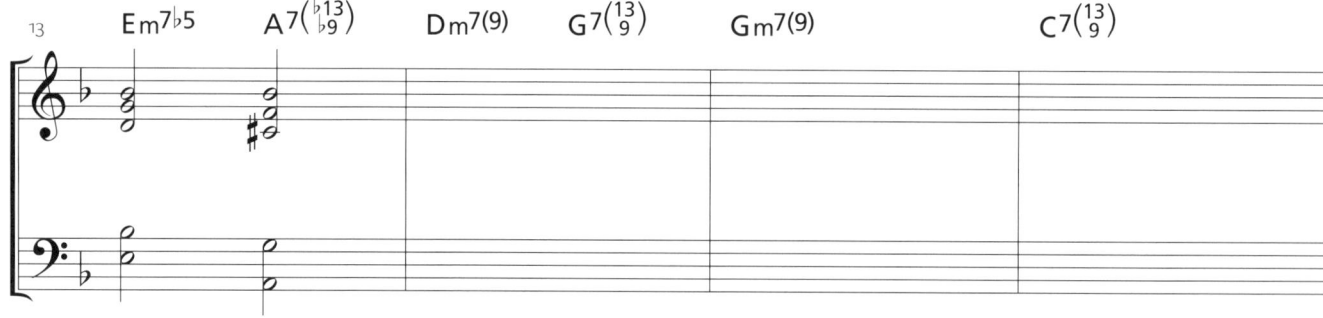

Summary: By now you should have learned the following:

- Diatonic chords built on all scale degrees in major
- II-V-I cadence with 3, 4, and 5 note spread voicings
- Practical use of the presented voicings

Chapter 3: Minor Diatonic

Diatonic Chords in Minor

Diatonic chords can be derived from a minor scale as well as from a major scale. There are different minor scales:

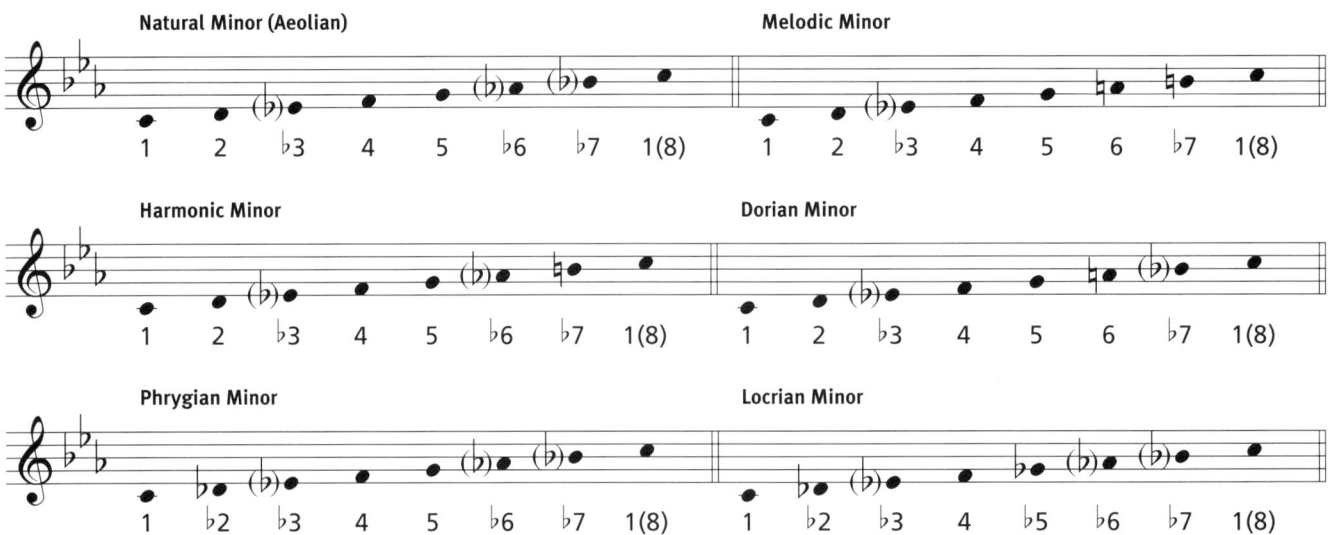

Modal Interchange

Many jazz standards, although written in a major key, use diatonic chords from a related minor scale. This substitution of diatonic chords is called modal interchange. Often the diatonic chords of the melodic minor scale are used.

Therefore it is recommended to know the diatonic chords of the melodic minor scale and to be able to play these using standard voicings.

Exercise:

- Play the diatonic chords of the **melodic minor** scale ascending and descending with the following voicings in all keys.
- Take as much time as you need and play, if necessary, out of tempo.
- Speak the degree of the scale and the chord name out loud before playing as demonstrated on track 7 of the CD.
- Keep track of your progress by using the check boxes again.

Root Position

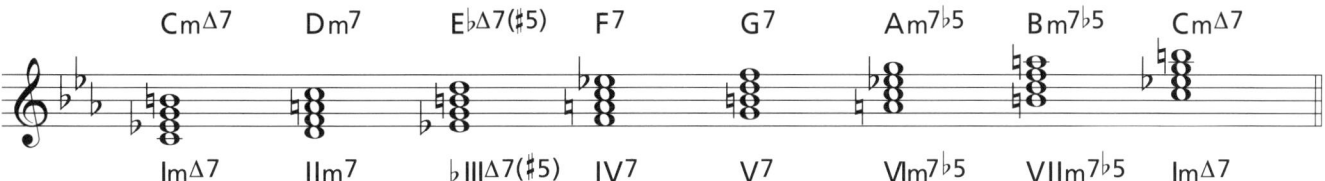

Check Boxes:

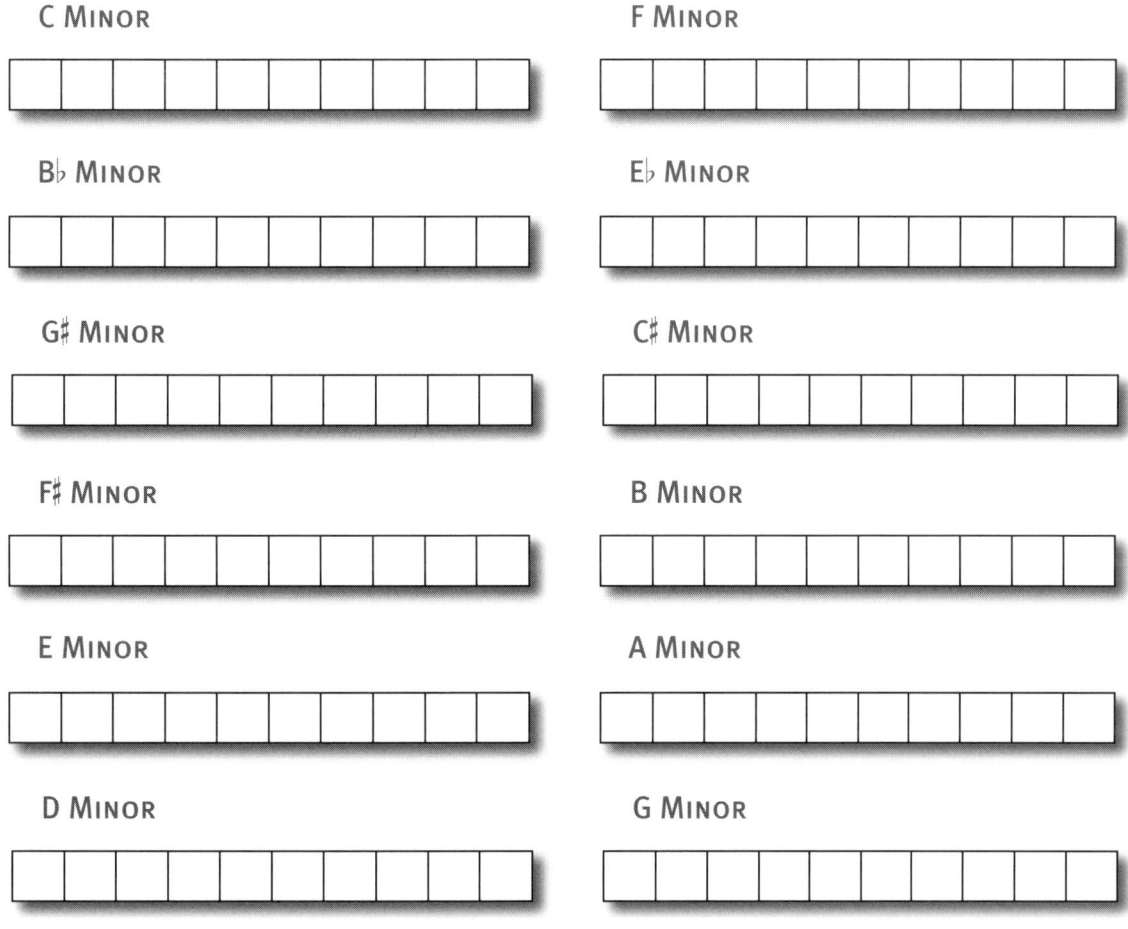

Exercise Tip:

Try to play the diatonic chords of the melodic minor scale as arpeggios as explained in the chapter *MAJOR DIATONIC*.

173 Voicing

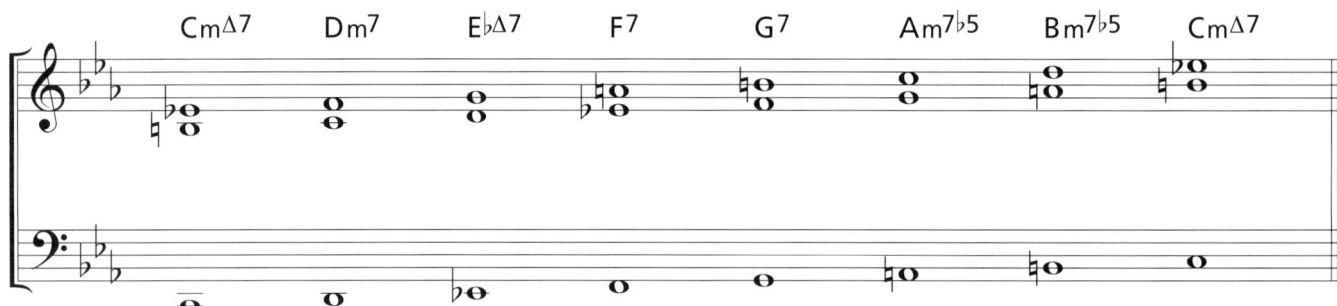

Check Boxes:

C Minor

F Minor

B♭ Minor

E♭ Minor

G♯ Minor

C♯ Minor

F♯ Minor

B Minor

E Minor

A Minor

D Minor

G Minor

137 Voicing

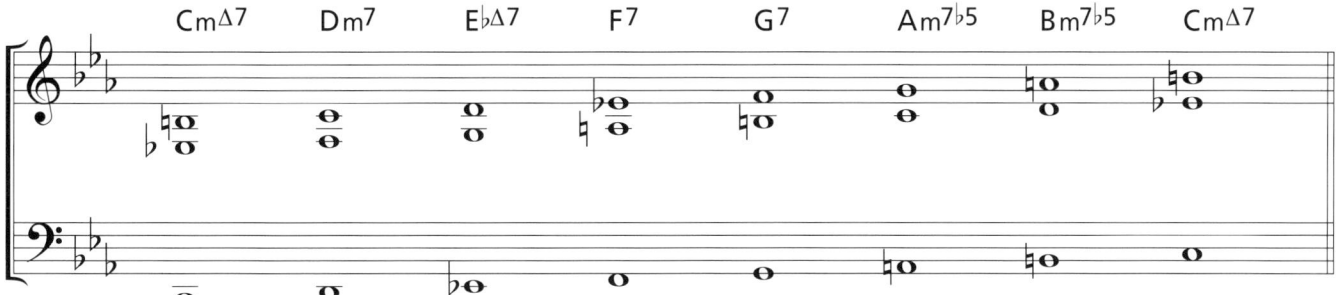

Check Boxes:

C Minor

F Minor

Bb Minor

Eb Minor

G# Minor

C# Minor

F# Minor

B Minor

E Minor

A Minor

D Minor

G Minor

1735 Voicing

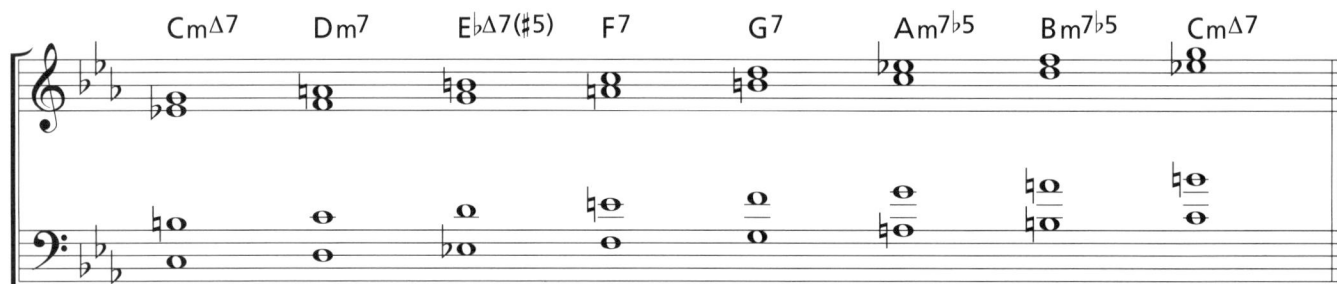

Check Boxes:

C Minor

F Minor

Bb Minor

Eb Minor

G# Minor

C# Minor

F# Minor

B Minor

E Minor

A Minor

D Minor

G Minor

1573 Voicing

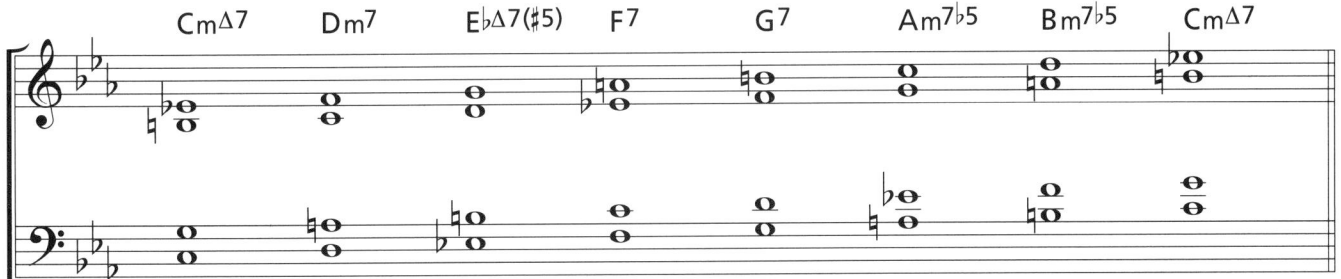

Check Boxes:

C Minor

F Minor

B♭ Minor

E♭ Minor

G♯ Minor

C♯ Minor

F♯ Minor

B Minor

E Minor

A Minor

D Minor

G Minor

II-V-I Cadence in Minor

The II-V-I cadence is often used in minor keys as well.

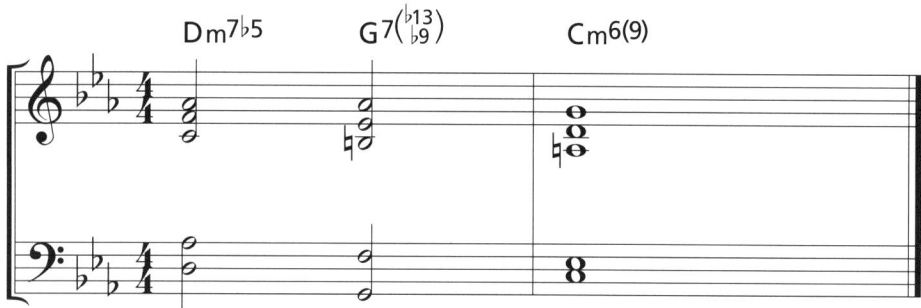

However, the seventh chords built on the second and fifth degrees are derived from the harmonic minor scale.

Diatonic chords in harmonic minor:

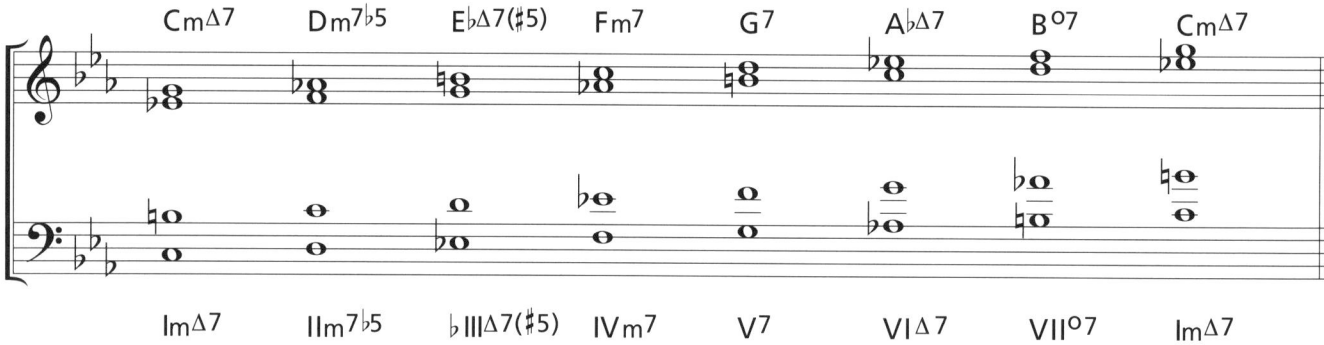

> **Tip:** It is common to use more than only one minor scale in a minor tune. It is also common to see both the major and minor seventh (in the key of C minor: B and B♭) in one bar. This ambivalence often contributes to the special feel of a composition in a minor key. Do not feel disturbed by the many possible variations.

II-V-I Cadence in Minor with 3 Note Spread Voicings

As already discussed in the *Major Diatonic* chapter, the II-V-I cadence should also be practiced with different spread voicings in minor keys. The chord built on the second degree can appear in four different voicings to emphasize its half-diminished character.

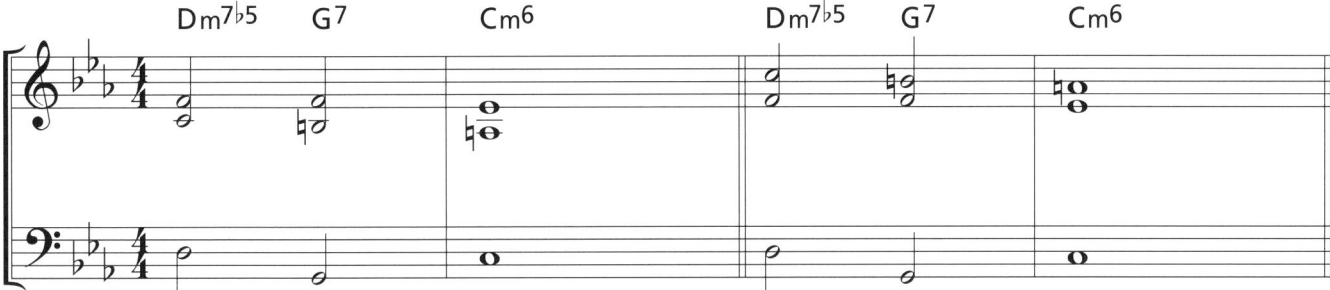

Exercise:

- Practice the four versions of the II-V-I cadence with 3 note spread voicings very slowly in all keys.
- Again, speak the chord name out loud before playing the chord.
- Then, try to play the voicings along to the following CD tracks.

Jazz Piano – Voicing Concepts

Tracks 23 & 24 ▸ II-V-I in Minor – Circle of Fifths

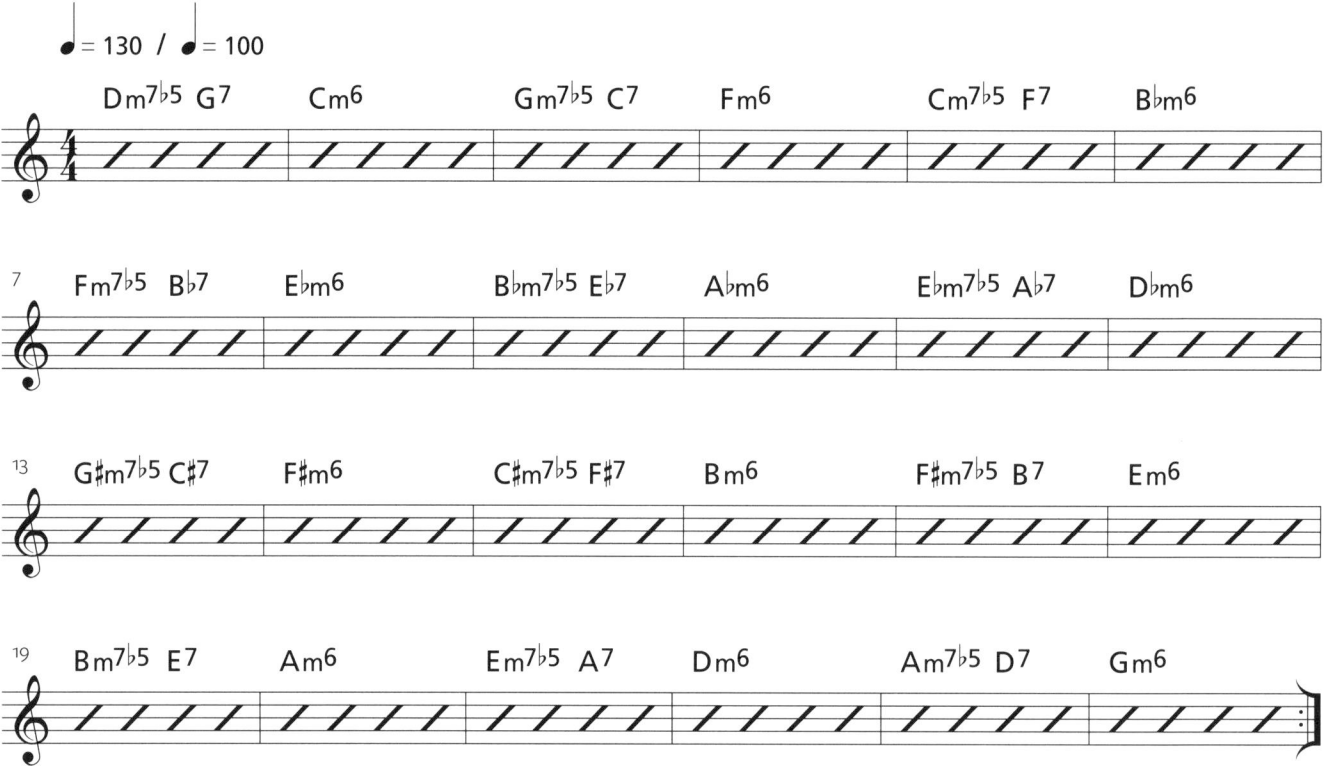

Note: On track 23, the three chords of the II-V-I cadence occur over the span of 8 bars. On track 24 the chords occur over the span of 4 bars!

Track 25 ▸ II-V-I in Minor – Whole Tone Descending 1

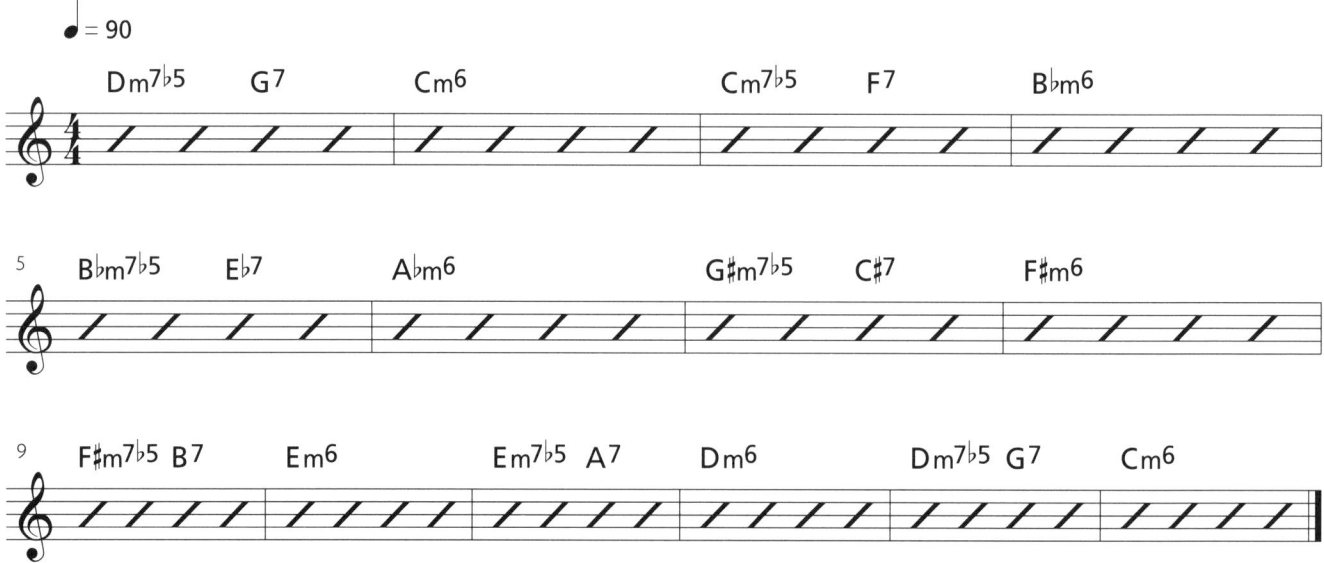

Track 26 ▶ II-V-I in Minor – Whole Tone Descending 2

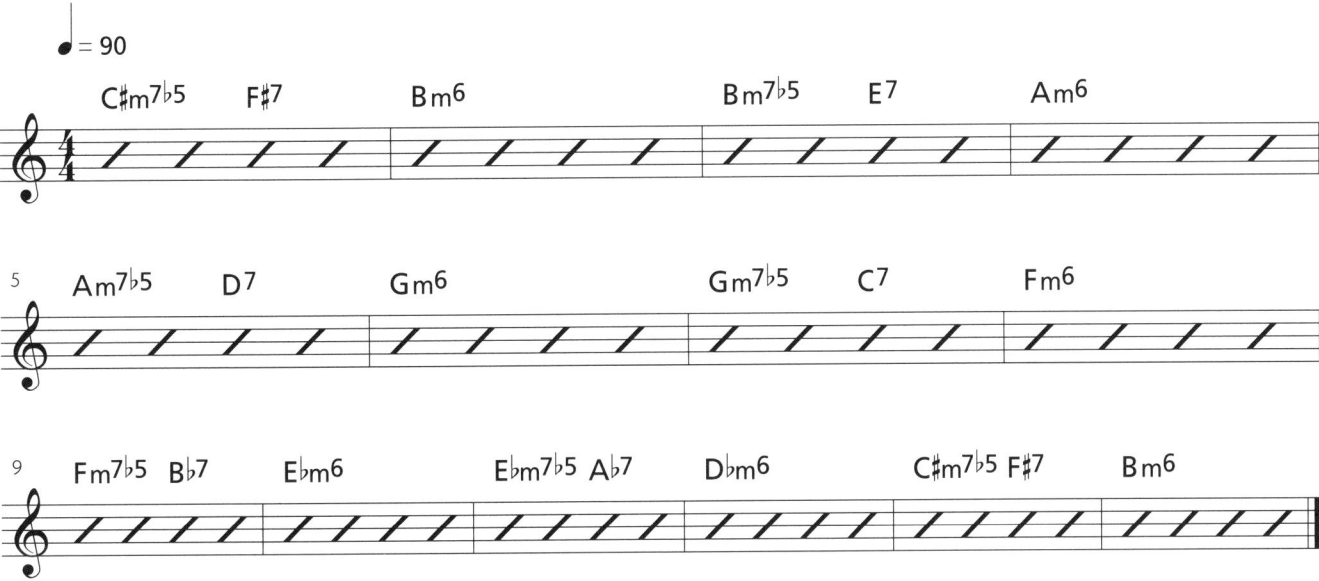

Track 27 ▶ II-V-I in Minor – Chromatically Descending

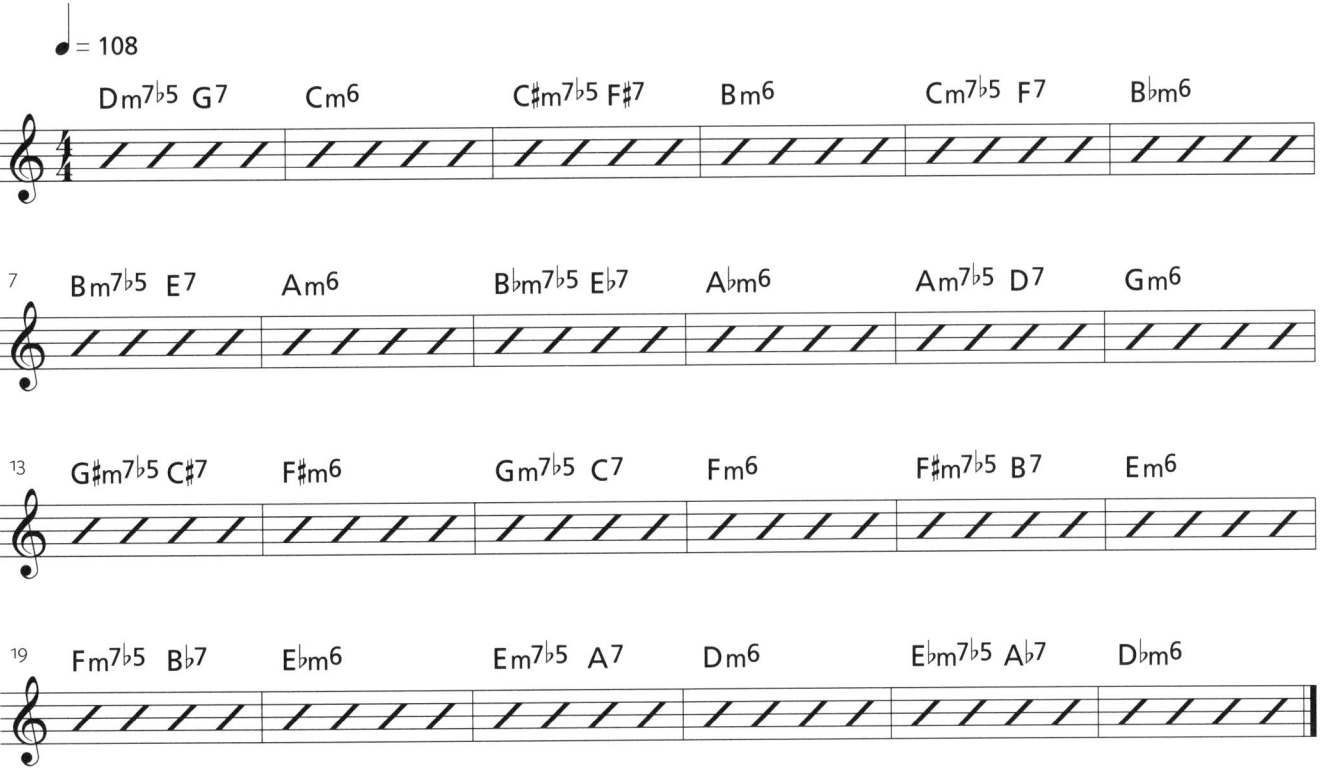

Track 28 ▸ II-V-I in Minor – Chromatically Ascending

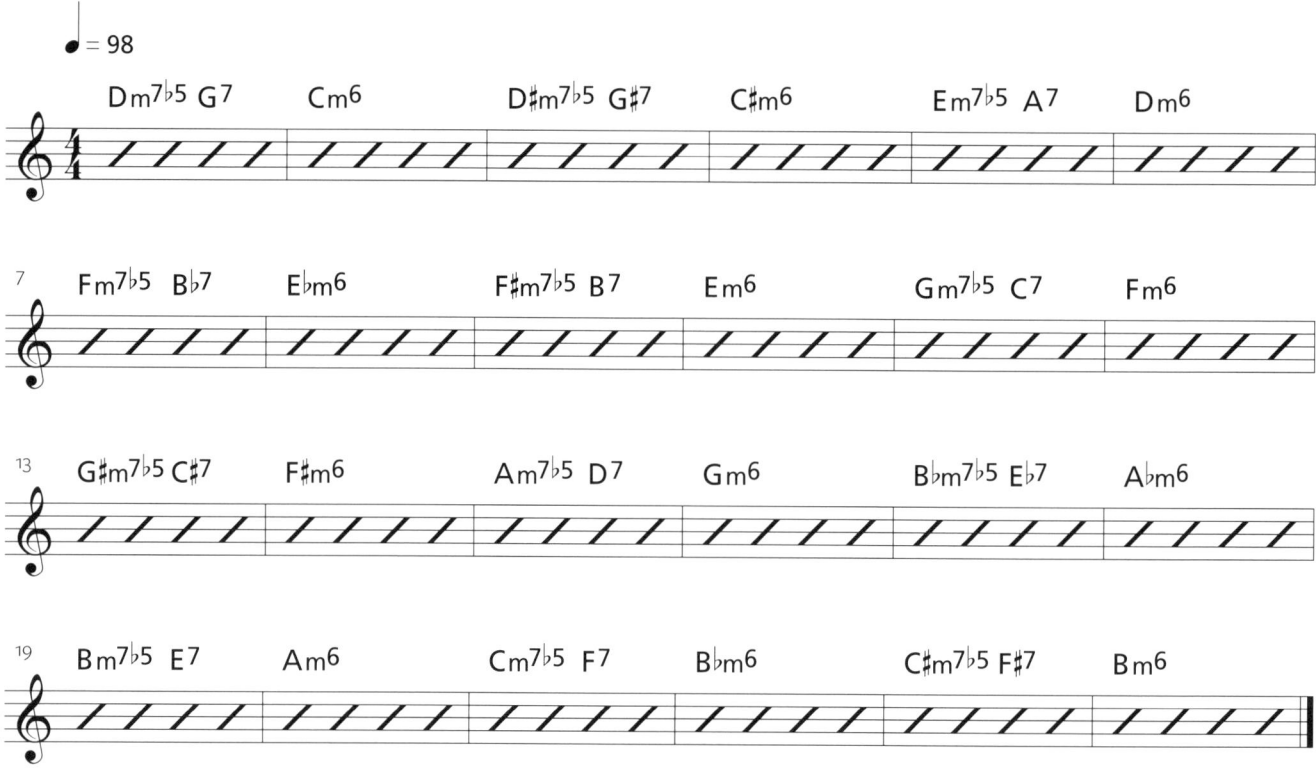

II-V-I Cadence in Minor with 3 Note Spread Voicings

Check Boxes:

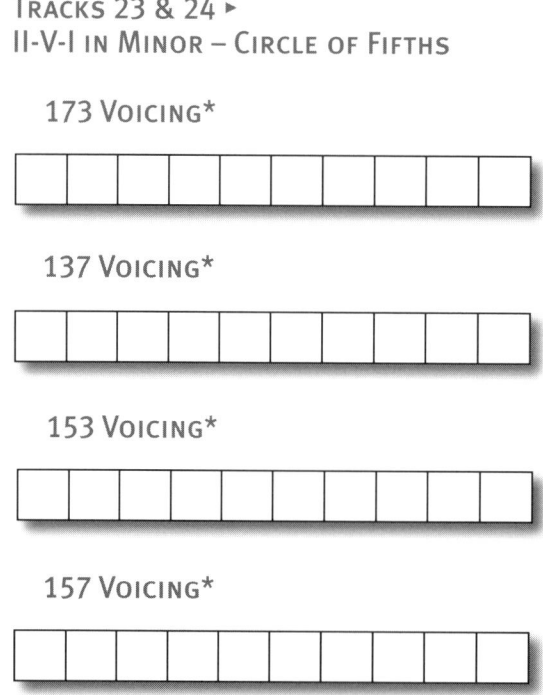

(*) Named after the chord type built on the second degree of the scale (m7/♭5).

Minor diatonic

Track 25 ▶
II-V-I in Minor – Whole Tone Descending 1

173 Voicing

137 Voicing

153 Voicing

157 Voicing

Track 27 ▶
II-V-I in Minor – Chromatically Descending

173 Voicing

137 Voicing

153 Voicing

157 Voicing

Track 26 ▶
II-V-I in Minor – Whole Tone Descending 2

173 Voicing

137 Voicing

153 Voicing

157 Voicing

Track 28 ▶
II-V-I in Minor – Chromatically Ascending

173 Voicing

137 Voicing

153 Voicing

157 Voicing

© 2007 by AMA Musikverlag

Exercise:

- Notate 3 note spread voicings for the given chords.
- Pay attention to smooth voice leading between the chords.
- Compare your version with the version in the Solution Key.
- Learn the chords by heart and play them along to the CD.

Track 29 ▸ Progression 7

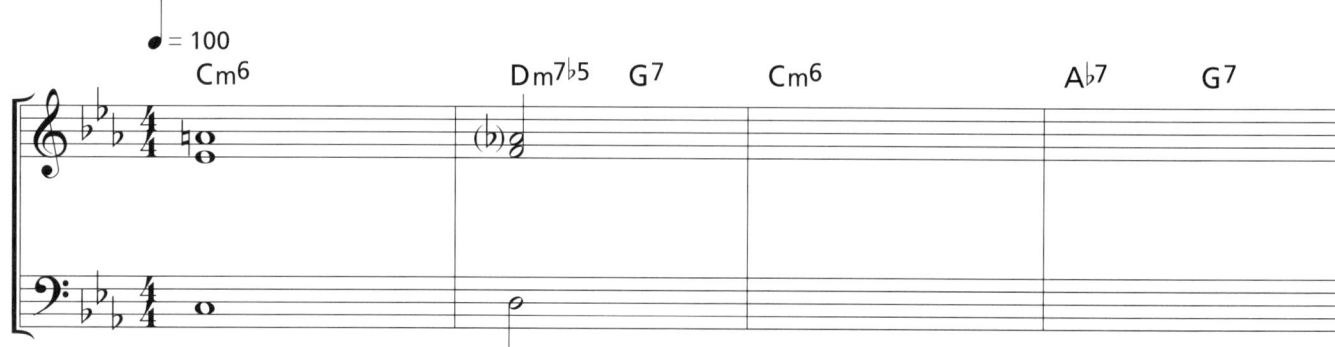

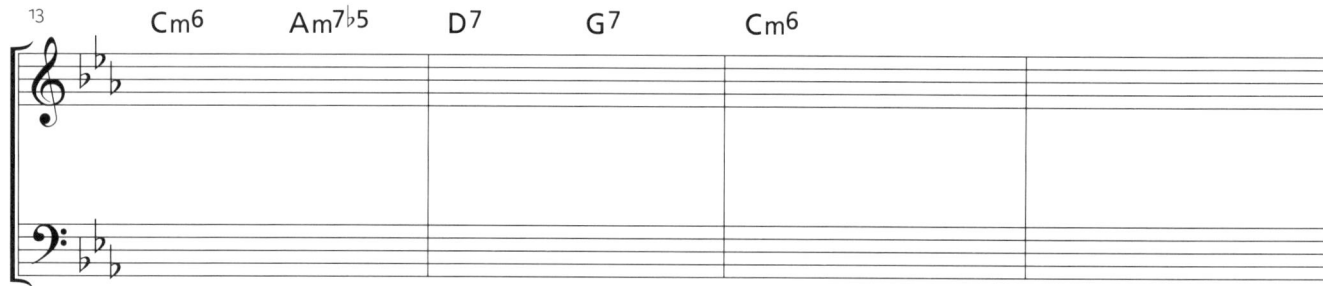

Minor diatonic

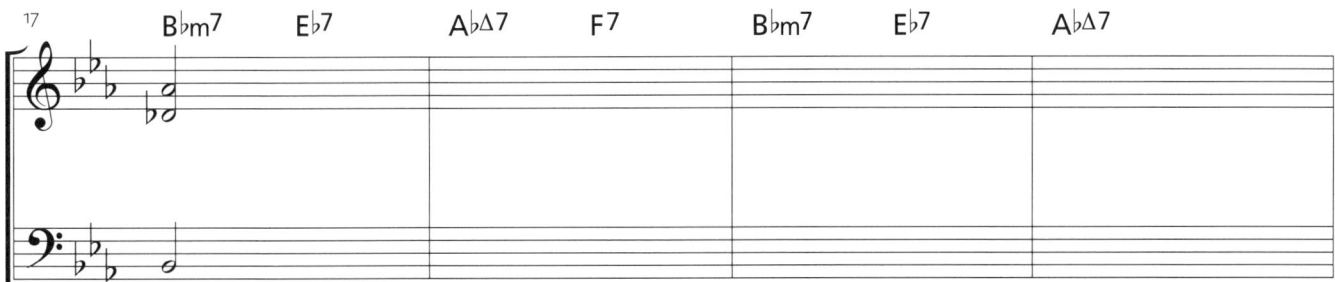
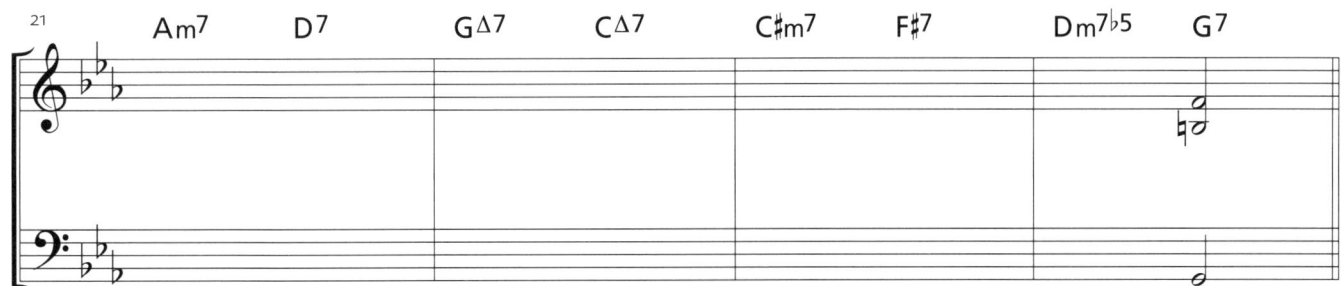
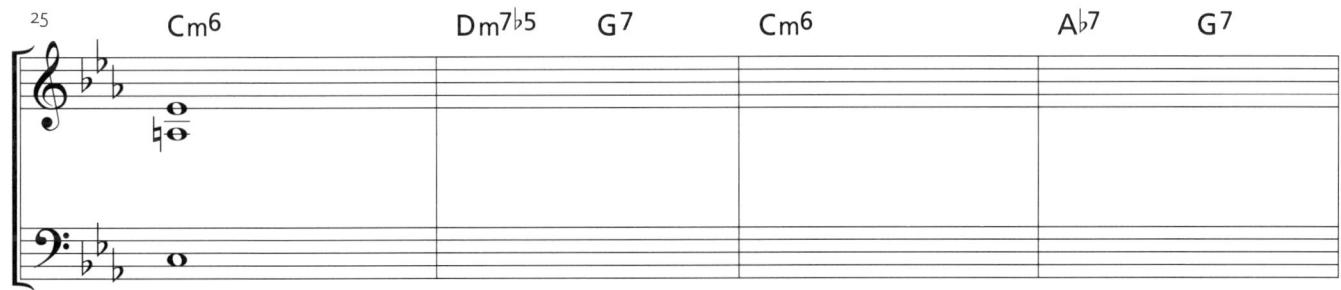
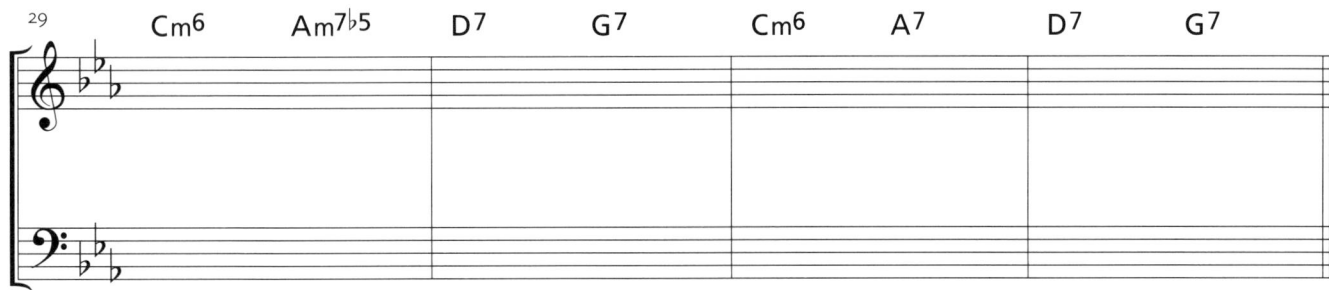

Exercise:

- Notate 3 note spread voicings for the given chords.
- Pay attention to smooth voice leading between the chords.
- Compare your version with the version in the Solution Key.
- Learn the chords by heart and play them along to the CD.

Track 30 ▸ Progression 8

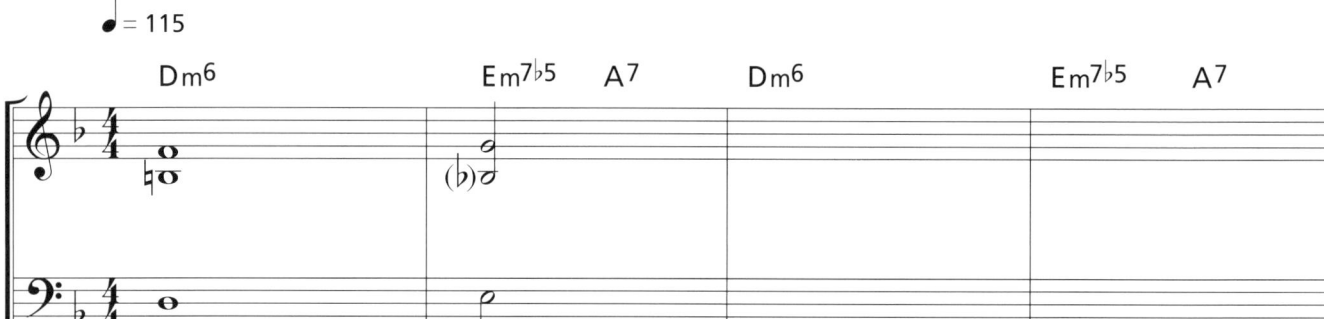

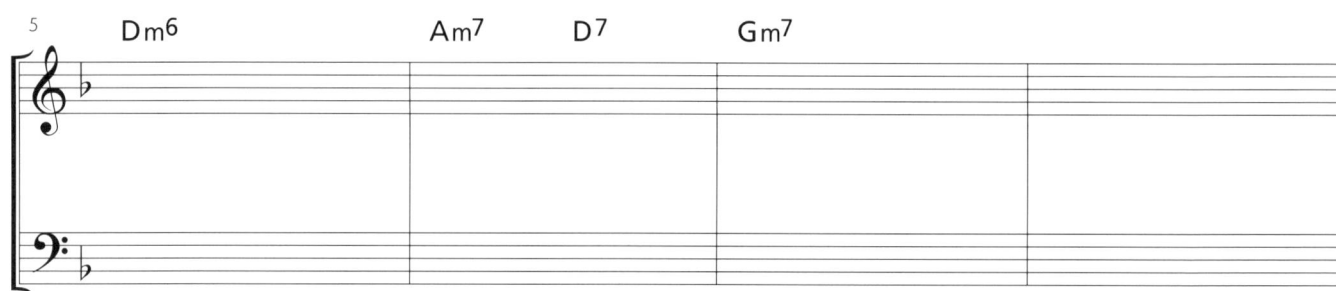

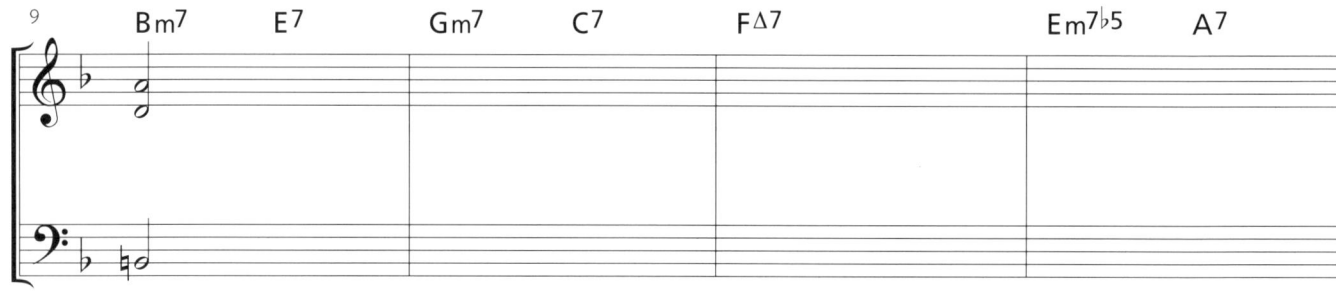

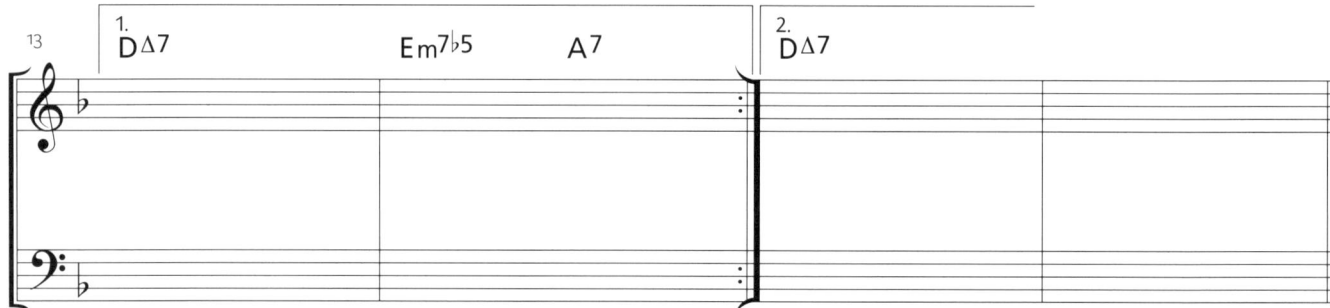

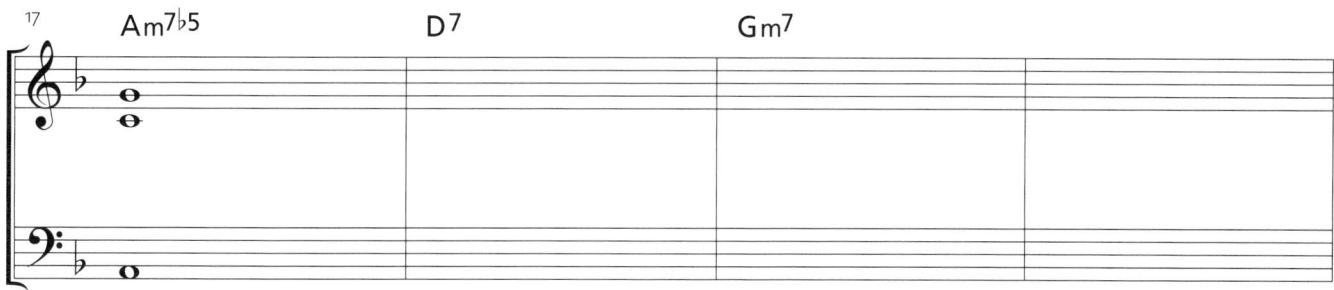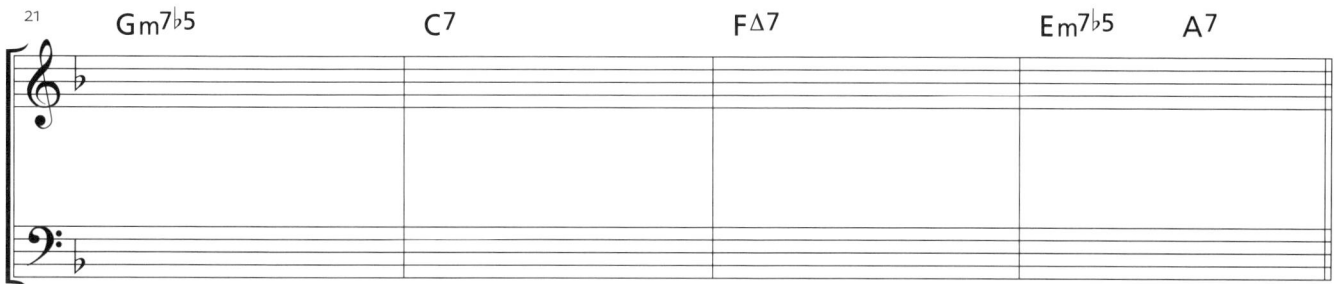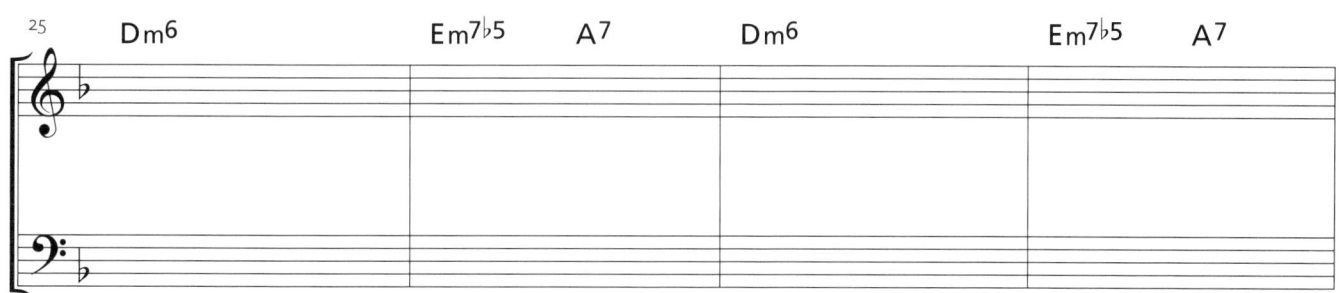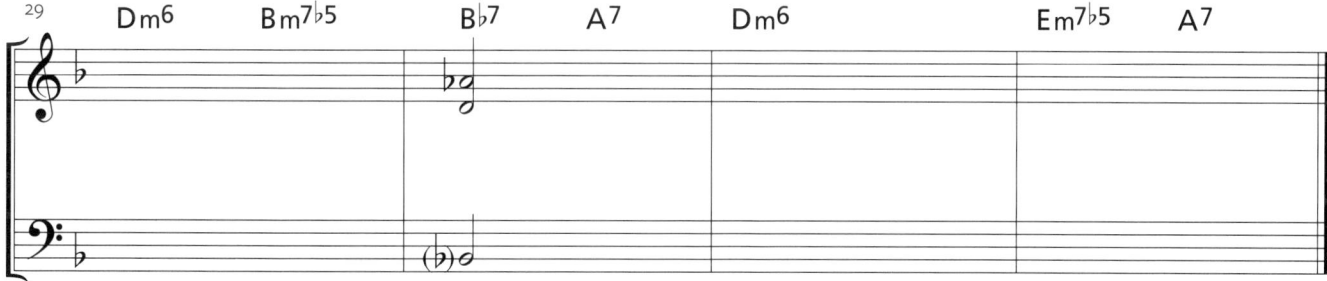

Jazz Piano – Voicing Concepts

II-V-I Cadence in Minor with 4 Note Spread Voicings

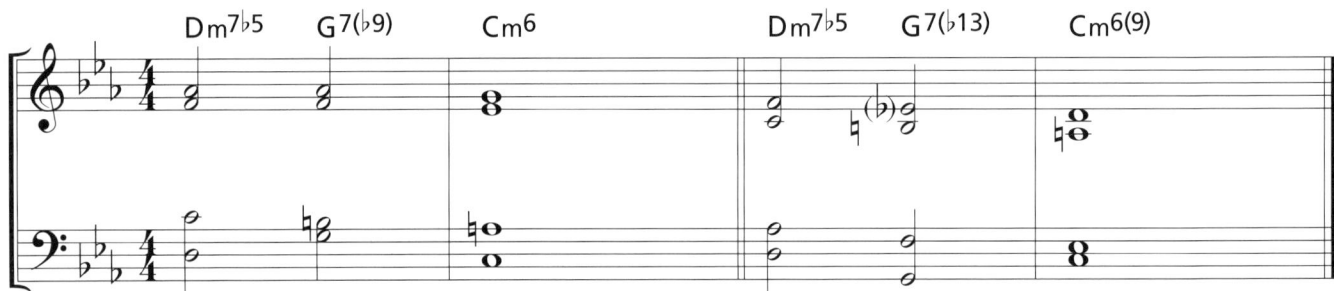

Exercise:

- Practice the II-V-I cadence with 4 note spread voicings slowly in all keys and later along to the practice tracks on the CD.

Check Boxes:

Tracks 23 & 24 ▸
II-V-I in Minor – Circle of Fifths

1735 Voicing*

1537 Voicing*

Track 25 ▸
II-V-I in Minor – Whole Tone Descending 1

1735 Voicing

1573 Voicing

Track 26 ▸
II-V-I in Minor – Whole Tone Descending 2

1735 Voicing

1573 Voicing

Track 27 ▸
II-V-I in Minor – Chromatically Descending

1735 Voicing

1573 Voicing

Track 28 ▸
II-V-I in Minor – Chromatically Ascending

1735 Voicing

1573 Voicing

(*) Named after the chord type built on the second degree of the scale (m7/♭5).

Exercise:

- Notate 4 note spread voicings for the given chords.
- Pay attention to smooth voice leading between the chords.
- Compare your version with the version in the Solution Key.
- Learn the chords by heart and play them along to the CD.

Track 31 ▸ Progression 9

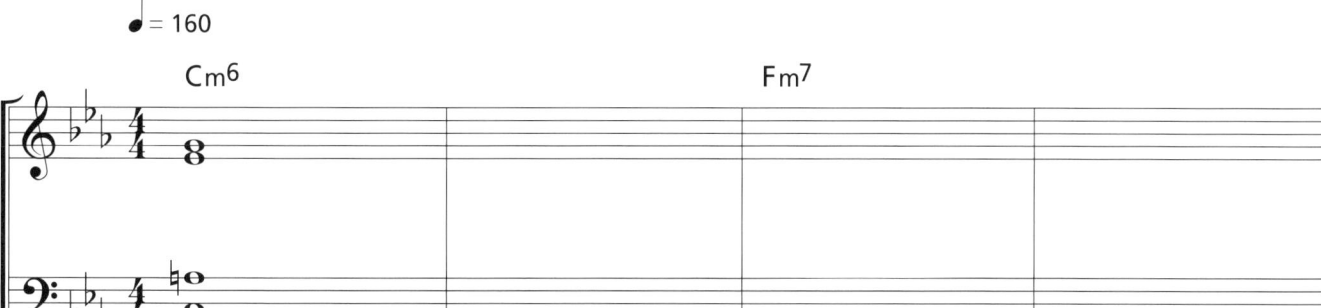

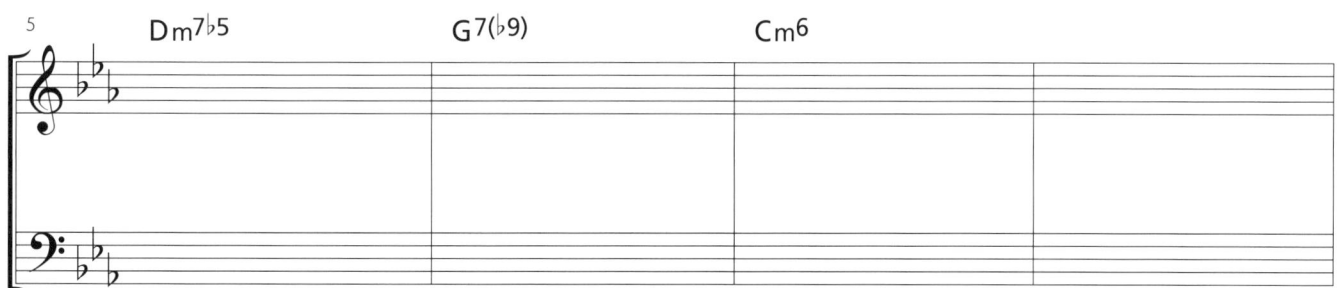

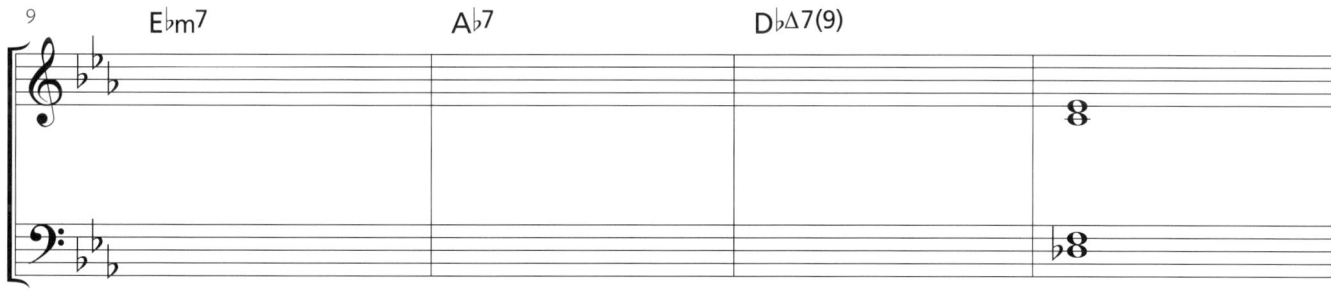

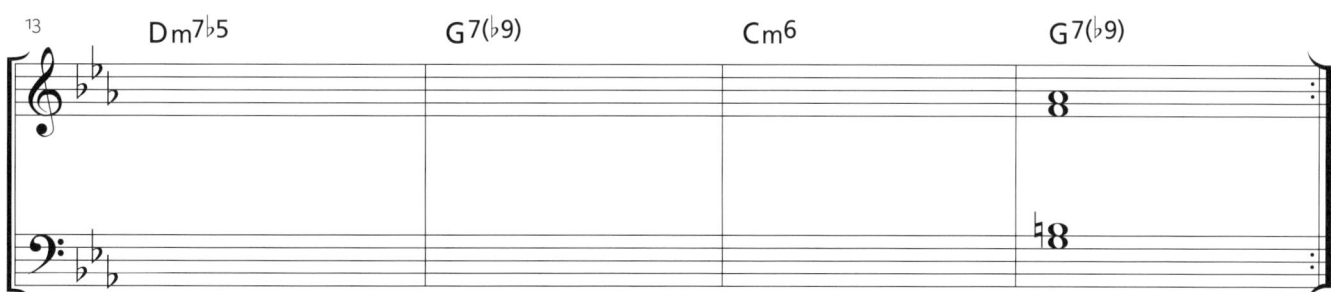

Jazz Piano – Voicing Concepts

Exercise:

- Notate 4 note spread voicings for the given chords.
- Pay attention to smooth voice leading between the chords.
- Compare your version with the version in the Solution Key.
- Learn the chords by heart and play them along to the CD.

Track 32 ▸ Progression 10

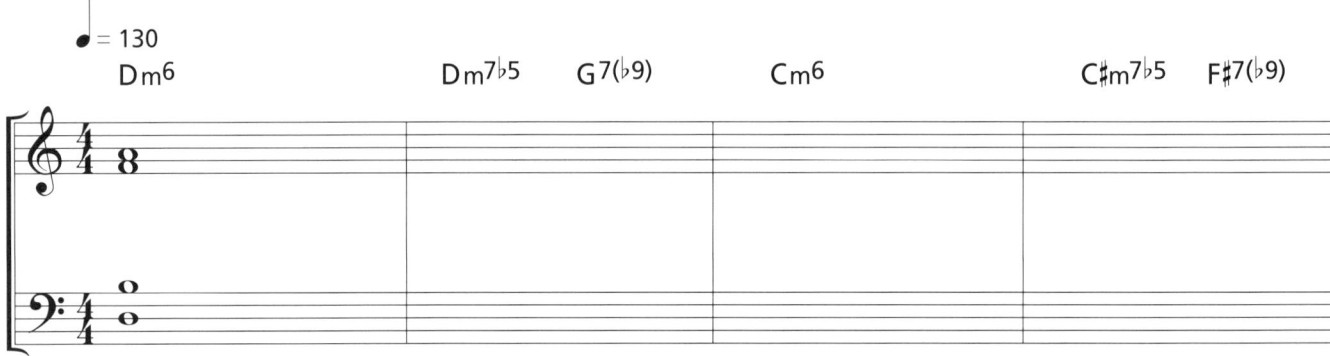

II-V-I Cadence in Minor with 5 Note Spread Voicings

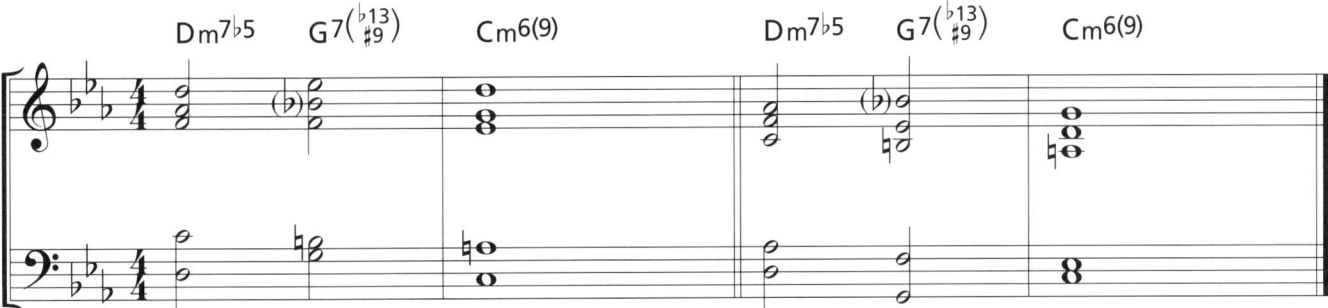

Alternatively, the minor II-V-I cadence can be played like this:

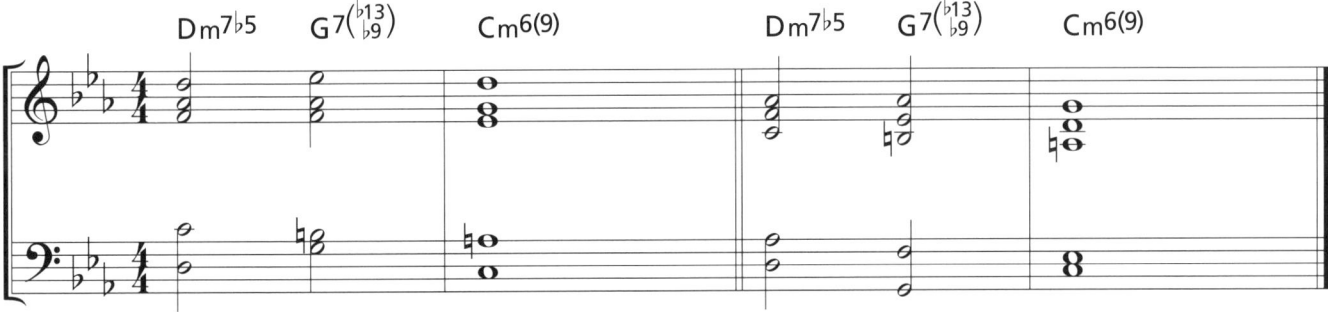

Tip: The 5 note spread voicing for m7/♭5 employs a doubled note here (root note or diminished fifth). This doubled note can later be replaced by the ninth or eleventh.
Half-diminished chords should be extended with care as a voicing might sound strange and stick out of the chord progression.

Example

(from *Jazz Piano – Solo Concepts*, "Black Nocturne", p. 22)

Jazz Piano – Voicing Concepts

Exercise:

- Play the II-V-I cadence with 5 note spread voicings slowly through all keys and then along to the corresponding practice tracks on the CD.
- Measure your progress using the check boxes.

II-V-I Cadence in Minor with 5 Note Spread Voicings

Check Boxes:

Tracks 23 & 24 ▸
II-V-I in Minor – Circle of Fifths

17351 Voicing*

15735 Voicing*

Track 25 ▸
II-V-I in Minor – Whole Tone Descending 1

17351 Voicing

15735 Voicing

Track 26 ▸
II-V-I in Minor – Whole Tone Descending 2

17351 Voicing

15735 Voicing

Track 27 ▸
II-V-I in Minor – Chromatically Descending

17351 Voicing

15735 Voicing

Track 28 ▸
II-V-I in Minor – Chromatically Ascending

17351 Voicing

15735 Voicing

(*) Named after the chord type built on the second degree of the scale (m7/♭5).

MINOR DIATONIC

EXERCISE:

- Notate 5 note spread voicings for the given chords.
- Compare your version with the version in the Solution Key.
- Learn the chords by heart and play them along with the CD.

TRACK 33 ▸ PROGRESSION 11

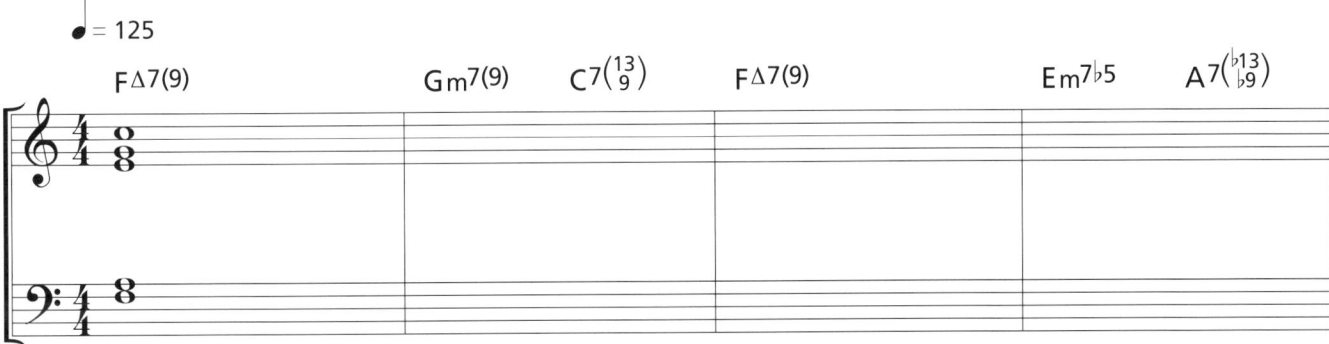

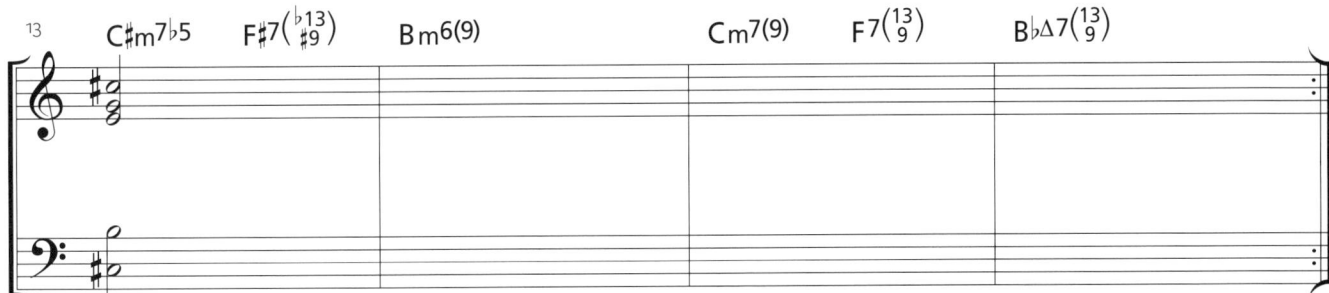

© 2007 by AMA Musikverlag

EXERCISE:

- Notate 5 note spread voicings for the given chords. The highest note of the voicing is supplied for some chords.
- Pay attention to smooth voice leading between the chords.
- Compare your version with the version in the Solution Key.
- Learn the chords by heart and then play along to the CD.

Track 34 – Progression 12

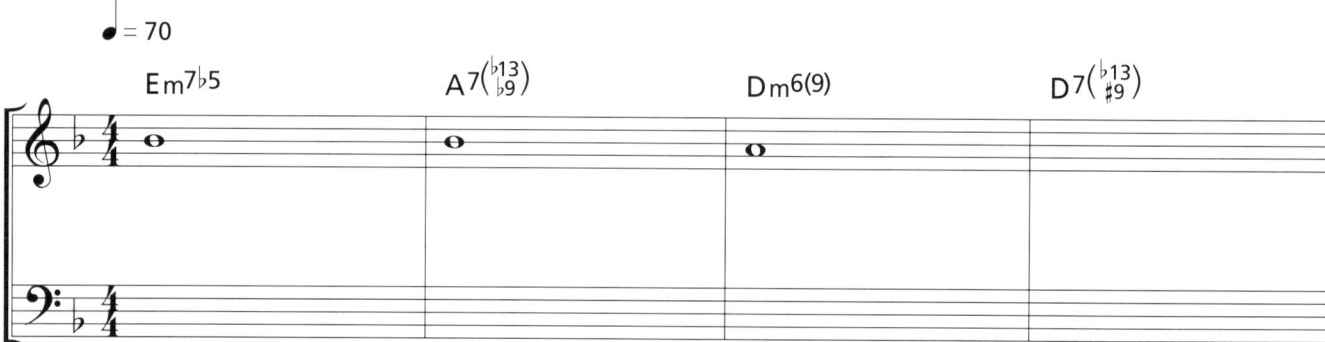

Minor diatonic

17 Em7♭5 | A7(♭13/♭9) | Dm6(9) | D7(♭13/♯9)

21 Gm7(9) | C7(13/9) | F△7(9) | A7(♭13/♭9)

25 Dm7(9) | Gm7(9) | B♭7(♯11/9) | A7(♭13/♭9)

29 Dm6(9) Bm7♭5 | B♭7(13) A7(♭13/♯9) | Dm6(9) |

> **Tip:** The following rule should be applied to the extension of dominant chords: if a dominant chord resolves into a **major chord** a fifth down, non-altered extensions are used (9 and/or 13). Resolving to a **minor chord**, altered chord-extensions are used (♭9, ♯9 and/or ♭13).

Summary: By now you should have learned the following:

- Diatonic chords on all degrees of the scale in melodic minor
- II-V-I cadence in minor with 3, 4 and 5 note spread voicings
- Practical application of the presented voicings

© 2007 by AMA Musikverlag

Chapter 4: Left Hand Voicings

In order to be able to play a melody or a solo accompaniment at the same time, there are several voicings that can be played with the left hand. These voicings are again built according to the voicing pyramid.

All examples refer to a C7 chord:

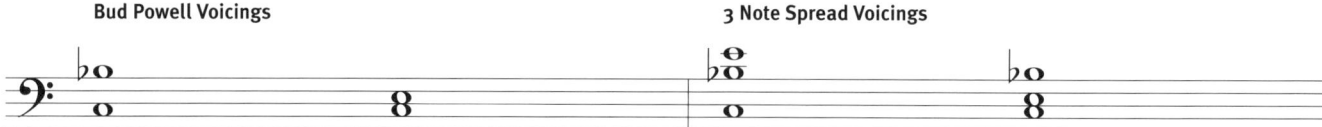

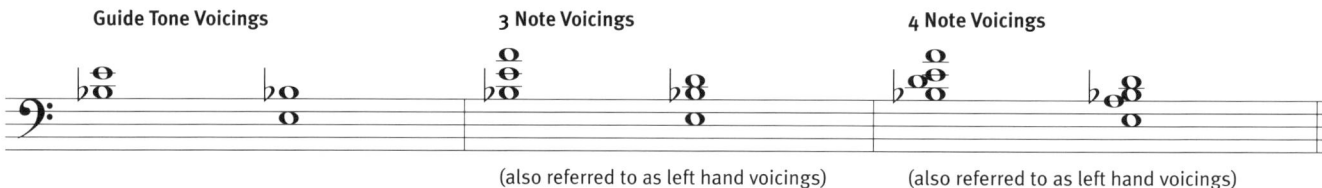

(also referred to as left hand voicings)   (also referred to as left hand voicings)

Bud Powell Voicings

This voicing, named after the jazz pianist Bud Powell (see *Jazz Piano – Solo Concepts*, p. 36), is composed of the root note and a guide tone. Being very simple in its structure, the voicing still supplies the sound character of the whole chord. The bass movement of a harmonic progression is supplied by the permanent presence of the root note as the lowest note.
The basic design of the Bud Powell voicing makes it easy to play and it is well suited for sight-reading unfamiliar jazz standards. The low interval limits for spread voicings apply again (see the chapter *Basics*).

> **Tip:** You already know the Bud Powell voicings: a 4 note spread voicing without the right hand!

II-V-I Major Cadence Using Bud Powell Voicings

EXERCISE:

- Play both versions of the II-V-I cadence using Bud Powell voicings slowly in all keys.
- Then, try to play the voicings along to the following CD tracks.
- Try to improvise along with the right hand. Use licks from *Jazz Piano – Improvisation Concepts*, p. 58 ff.

CHECK BOXES:

TRACKS 12 & 13 ▸
II-V-I in Major – Circle of Fifths

17 Voicing

13 Voicing

TRACK 15 ▸
II-V-I in Major – Chromatically Descending

17 Voicing

13 Voicing

TRACK 14 ▸
II-V-I in Major – Whole Tone Descending

17 Voicing

13 Voicing

TRACK 16 ▸
II-V-I in Major – Chromatically Ascending

17 Voicing

13 Voicing

© 2007 by AMA Musikverlag

II-V-I Minor Cadence Using Bud Powell Voicings

EXERCISE:

- Play the four versions of the II-V-I cadence using Bud Powell voicings slowly in all keys.
- Then, try to play the voicings along to the following CD tracks.

CHECK BOXES:

TRACKS 23 & 24 ▶
II-V-I IN MINOR – CIRCLE OF FIFTHS

17 VOICING

15 VOICING – VERSION 1

13 VOICING

15 VOICING – VERSION 2

TRACK 25 ▶
II-V-I IN MINOR – WHOLE TONE DESCENDING 1

17 VOICING

13 VOICING

15 VOICING – VERSION 1

15 VOICING – VERSION 2

TRACK 26 ▶
II-V-I IN MINOR – WHOLE TONE DESCENDING 2

17 VOICING

13 VOICING

15 VOICING – VERSION 1

15 VOICING – VERSION 2

Left Hand Voicings

TRACK 27 ▸
II-V-I IN MINOR – CHROMATICALLY DESCENDING

17 VOICING

13 VOICING

15 VOICING – VERSION 1

15 VOICING – VERSION 2

TRACK 28 ▸
II-V-I IN MINOR – CHROMATICALLY ASCENDING

17 VOICING

13 VOICING

15 VOICING – VERSION 1

15 VOICING – VERSION 2

EXERCISE:

- Notate Bud Powell voicings for the given chord progressions.
- Again, pay attention to smooth voice leading.
- Compare your version with the version in the Solution Key.
- Learn the progression by heart and play it along to the CD.

TRACK 35 ▸ PROGRESSION 13

© 2007 by AMA Musikverlag

77

EXERCISE:

- Notate Bud Powell voicings for the given chord progressions.
- Compare your version with the version in the Solution Key.
- Learn the progression by heart and play it along to the CD.

Track 36 ▸ Progression 14

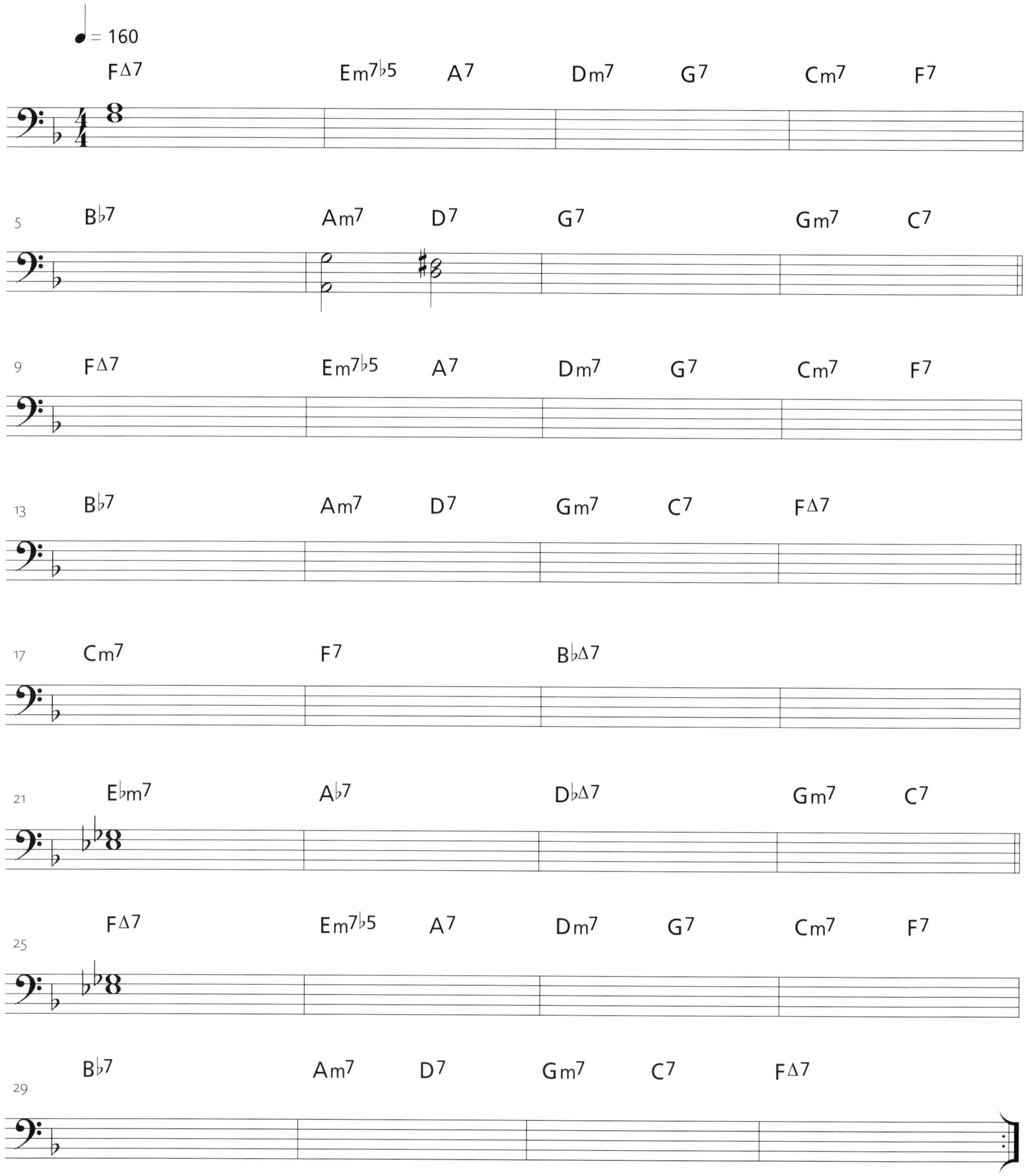

♩ = 160

| FΔ7 | Em7♭5 A7 | Dm7 G7 | Cm7 F7 |

| B♭7 | Am7 D7 | G7 | Gm7 C7 |

| FΔ7 | Em7♭5 A7 | Dm7 G7 | Cm7 F7 |

| B♭7 | Am7 D7 | Gm7 C7 | FΔ7 |

| Cm7 | F7 | B♭Δ7 | |

| E♭m7 | A♭7 | D♭Δ7 | Gm7 C7 |

| FΔ7 | Em7♭5 A7 | Dm7 G7 | Cm7 F7 |

| B♭7 | Am7 D7 | Gm7 C7 | FΔ7 |

Earl Kenneth Father *(Fatha)* Hines (* December 28, 1903, † April 22, 1983) started playing cornet first but later changed to piano. He moved from Pittsburgh to Chicago in 1924. Here he met Louis Armstrong whom he admired deeply and recorded two milestones of jazz history with him in 1928: *West End Blues* and *Weather Bird*. As a bandleader he signed-on some of the leading jazz musicians of the 1930s. In the early 1940s, a still unknown Dizzy Gillespie, Charlie Parker and Billy Eckstine played in his band and each would earn a world renowned reputation later. This gave Hines' band the reputation of being the cradle of Bebop. Hines played the so-called trumpet style, reproducing Armstrong's lines on the piano. This made him one of the precursors of the swing piano style that was later perfected by Teddy Wilson. Earl Hines was a big influence on the development of jazz piano and is considered one of the best players of all time. His style is an important link between traditional and modern jazz.

Tip: Try to learn a new jazz standard each week and play it by heart!

3 Note Spread Voicings for the Left Hand

3 note spread voicings are the "bread and butter" of solo jazz piano playing. These voicings supply the full harmonic progression only using the left hand. The right hand can be used for themes or improvisation. All great jazz pianists use these voicings.

One distinguishes between "big" (173) and "small" (137) 3 note spread voicings.

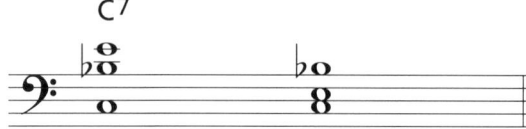

Tip: Pianists with small hands cannot play the 173 voicing as one chord. Play the root note already an eighth note before the actual chord change and the two guide-notes on beat 1. This playing aid should only be used for voicings that, in fact, cannot be played with small hands. All others should always be played as one chord.

Do not practice these voicings longer than 20 minutes at a time as your left hand might cramp up.

II-V-I Cadence in Major Using 3 Note Spread Voicings

EXERCISE:

- Play both versions of the II-V-I cadence using 3 note spread voicings slowly in all keys.
- Then, try to play these voicings along to the following CD tracks.

Check Boxes:

Tracks 12 & 13 ▶
II-V-I in Major – Circle of Fifths

173 Voicing

137 Voicing

Track 14 ▶
II-V-I in Major – Whole Tone Descending

173 Voicing

137 Voicing

Track 15 ▶
II-V-I in Major – Chromatically Descending

173 Voicing

137 Voicing

Track 16 ▶
II-V-I in Major – Chromatically Ascending

173 Voicing

137 Voicing

Jazz Piano – Voicing Concepts

II-V-I Cadence in Minor Using 3 Note Spread Voicings

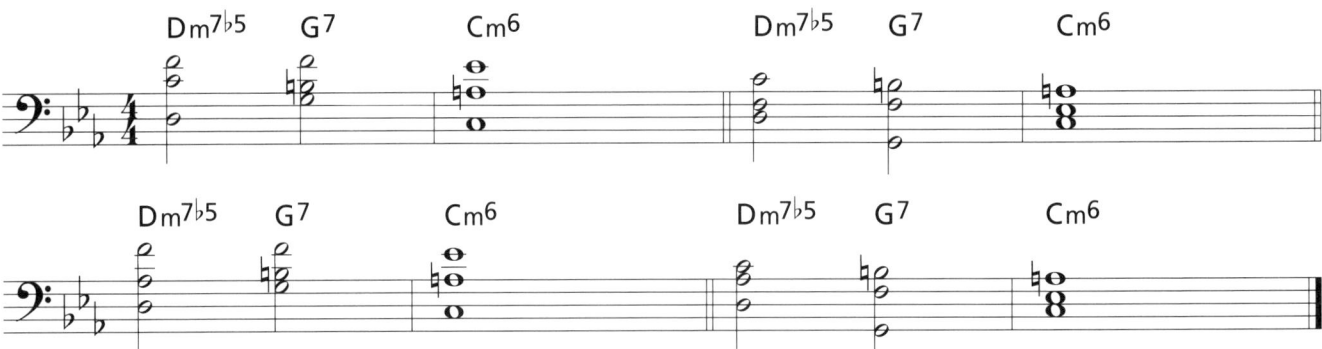

EXERCISE:

- Play the four versions of the II-V-I cadence using 3 note spread voicings very slowly in all keys.
- Again, say the chord name out loud before playing the chord.
- Then, try to play the voicings along to the following CD tracks.

CHECK BOXES:

TRACKS 23 & 24 ▶
II-V-I in Minor – Circle of Fifths

173 Voicing

153 Voicing-Version

137 Voicing

157 Voicing-Version

TRACK 25 ▶
II-V-I in Minor – Whole Tone Descending 1

173 Voicing

137 Voicing

153 Voicing-Version

157 Voicing-Version

TRACK 26 ▶
II-V-I in Minor – Whole Tone Descending 2

173 Voicing

137 Voicing

153 Voicing-Version

157 Voicing-Version

Left Hand Voicings

Track 27 ▸
II-V-I in Minor – Chromatically Descending

173 Voicing

137 Voicing

153 Voicing-Version

157 Voicing-Version

Track 28 ▸
II-V-I in Minor – Chromatically Ascending

173 Voicing

137 Voicing

153 Voicing-Version

157 Voicing-Version

EXERCISE:

- Notate 3 note spread voicings for the given chord progressions.
- Compare your version with the version in the Solution Key.
- Learn the progression by heart and play it along to the CD.

Track 37 ▸ Progression 15

Tip: The chord progression above employs so-called SubV chords. These substitute the dominant chord with another dominant chord that uses the same guide tones. For example: Em7 A7 becomes Em7 Eb7. A7 and Eb7 use the same enharmonically equivalent guide tones (see the chapter *Reharmonization*).

© 2007 by AMA Musikverlag

EXERCISE:

- Notate 3 note spread voicings for the given chord progressions.
- Compare your version with the version in the Solution Key.
- Learn the progression by heart and play it along with the CD.

Track 38 ▸ Progression 16

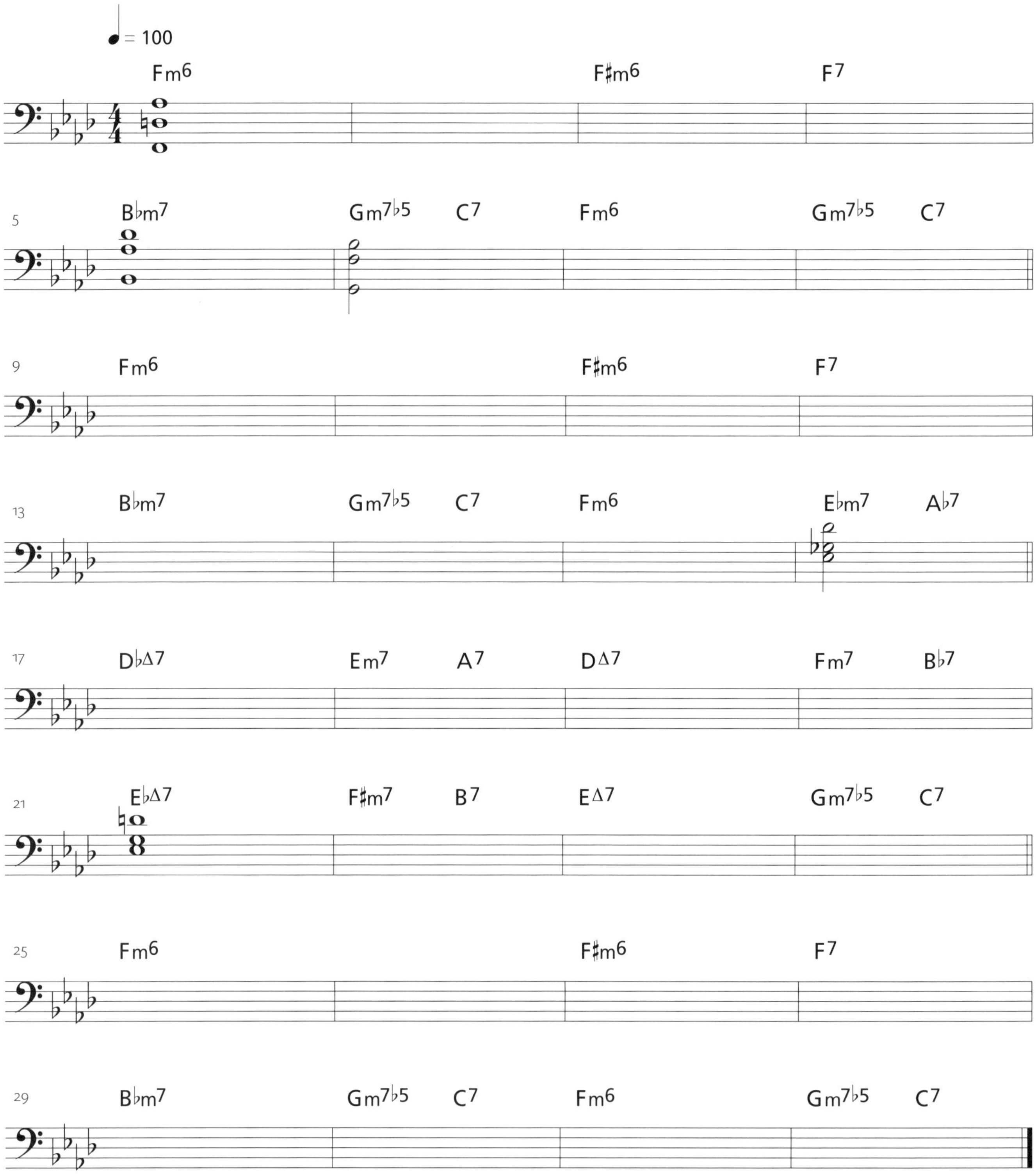

♩ = 100

| Fm6 | | F#m6 | F7 |

5 | B♭m7 | Gm7♭5   C7 | Fm6 | Gm7♭5   C7 |

9 | Fm6 | | F#m6 | F7 |

13 | B♭m7 | Gm7♭5   C7 | Fm6 | E♭m7   A♭7 |

17 | D♭△7 | Em7   A7 | D△7 | Fm7   B♭7 |

21 | E♭△7 | F#m7   B7 | E△7 | Gm7♭5   C7 |

25 | Fm6 | | F#m6 | F7 |

29 | B♭m7 | Gm7♭5   C7 | Fm6 | Gm7♭5   C7 |

Guide Tone Voicings

If one is accompanied by a bass player, the root note can be left out in the left hand. This offers the left hand the chance to add extra notes (i.e. chord extensions). Now the right hand is free to play a melody or improvise over this complex and full harmonic accompaniment of the left hand together with the bass player.

Guide tone voicings are made up of the two guide notes, the third and the seventh. Guide tone voicings need only little attention due to their simple structure yet they still possess the character of the full chord so that all concentration can be focused on the right hand.

Guide Tone Voicings

Ray Charles (* September 23, 1930, † June 10, 2004) grew up in poverty and segregation and lost his sight at the age of seven when white doctors refused to treat him. He moved to Seattle (Washington) in 1947 and recorded his first record *Baby, Let Me Hold Your Hand* in 1951. His first recordings were rhythm and blues and imitated Charles Brown and Nat King Cole. Only with Atlantic Records (1952–1959) did his music take on its in many ways unmistakable style (vocals, instrumental style, composition, arrangement) through emphasizing his gospel and jazz influences. This made him the most important precursor of soul. In 1959 he switched to ABC records and more pop music elements entered into his music resulting in songs like *Unchain My Heart* and *Hit The Road, Jack*. He had an unforgettable appearance in 1979 in the cult movie *Blues Brothers* playing the song *Shake Your Tailfeather*. The first half of his life was adapted for screen in 2004 and starred Jamie Foxx.

II-V-I Major Cadence with Guide Tone Voicings

[Musical notation: Bass clef, 4/4 time. Measure 1: Dm7, G7, C△7. Measure 2: Dm7, G7, C△7.]

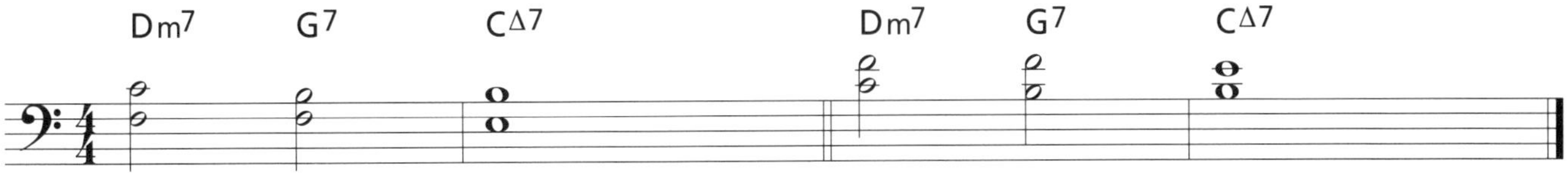

EXERCISE:

- Play both versions of the II-V-I cadence with guide tone voicings slowly in all keys.
- Then, try to play these voicings along to the following CD tracks.
- Try to improvise along with the right hand. Use different licks from *Jazz Piano – Improvisation Concepts*, p. 58 ff.

Check Boxes:

Tracks 12 & 13 ▸
II-V-I in Major – Circle of Fifths

37 Voicing

73 Voicing

Track 14 ▸
II-V-I in Major – Whole Tone Descending

37 Voicing

73 Voicing

Track 15 ▸
II-V-I in Major – Chromatically Descending

37 Voicing

73 Voicing

Track 16 ▸
II-V-I in Major – Chromatically Ascending

37 Voicing

73 Voicing

II-V-I Minor Cadence with Guide Tone Voicings

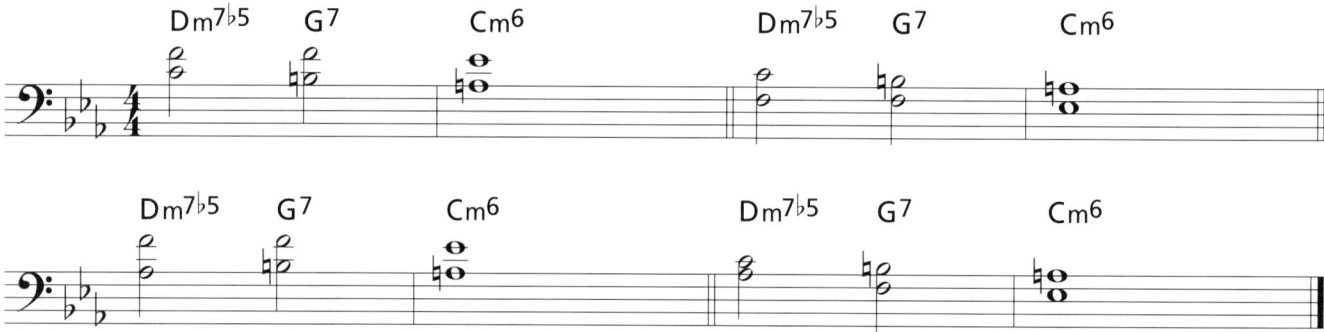

EXERCISE:

- Play the four versions of the II-V-I cadence with guide tone voicings slowly in all keys.
- Then, try to play these voicings along to the following CD tracks.

Check Boxes:

Tracks 23 & 24 ▶
II-V-I in Minor – Circle of Fifths

73 Voicing

37 Voicing

53 Voicing

57 Voicing

Left Hand Voicings

Track 25 ▸
II-V-I in Minor – Whole Tone Descending 1

73 Voicing

37 Voicing

53 Voicing

57 Voicing

Track 26 ▸
II-V-I in Minor – Whole Tone Descending 2

73 Voicing

37 Voicing

53 Voicing

57 Voicing

Track 27 ▸
II-V-I in Minor – Chromatically Descending

73 Voicing

37 Voicing

53 Voicing

57 Voicing

Track 28 ▸
II-V-I in Minor – Chromatically Ascending

73 Voicing

37 Voicing

53 Voicing

57 Voicing

© 2007 by AMA Musikverlag

Jazz Piano – Voicing Concepts

EXERCISE:

- Notate the guide tone voicings for the given chord progressions.
- Compare your version with the version in the Solution Key.
- Learn the progression by heart and play it along to the CD.

Track 39 ▸ Progression 17

Tip: Guide tone voicings (as well as 3 note spread voicings) are perfect for sight-reading!

EXERCISE:

- Notate the guide tone voicings for the given chord progressions.
- Compare your version with the version in the Solution Key.
- Learn the progression by heart and play it along to the CD.

Track 40 ▸ Progression 18

Left Hand Voicings

3 Note Voicings (3 Note Left Hand Voicings)

3 note voicings consist of two guide tones and an additional note **on top** of the guide tones. These well-balanced voicings are preferred by many pianists and often played with the left hand to accompany a melody or an improvisation.

3 Note Voicing

Example

(from *Jazz Piano – Solo Concepts*, "*Black Nocturne*", p. 21)

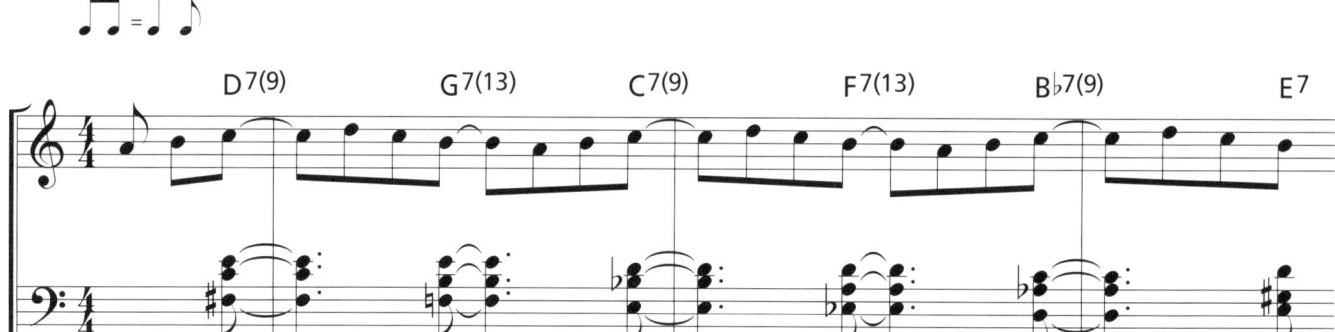

II-V-I Major Cadence with 3 Note Voicings

EXERCISE:

- Play both versions of the II-V-I cadence with 3 note voicings slowly in all keys.
- Then, try to play these voicings along to following CD tracks.

Check Boxes:

Tracks 12 & 13 ▸
II-V-I in Major – Circle of Fifths

379 Voicing

735 Voicing

Track 14 ▸
II-V-I in Major – Whole Tone Descending

379 Voicing

735 Voicing

Track 15 ▸
II-V-I in Major – Chromatically Descending

379 Voicing

735 Voicing

Track 16 ▸
II-V-I in Major – Chromatically Ascending

379 Voicing

735 Voicing

© 2007 by AMA Musikverlag

II-V-I Minor Cadence with 3 Note Voicings

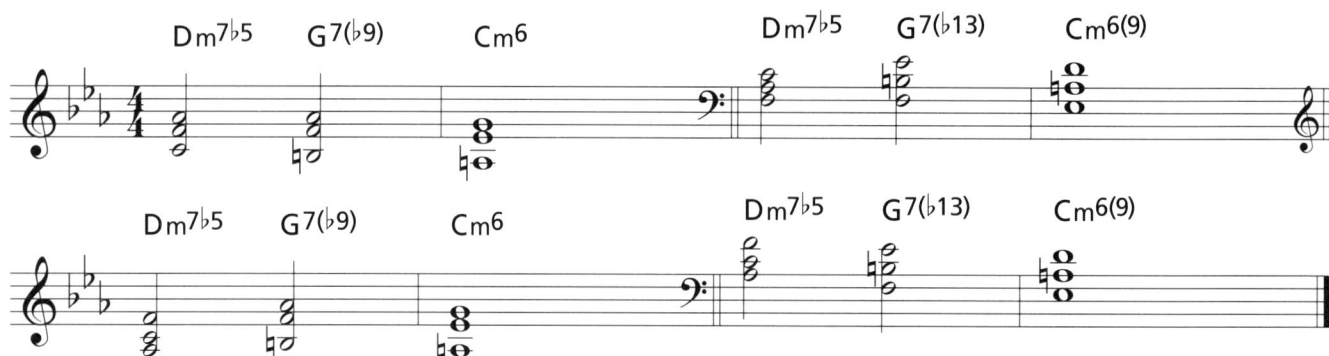

EXERCISE:

- Play all four versions of the II-V-I cadence with 3 note voicings slowly in all keys.
- Then, try to play these voicings along to following CD tracks.

CHECK BOXES:

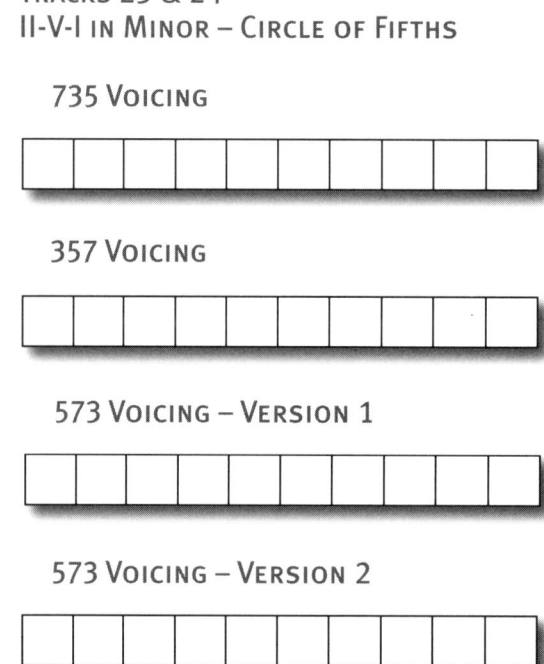

LEFT HAND VOICINGS

TRACK 25 ▶
II-V-I IN MINOR – WHOLE TONE DESCENDING 1

735 VOICING

357 VOICING

573 VOICING – VERSION 1

573 VOICING – VERSION 2

TRACK 27 ▶
II-V-I IN MINOR – CHROMATICALLY DESCENDING

735 VOICING

357 VOICING

573 VOICING – VERSION 1

573 VOICING – VERSION 2

TRACK 26 ▶
II-V-I IN MINOR – WHOLE TONE DESCENDING 2

735 VOICING

357 VOICING

573 VOICING – VERSION 1

573 VOICING – VERSION 2

TRACK 28 ▶
II-V-I IN MINOR – CHROMATICALLY ASCENDING

735 VOICING

357 VOICING

573 VOICING – VERSION 1

573 VOICING – VERSION 2

Jazz Piano – Voicing Concepts

EXERCISE:

- Notate the 3 note voicings for the given chord progressions.
- Compare your version with the version in the Solution Key.
- Learn the progression by heart and play it along to the CD.

Track 41 ▸ Progression 19

♩ = 126

| F6(9) | D7(♯9) | Gm7 | C7(9) |

| Am7 | D7(9) | A♭m7 D♭7(9) | Gm7 C7(9) |

| F∆7(13) | E♭7(9) | D7(♯9) | D7(♭9) |

| G7(13) | C7(9) | B♭m7 | E♭7(9) |

LEFT HAND VOICINGS

EXERCISE:

- Notate the 3 note voicings for the given chord progressions.
- Compare your version with the version in the Solution Key.
- Learn the progression by heart and play it along to the CD.

TRACK 42 ▸ PROGRESSION 20

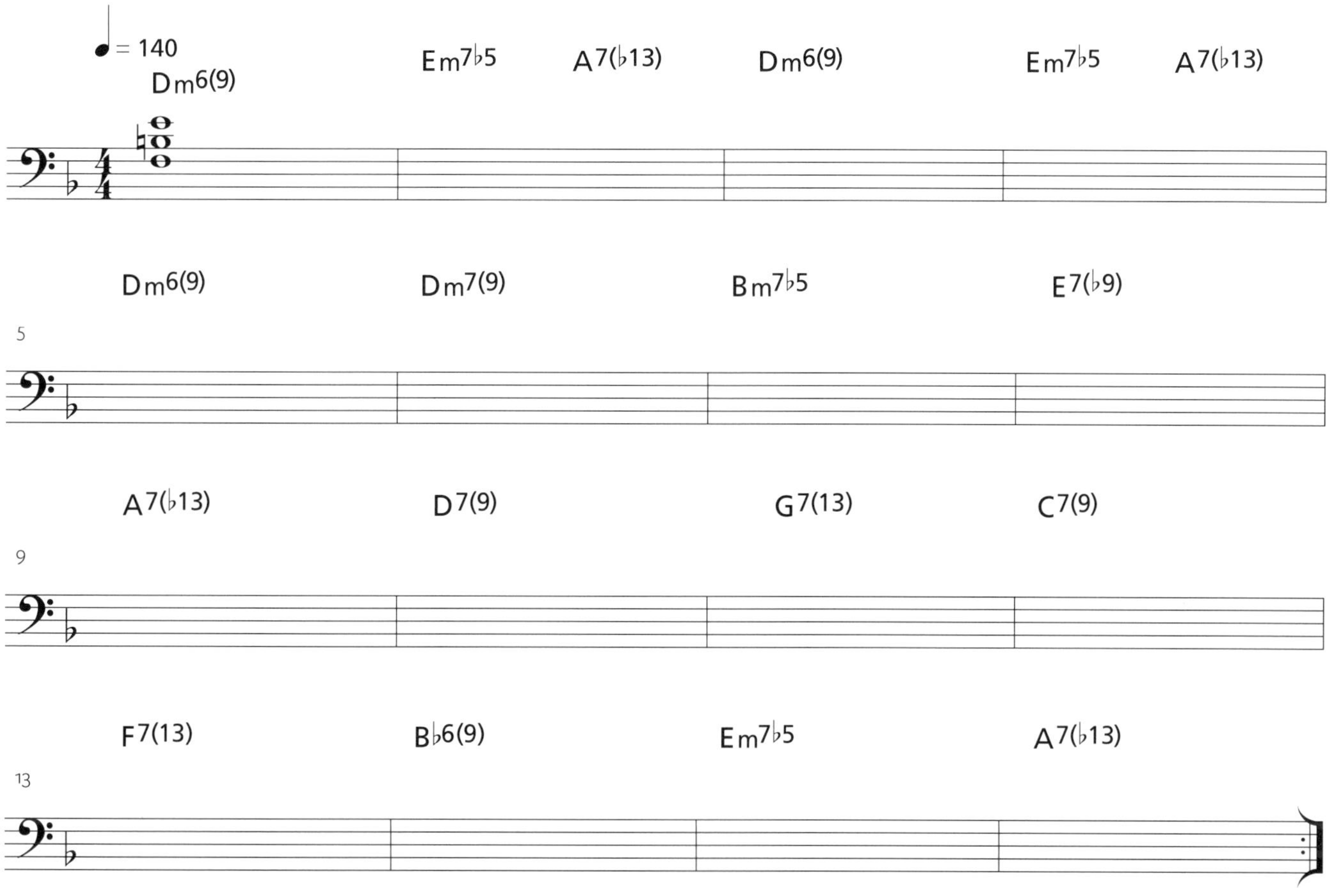

♩ = 140

| Dm6(9) | Em7♭5 | A7(♭13) | Dm6(9) | Em7♭5 | A7(♭13) |

| Dm6(9) | Dm7(9) | Bm7♭5 | E7(♭9) |

| A7(♭13) | D7(9) | G7(13) | C7(9) |

| F7(13) | B♭6(9) | Em7♭5 | A7(♭13) |

4 Note Voicings (4 Note Left Hand Voicings)

4 note voicings are the most common left hand voicings. They are also called "jazz voicings". These voicings employ the guide tones again plus one chord extension on top of each guide tone. There is probably no serious jazz pianist that did not strain his brain and fingers over these voicings because it takes a lot of practice to have these at one's disposal at any given time.

4 Note Voicings

Example

(from *Jazz Piano – Solo Concepts*, "*Sunrise*", p. 75)

LEFT HAND VOICINGS

II-V-I Major Cadence with 4 Note Voicings

EXERCISE:

- Play both versions of the II-V-I cadence with guide tone voicings slowly in all keys.
- Then, try to play these voicings along to following CD tracks.

Check Boxes:

Tracks 12 & 13 ▸
II-V-I in Major – Circle of Fifths

3579 Voicing

7935 Voicing

Track 14 ▸
II-V-I in Major – Whole Tone Descending

3579 Voicing

7935 Voicing

Track 15 ▸
II-V-I in Major – Chromatically Descending

3579 Voicing

7935 Voicing

Track 16 ▸
II-V-I in Major – Chromatically Ascending

3579 Voicing

7935 Voicing

II-V-I Minor Cadence with 4 Note Voicings

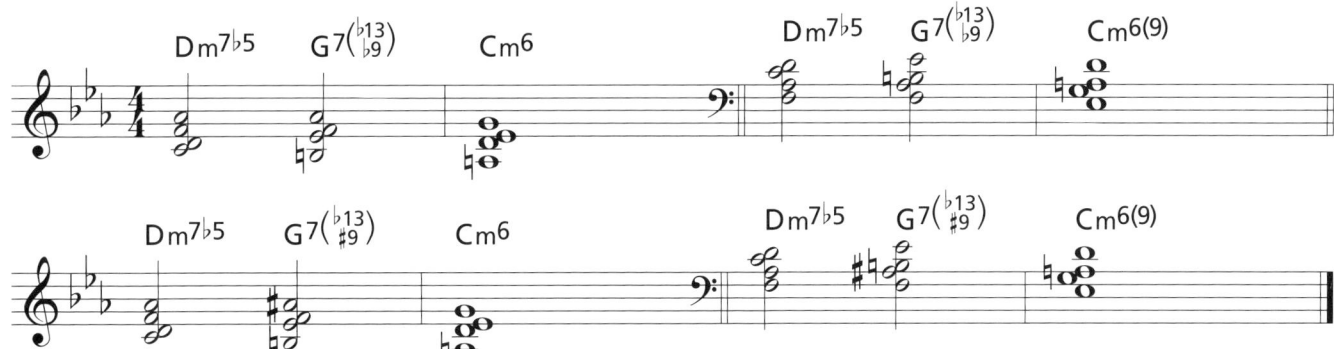

EXERCISE:
- Play the versions of the II-V-I cadence with 4 note voicings slowly in all keys.
- Then, try to play these voicings along to following CD tracks.

Check Boxes:

Tracks 23 & 24 ▸
II-V-I in Minor – Circle of Fifths

7135 Voicing

3571 Voicing

Tip: As mentioned before, a dominant chord can have different chord extensions. In the example above the ♭9 is replaced by the optional ♯9. Whichever chord extension is used is determined first by the chord symbol and second by your own personal taste. The chord symbol X8(alt) is often seen, too. "Alt" stands for altered and the following optional extensions can be used: ♭9, ♯9, ♯11, ♭5, ♯5 or ♭13.

Track 25 ▸
II-V-I in Minor – Whole Tone Descending 1

7135 Voicing

3571 Voicing

Track 26 ▸
II-V-I in Minor – Whole Tone Descending 2

7135 Voicing

3571 Voicing

Track 27 ▸
II-V-I in Minor – Chromatically Descending

7135 Voicing

3571 Voicing

Track 28 ▸
II-V-I in Minor – Chromatically Ascending

7135 Voicing

3571 Voicing

© 2007 by AMA Musikverlag

Jazz Piano – Voicing Concepts

EXERCISE:

- Notate the 4 note voicings for the given chord progressions.
- Compare your version with the version in the Solution Key.
- Learn the progression by heart and play it along to the CD.

Track 43 ▸ Progression 21

EXERCISE:

- Notate the 4 note voicings for the given chord progressions.
- Compare your version with the version in the Solution Key.
- Learn the progression by heart and play it along to the CD.

Track 44 – Progression 22

Tip: Practice all the explained techniques with every progression and standard progression that are covered in this book. You can find more progressions for practicing in the Solution Key of *Jazz Piano – Improvisation Concepts*. The appendix also provides a checklist so you can keep track of your progress.

Summary: By now you should have learned the following:
- Bud Powell Voicings
- 3 note spread voicings for the left hand
- Guide tone Voicings
- 3 note voicings
- 4 note voicings
- II-V-I cadence in major and minor using the given voicings
- Practical application of the presented voicings

© 2007 by AMA Musikverlag

Chapter 5: Two Hand Voicings

Two hand voicings (locked hand voicings) are used when you play with a rhythm section. The bass player plays the root note so that the pianist can include additional chord extensions in his voicings. Although similar to the left hand voicings, there are different voicings that are used:

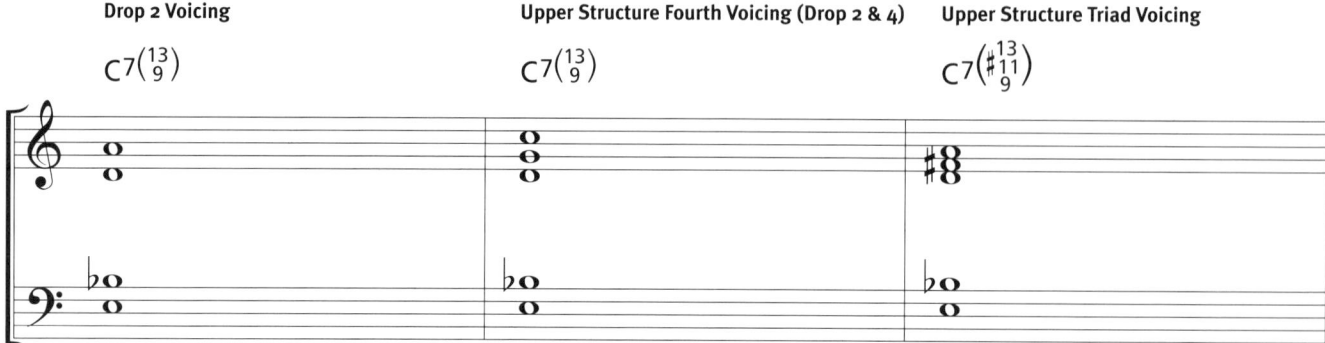

♭9 Interval in a Voicing

When playing two hand voicings or voicings with several notes in general, avoid using a ♭9 interval between two notes as this does not sound good (with the only exception being the dominant(♭9)-chord).

Avoid these voicings:

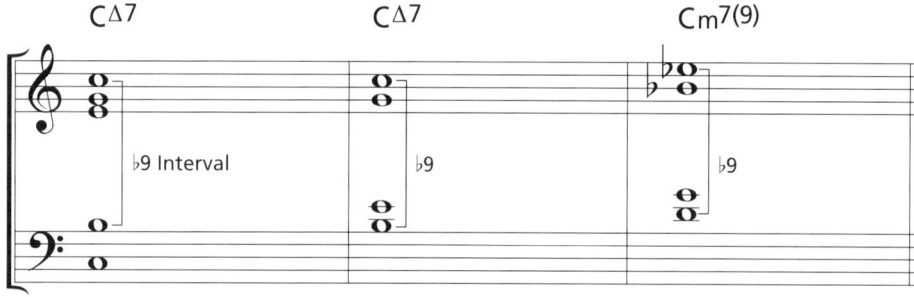

Drop 2 Voicings

Drop 2 voicings are excellent to accompany in a melodic fashion. In contrast to the voicings introduced up till now, drop 2 voicings are built **from top to bottom**.

The foundation of a drop 2 voicing is a simple seventh chord in a closed position. The second voice from the top is dropped an octave down, hence the name "drop 2".

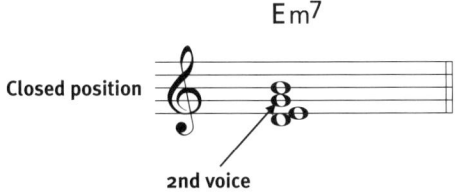

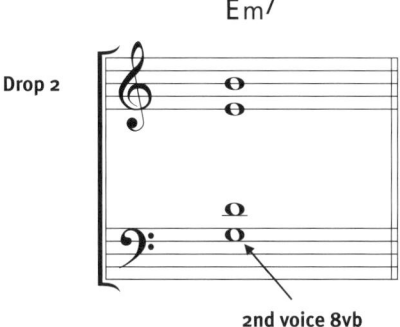

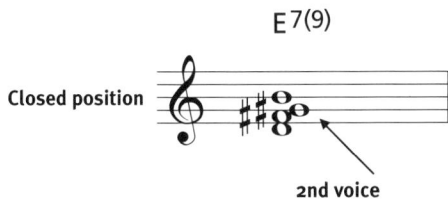

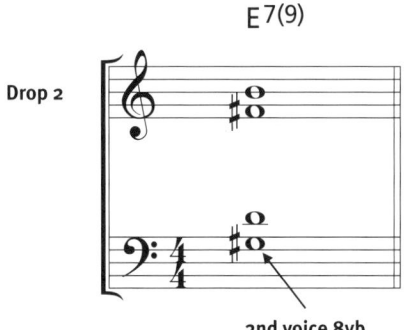

Jazz Piano – Voicing Concepts

EXERCISE:

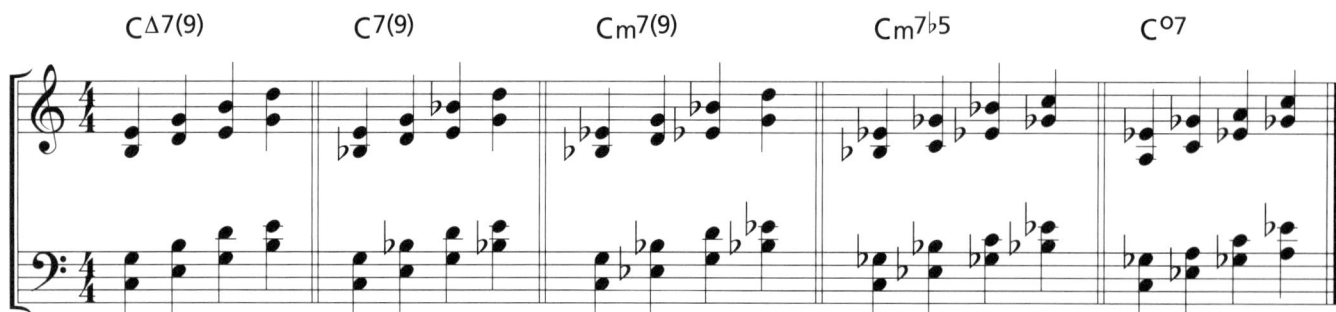

- In order to memorize the structure and pattern of the drop 2 voicing, play the seventh chords above as notated in all keys.
- Play two notes with each hand.
- Use the sustain pedal to create smooth transitions between the chords.
- Play slowly, ascending and descending through several octaves.
- Keep track of your progress using the familiar check boxes.
- If you feel like it, play the voicings along to CD tracks 1–6.

Check Boxes:

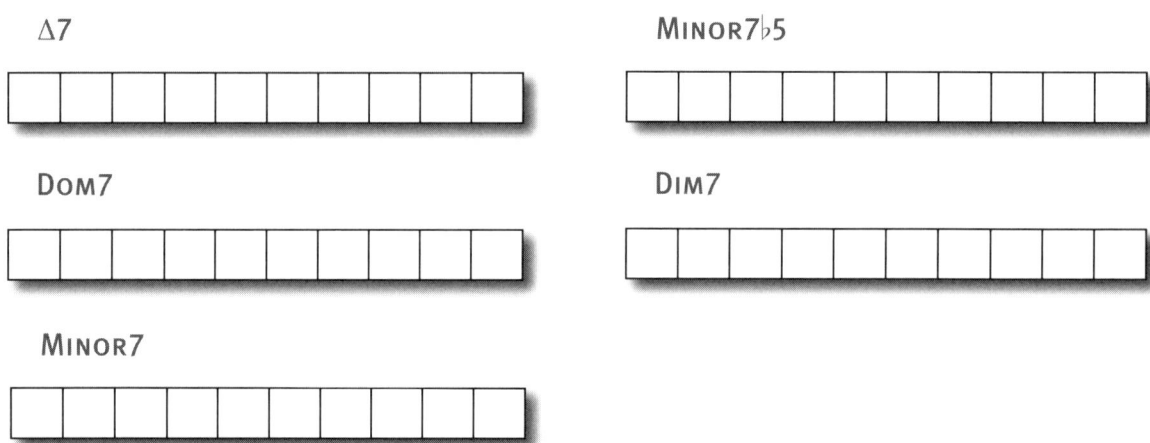

Tip: Learning drop 2 voicings takes some patience. Make sure you practice consciously and slowly as this is the only way to get these voicings into your head and fingers.

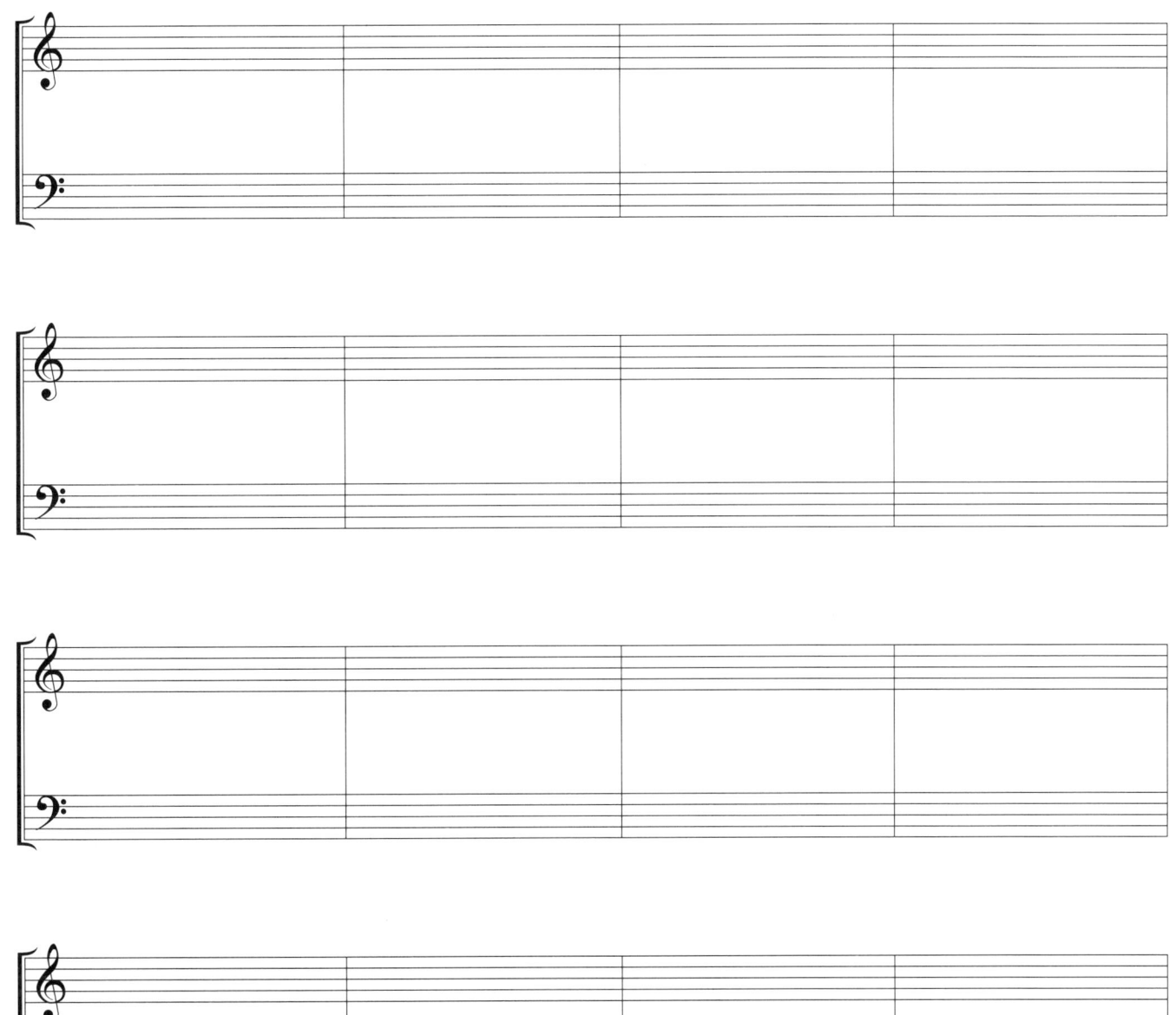

Jazz Piano – Voicing Concepts

II-V-I Major Cadence with Drop 2 Voicings

EXERCISE:

- Play all four versions of the II-V-I cadence with drop 2 voicings very slowly in all keys and later along to the CD.
- Using the fifth and the ninth as the highest notes are common variations. You should memorize these first.

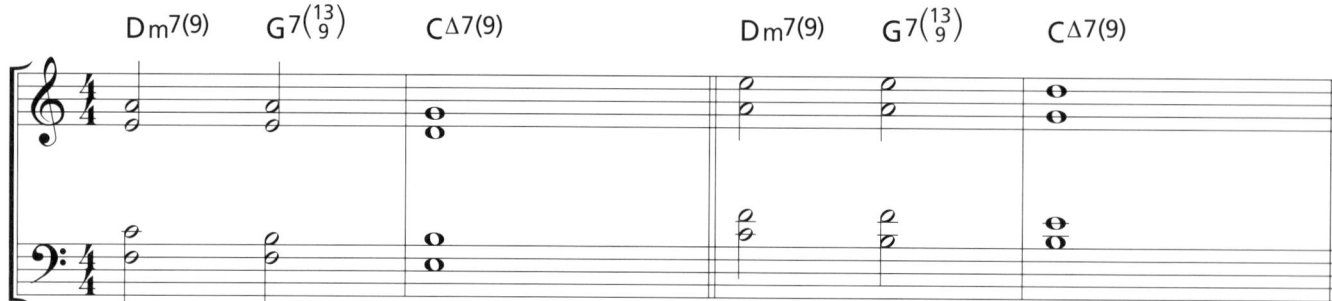

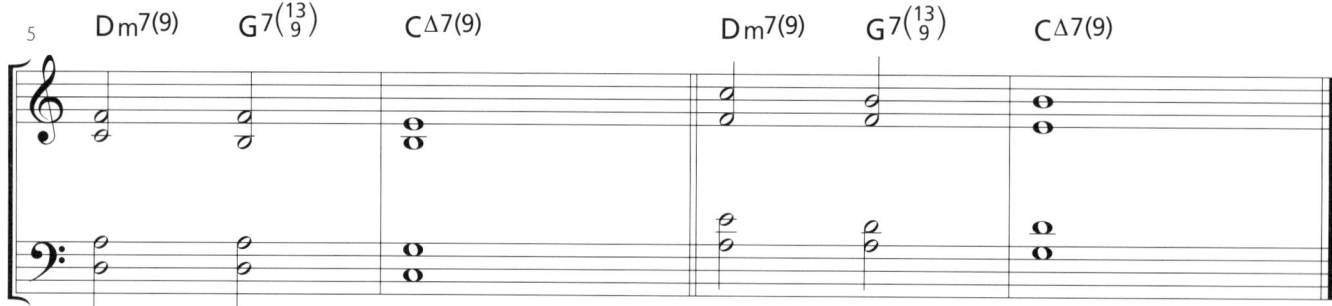

Check Boxes:

Tracks 12 & 13 ▶
II-V-I in Major – Circle of Fifths

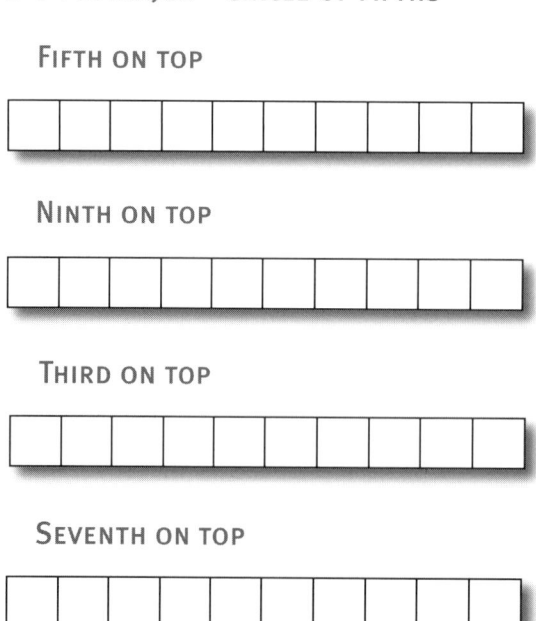

TRACK 14 ►
II-V-I IN MAJOR – WHOLE TONE DESCENDING

FIFTH ON TOP

NINTH ON TOP

THIRD ON TOP

SEVENTH ON TOP

TRACK 15 ►
II-V-I IN MAJOR – CHROMATICALLY DESCENDING

FIFTH ON TOP

NINTH ON TOP

THIRD ON TOP

SEVENTH ON TOP

TRACK 16 ►
II-V-I IN MAJOR – CHROMATICALLY ASCENDING

FIFTH ON TOP

NINTH ON TOP

THIRD ON TOP

SEVENTH ON TOP

Jazz Piano – Voicing Concepts

II-V-I Major Cadence in Minor with Drop 2 Voicings

EXERCISE:

- Play all four versions of the II-V-I cadence with drop 2 voicings very slowly in all keys and later along to the CD.
- Using the fifth and the octave as the highest notes are common variations. You should memorize these first.

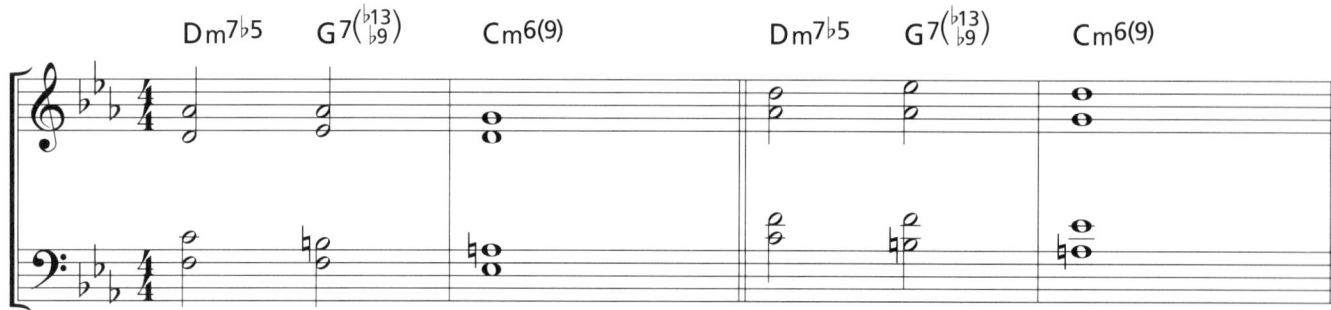

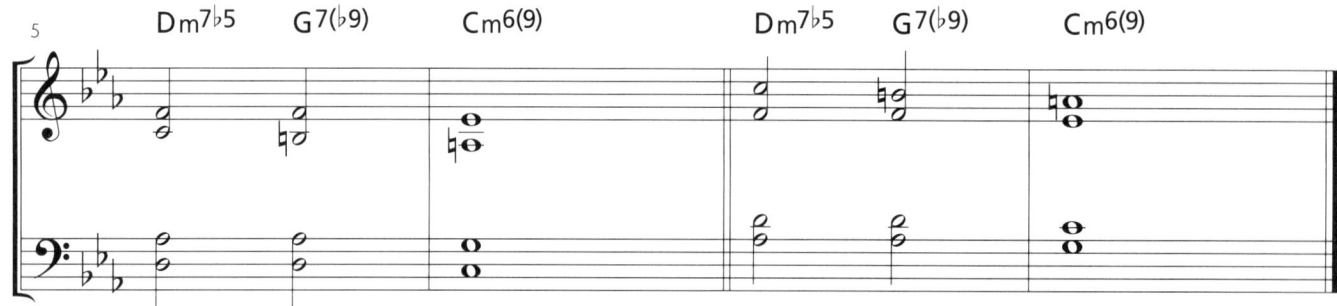

CHECK BOXES:

Tracks 23 & 24 ▶
II-V-I in Minor – Circle of Fifths

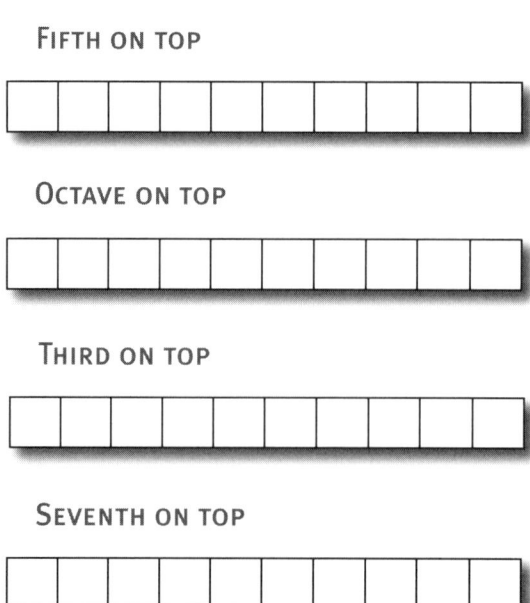

© 2007 by AMA Musikverlag

Two Hand Voicings

Track 25 ▸
II-V-I in Minor – Whole Tone Descending 1

Fifth on top

Octave on top

Third on top

Seventh on top

Track 26 ▸
II-V-I in Minor – Whole Tone Descending 2

Fifth on top

Octave on top

Third on top

Seventh on top

Track 27 ▸
II-V-I in Minor – Chromatically Descending

Fifth on top

Octave on top

Third on top

Seventh on top

Track 28 ▸
II-V-I in Minor – Chromatically Ascending

Fifth on top

Octave on top

Third on top

Seventh on top

EXERCISE:

- Notate drop 2 voicings under the given notes.
- Make sure that two notes are written on each staff.
- Compare your version with the version in the Solution Key.
- Learn the voicings by heart and play them along to the CD.

TRACK 45 ▸ PROGRESSION 23

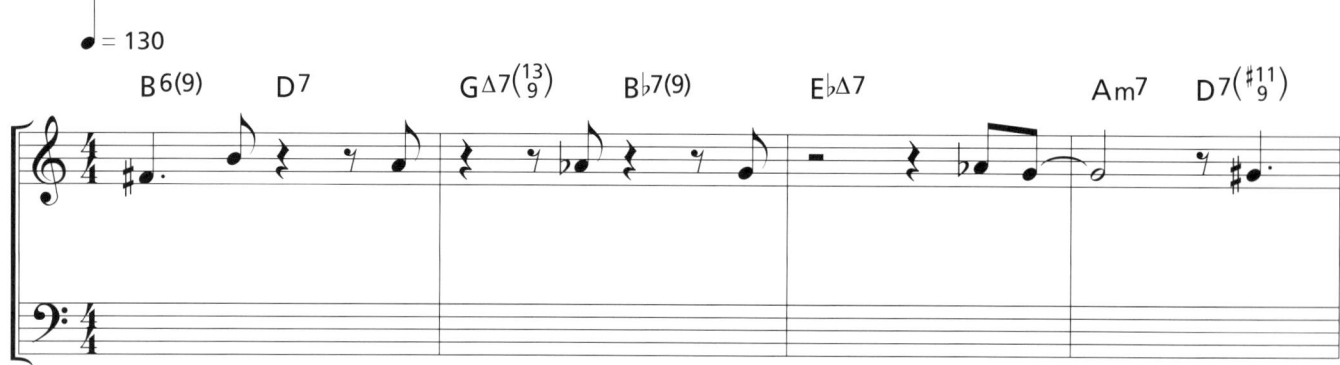

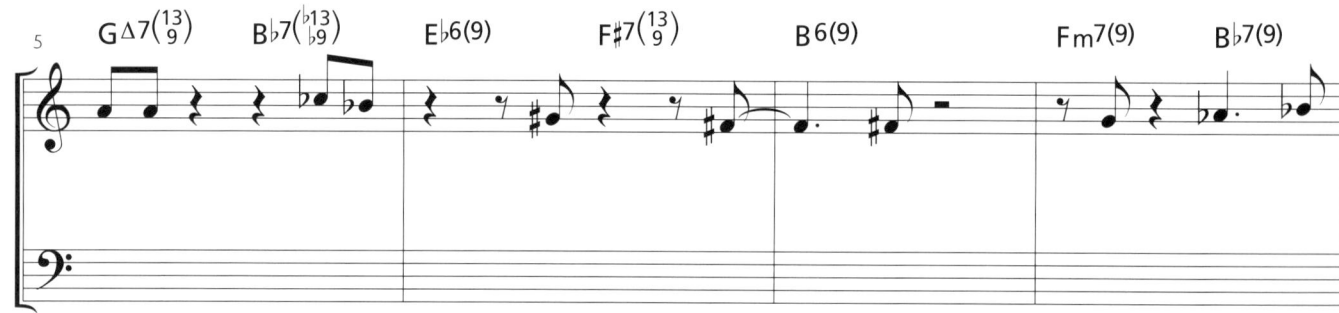

Two Hand Voicings

EXERCISE:

- Notate drop 2 voicings under the given notes.
- Make sure that two notes are written on each staff.
- Compare your version with the version in the Solution Key.
- Learn the voicings by heart and play them along to the CD.

Track 46 ▸ Progression 24

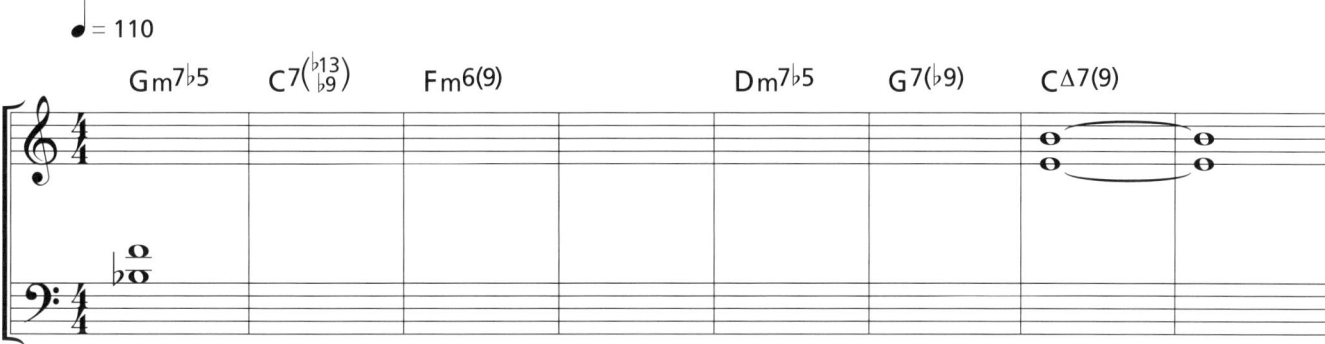

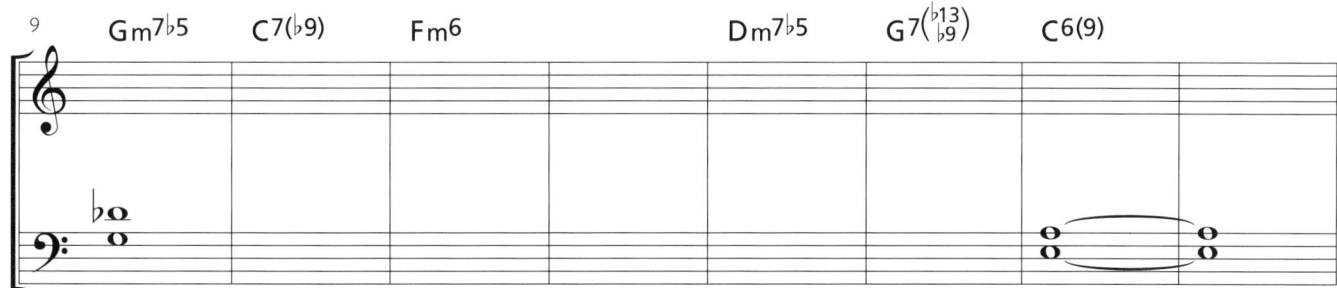

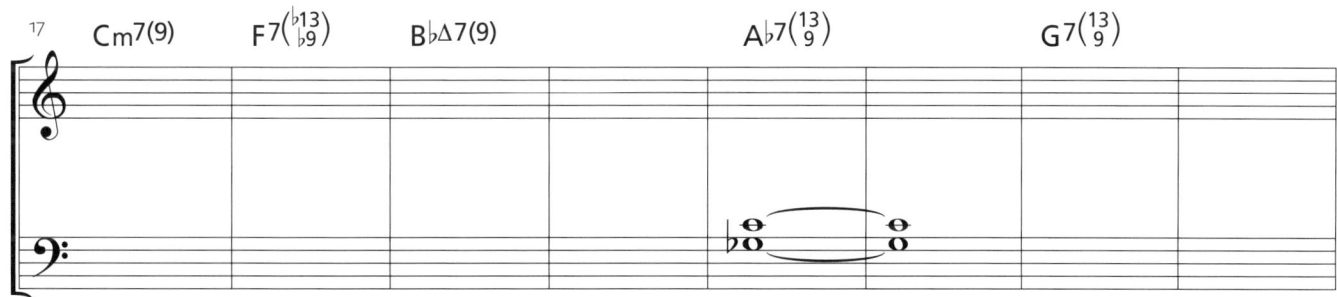

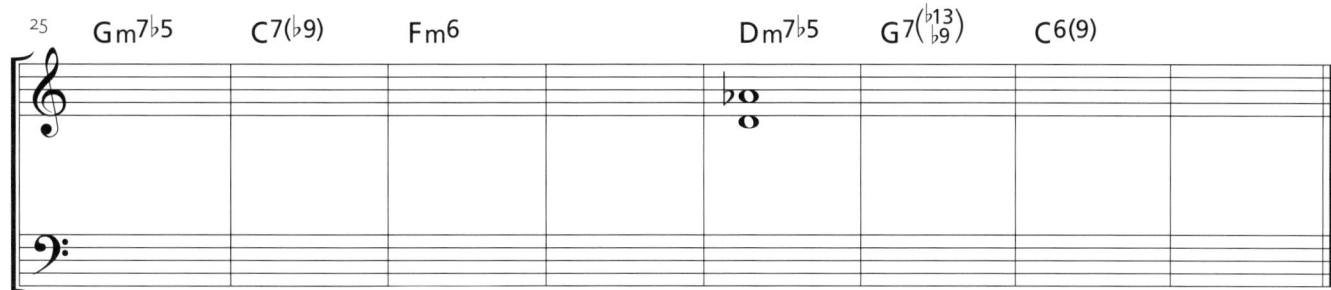

Tip: Talk to guitar players as some guitar voicings (e.g. drop 2 voicings) can be easily transferred to the piano.

© 2007 by AMA Musikverlag

Upper Structure Voicings

Another kind of two handed voicing is the "upper structure voicing". It usually consists of two guide tones played with the left hand and an ordered upper structure of notes (a triad or structure of fourths). The upper structure usually consists of several chord extensions and is played with the right hand.

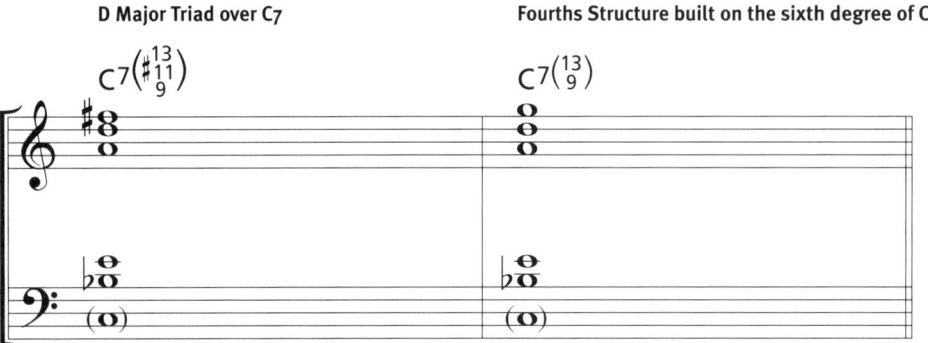

An upper structure voicing must have **at least one chord extension**:

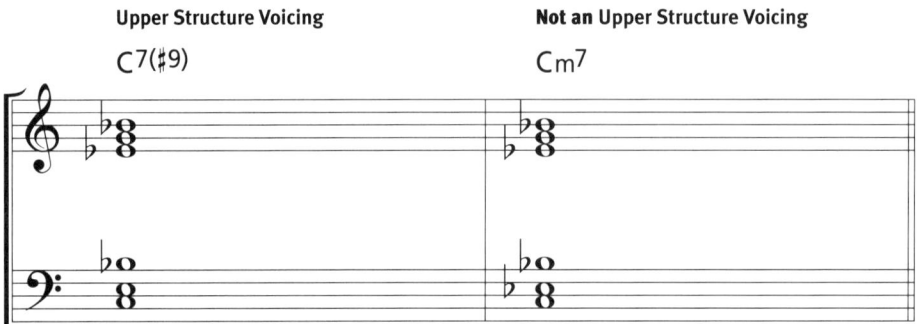

It is possible to use a guide tone in the upper structure. To avoid doubled notes (especially doubled thirds) it can be recommended to play the root note with the left hand.

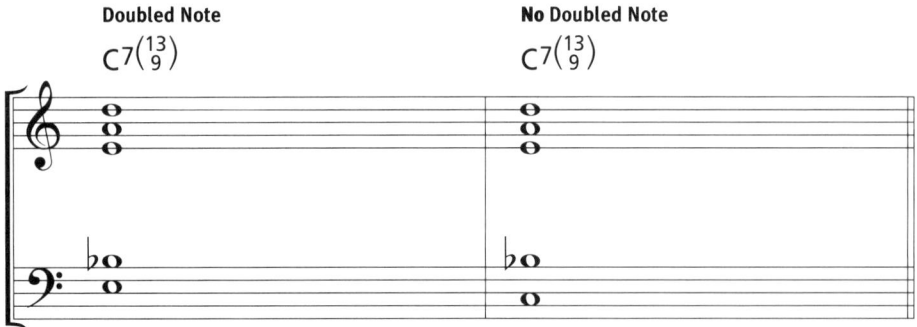

Tip: Try to play the lowest note of the upper structure no further away than a sixth from the uppermost guide tone. Otherwise the sound of the upper structure will get lost. The upper structure triads can obviously be played in other inversions than those notated above.

Two Hand Voicings

Example

(from *Jazz Piano – Solo Concepts*, "Tender Moments", p. 43)

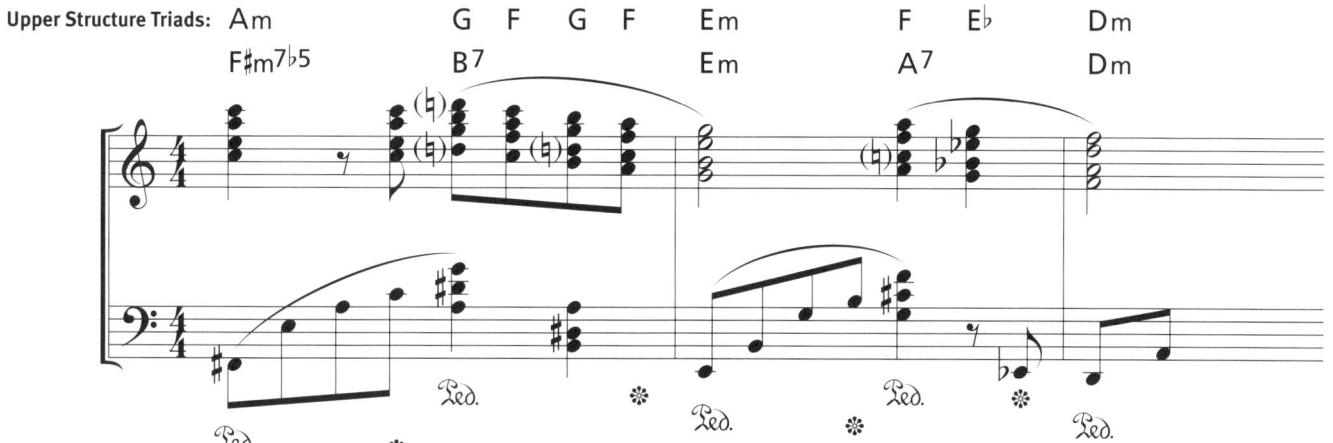

Joe Zawinul (born July 7, 1932 in Vienna) is considered by experts to be one of the greatest innovators when it comes to the electrification of keyboard playing. Jazz historians note that, apart from his influence while playing with Cannonball Adderley, he was instrumental in the seminal phase of the development of the fusion style that he developed together with Miles Davis in the late 1960s. His biggest commercial success was in the 1970s with his band Weather Report. With his band The Zawinul Syndicate, he has developed a unique style in recent years that crosses over between jazz, world and dance music. Over the years he has received numerous awards for his work which include several Grammys, countless Downbeat Reader Poll #1 nominations, the Amadeus and Hans Koller Awards, the Golden Ring of the City of Vienna, the Miles Davis Award etc.

EXERCISE:

- Play the following upper structure voicings slowly in all keys.
- In order to hear the voicings with a root note you should play following variations as well:

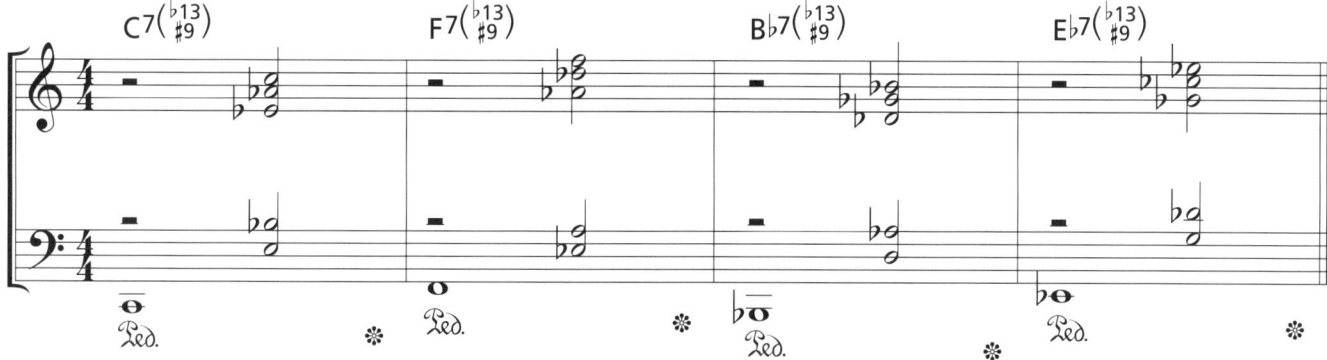

© 2007 by AMA Musikverlag

Δ7

Track 7

Dom7

Track 8

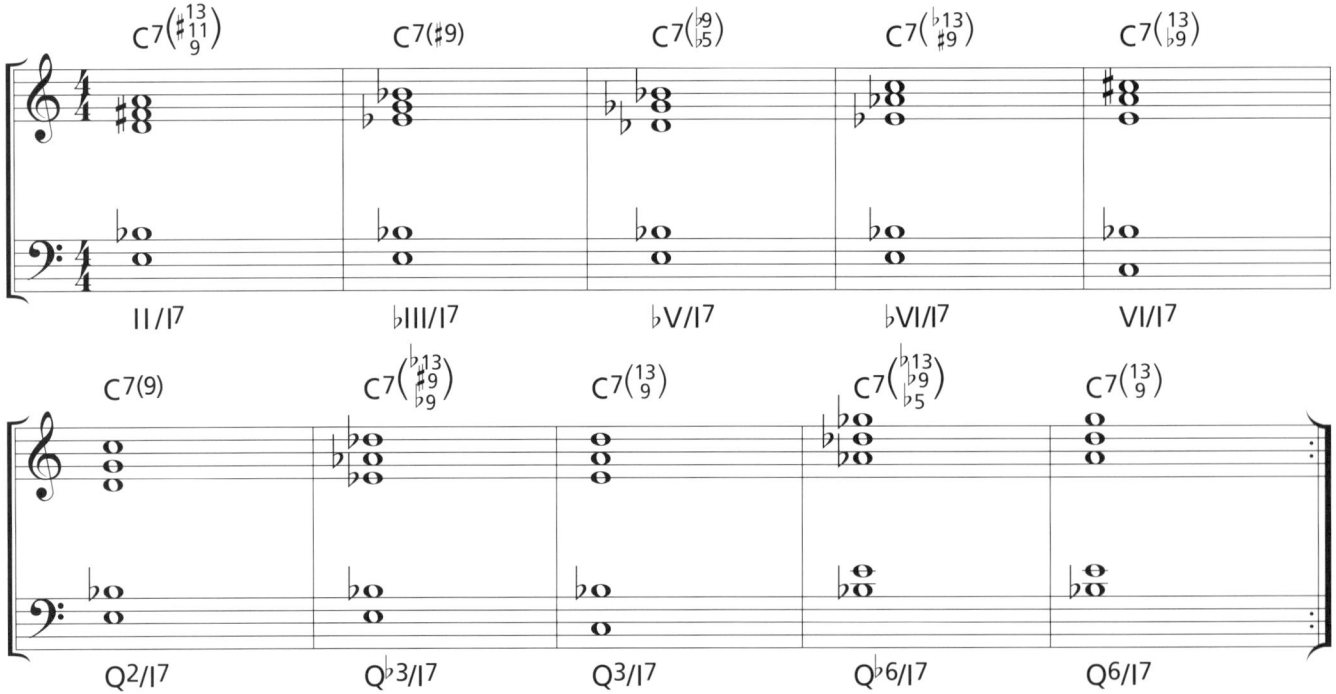

m7

Track 9

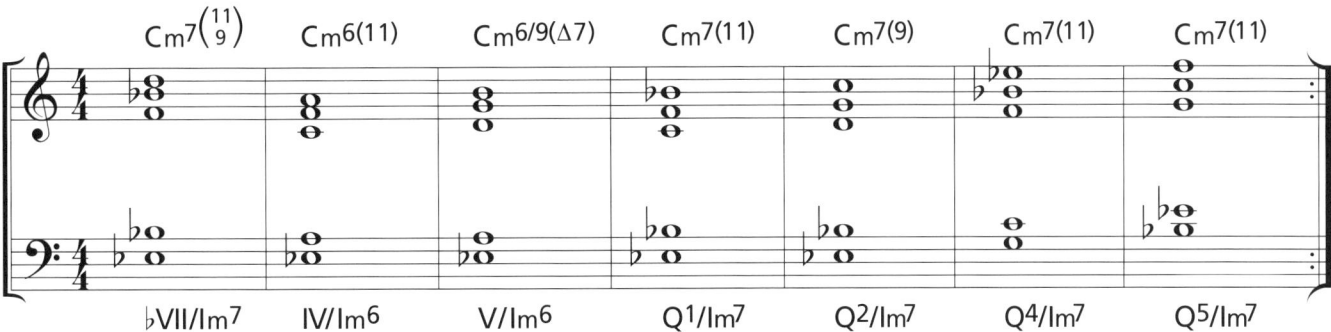

m7♭5

Track 10

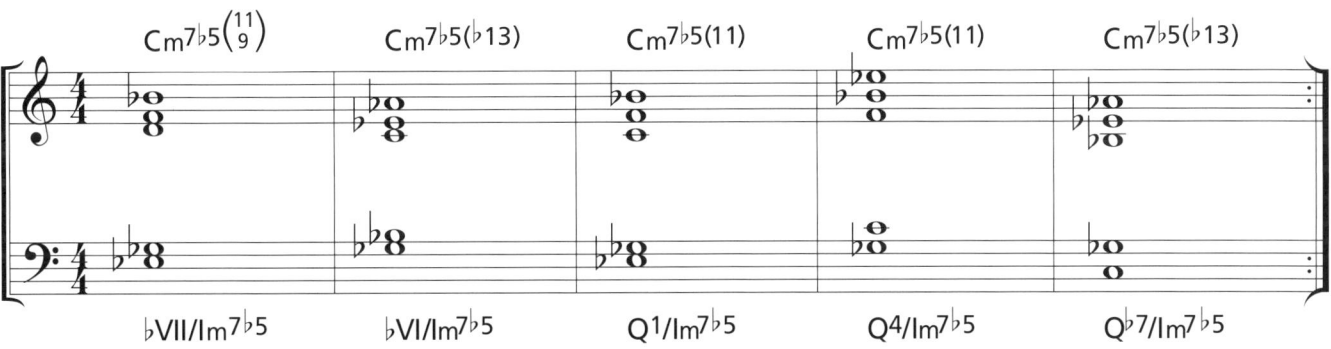

Note: V/IΔ7 means that the fifth degree triad is played over the Δ7 chord. Ex.: G major triad over CΔ7. Q3/IΔ7 means that a fourth structure built on the third degree is played over a Δ7 chord, i.e. e–a–d over CΔ7.

EXERCISE:

- Play the following upper structure voicings along to the already well-known II-V-I cadences on the CD.

II-V-I in Major

Tracks 12–16

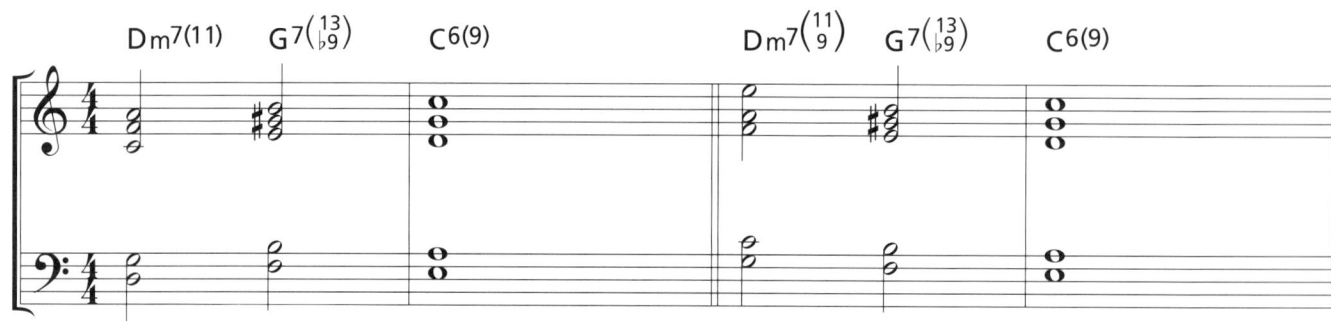

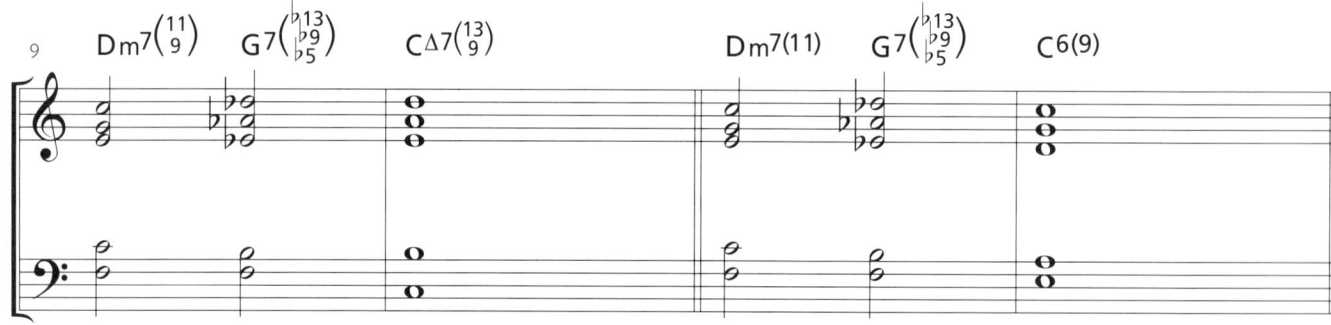

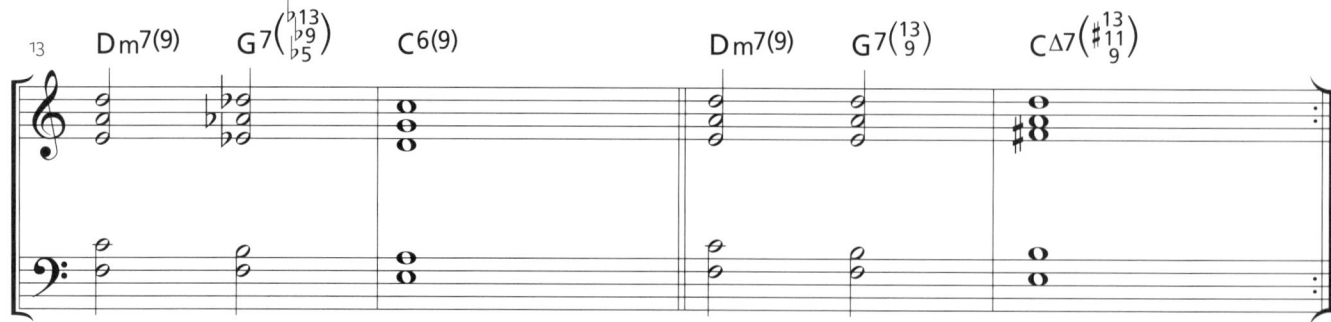

II-V-I in Minor

Tracks 23–28

Tip: All the upper structure voicings shown can be combined within the II-V-I cadence. This offers many variations in which to play the II-V-I cadence using upper structure voicings. That's why we're not using check boxes here. Combine the voicings shown and practice at least three variations carefully in all keys.

EXERCISE:

- Notate upper structure voicings under the given notes.
- Make sure that two notes are written on each staff.
- Compare your version with the version in the Solution Key.
- Learn the voicings by heart and play them along to the CD.

Track 47 ▸ Progression 25

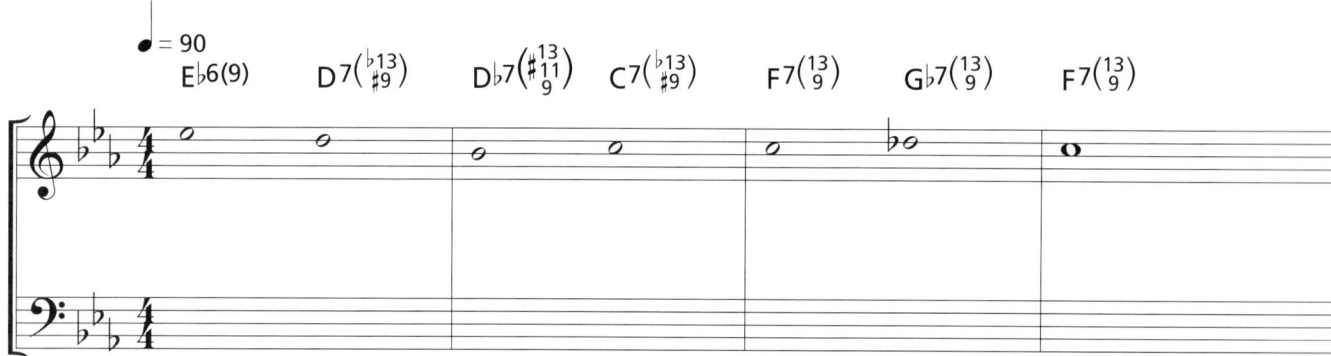

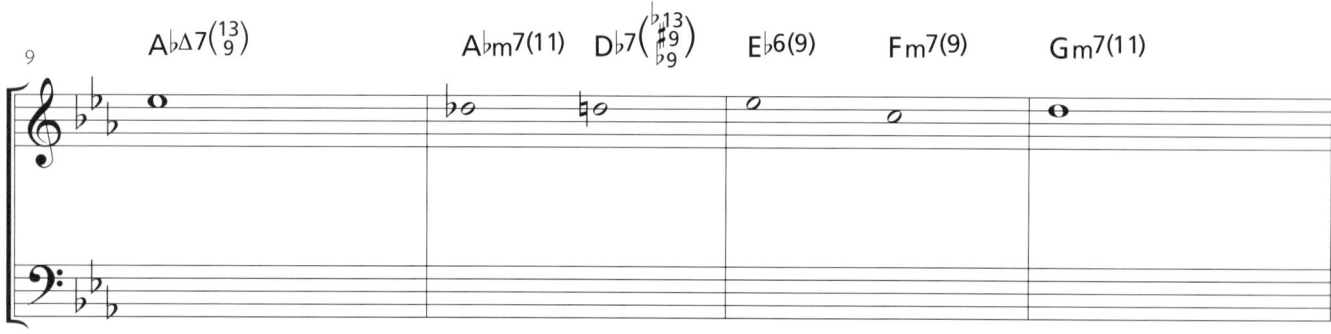

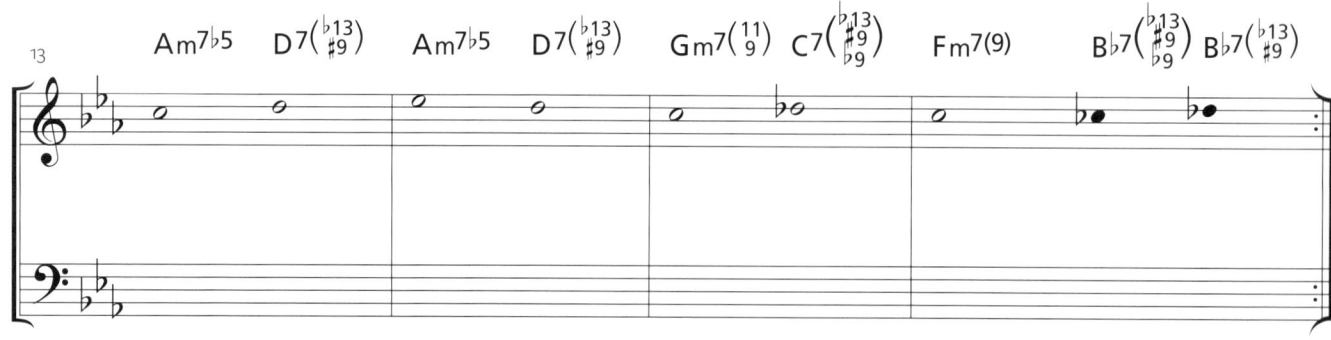

EXERCISE:

- Notate upper structure voicings under the given notes.
- Make sure that two notes are written on each staff.
- Compare your version with the version in the Solution Key.
- Learn the voicings by heart and play them along to the CD.

Track 48 ▸ Progression 26

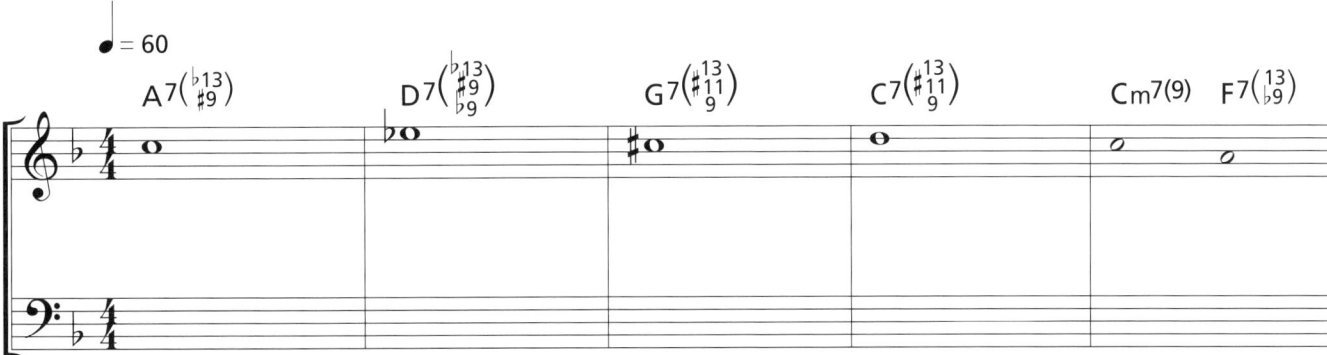

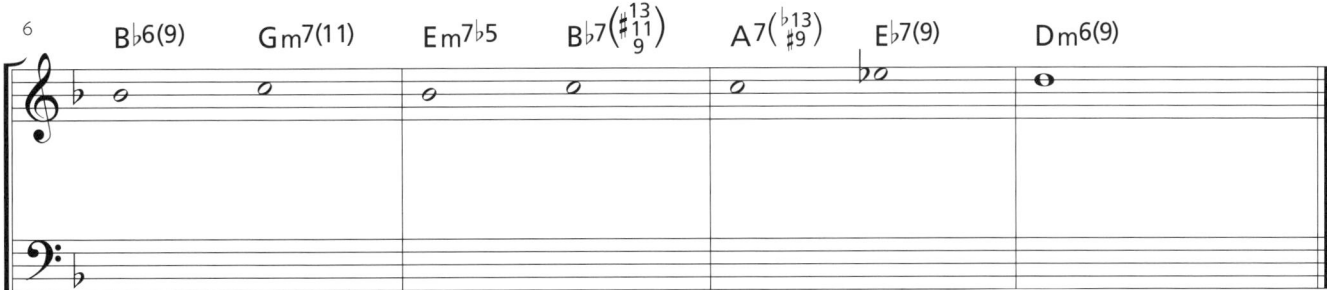

Summary: By now you should have learned the following:

- Seventh chords with drop 2 voicings
- II-V-I cadence in major and minor with drop 2 voicings
- Seventh chords with upper structure voicings
- II-V-I cadence in major and minor with upper structure voicings
- Practical application of the presented voicings

Chapter 6: Reharmonization

To bring more variety into an existing harmonic progression, it is common in jazz to change it according to the individual taste of the performer. Experienced jazz pianists use different reharmonization techniques (reharmonization: new harmonization or invention of new chord progressions). The five most common techniques are introduced here:

- Dominant substitution (SubV)
- IIm7 addition
- Chromatic approach
- Chord substitution
- Pedal point
- Contrary motion

The intent of a new harmonization should be to interpret a familiar tune in a new and fresh way. In conclusion, reharmonization should have the following effects:

- To bring density to existing progressions, i.e. add chords
- To alter existing chords, i.e to create new sound colors

Tip: The following techniques will not be investigated as deeply as before because as there are simply too many variations of these reharmonization techniques. Practice the principles of these techniques and experiment with jazz standards and your original compositions.

Example

(from *Jazz Piano – Solo Concepts*, "*Jazz Flowers*", p. 62 ff.)

Compare the original with the new harmonic arrangement. Not only were chords added but the melody has been adapted to fit the swing style.

Tip: "If it ain't broke, don't fix it." Remember this adage and it will save you a lot of work! Only change a harmonic progression or single chords when the change leads to musical improvement. Before changing things, one should be certain about the purpose of the change.

Dominant Substitution (SubV)

A popular tool for the expansion of any given chord progression is the so-called SubV chord (spoken "sub-five"). Consider the following theoretical background:

The guide tones (third and seventh) of a dominant chord form the interval of a diminished fifth or tritone. Taken alone and with their enharmonic equivalents, we discover that two dominant chords use the same guide tones:

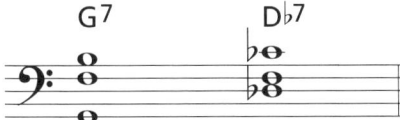

As these chords use the same guide tones, they are interchangeable and can be substituted accordingly. They are either called "dominant substitutions" (short: SubV) or "tritone substitutions" as both chords are a tritone (three whole notes) apart.

The harmonic rhythm can be expanded by letting a SubV follow a dominant chord. Thereby, the space that was previously occupied by only one chord is now occupied by two chords.

II-V-I Original Cadence:

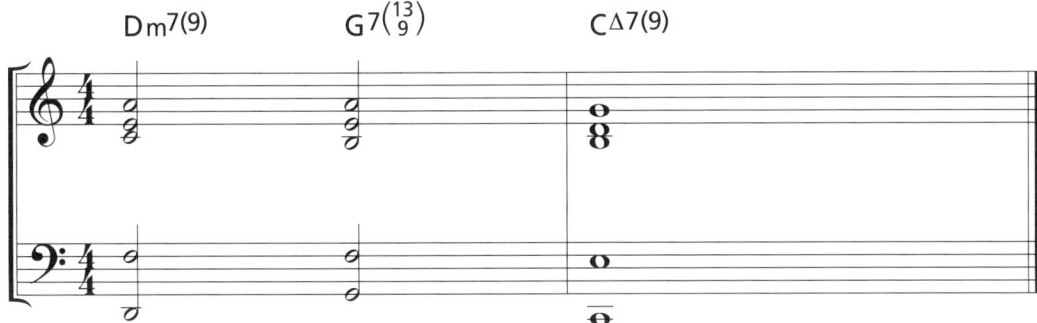

II-V-I Cadence with Additional SubV-Chord:

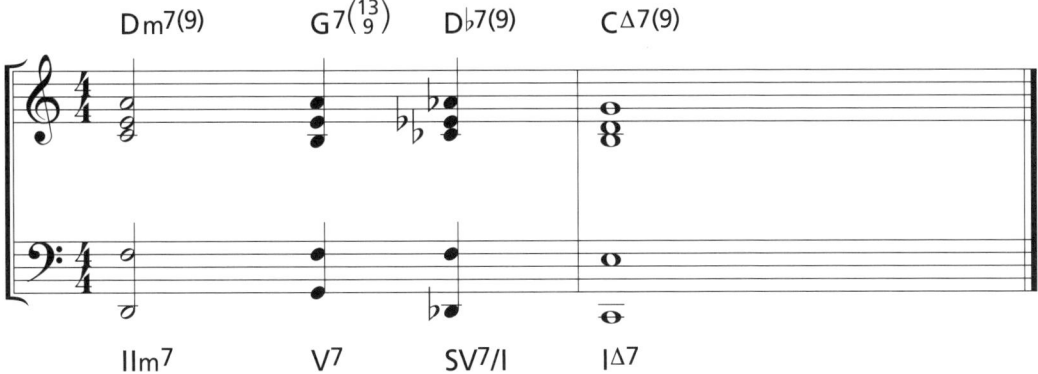

EXERCISE:

- Play the II-V-I cadence above in all keys.

EXERCISE:

- Add an additional SubV after each dominant chord.
- Compare your version with the version in the Solution Key.
- Play the progression using standard spread voicings.

It's also possible to put a dominant or SubV chord in front of any chord. Here the following thought has to be taken into account:

A preceding dominant chord is always **a fifth higher** than the target chord (secondary dominant). A SubV chord is always **one half step higher** than the target chord.

EXERCISE:

- Put a SubV chord **in front of every** chord (half step higher than the target chord, see bar 1–3).
- Compare your version with the version in the Solution Key.
- Play the progression using standard voicings.

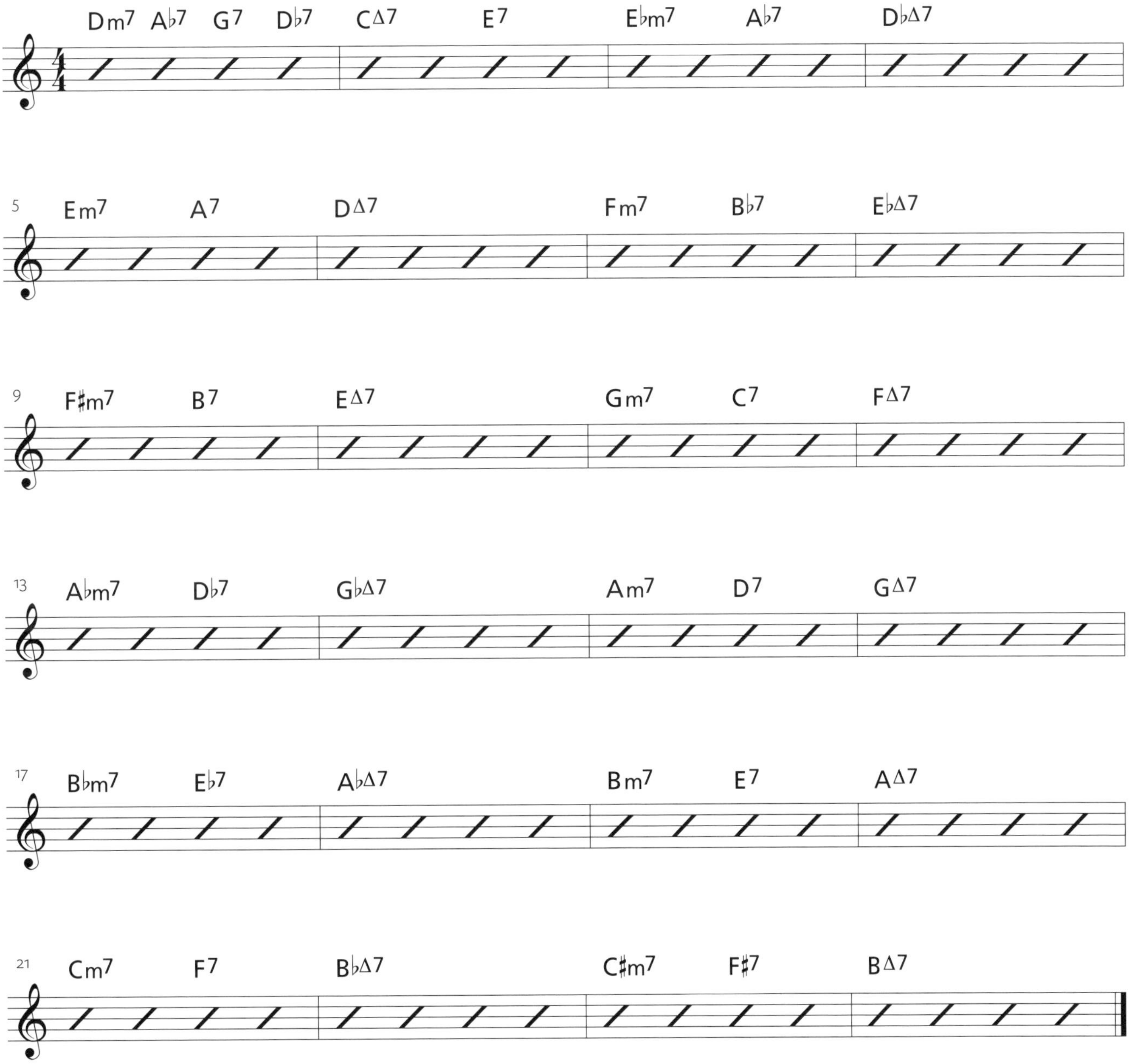

Jazz Piano – Voicing Concepts

EXERCISE:

- Notate 4 note spread voicings for the given harmonic progression.
- Notate an additional SubV voicing and its chord symbol in front of every chord.
- Compare your version with the version in the Solution Key.

Tip: SubV chords usually use the mixolydian♯11 scale plus the following chord extensions:

9, ♯11, 13.

The exception proves the rule!

Reharmonization

IIm7 Extension

> "Where there's a V7, there's a IIm7!"

Every dominant chord can be preceded by a minor7 chord a fifth higher (II-V cadence). Example:

Original Chord Progression:

Chord Progression Extended by IIm7:

EXERCISE:

- Add IIm7 chords to the chord progression on the next page.
- Notate the chord symbols above the given harmonic progression.
- Compare your version with the version in the Solution Key.
- Play the chord progression using standard voicings.

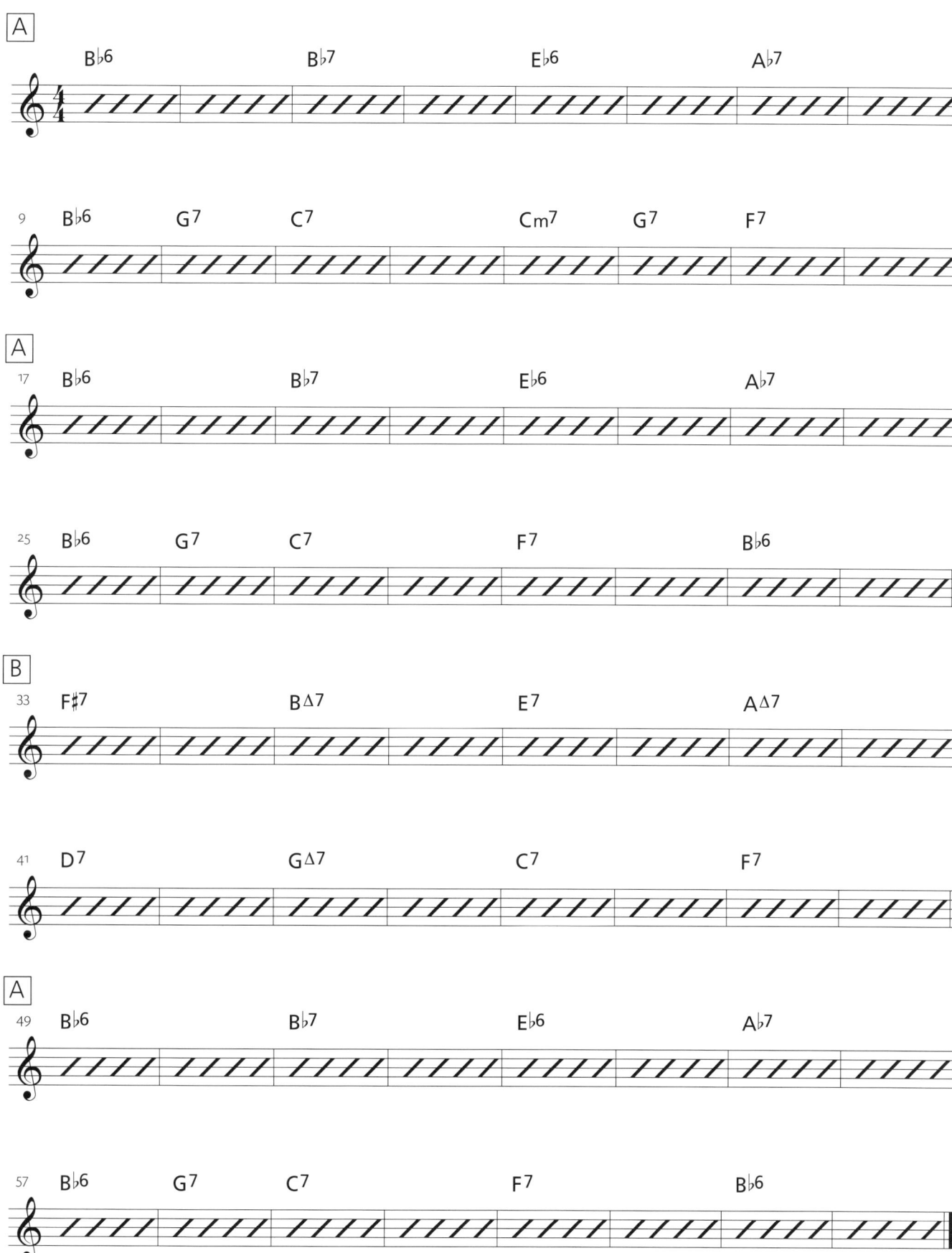

Chromatic Approach

One way to become rhythmically and harmonically more active is to use a chromatic approach to chords. Similar to the SubV chord, every chord can be approached chromatically from above or below. The same voicing is simply moved chromatically.

Chromatically from above:

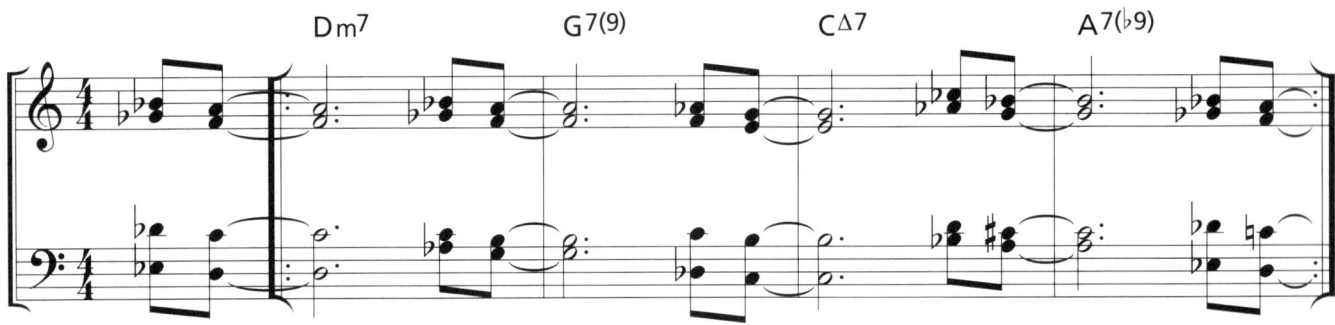

Chromatically from below:

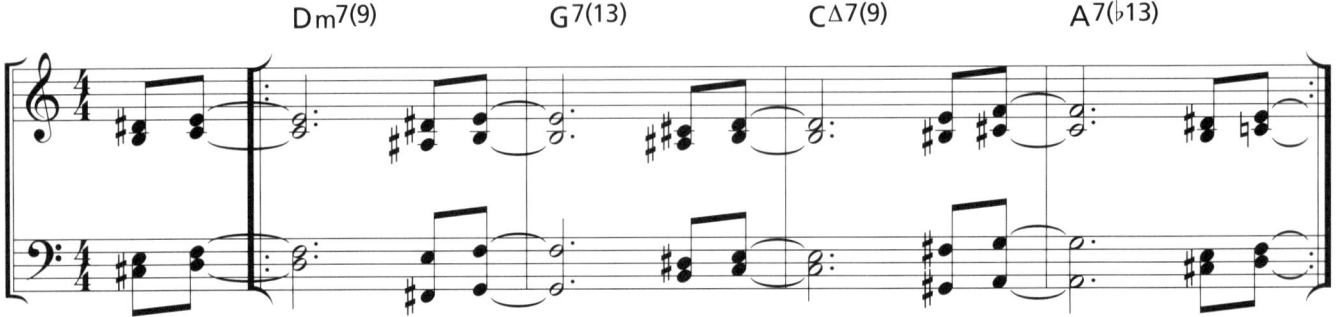

EXERCISE:

- Apply this technique to the previous tunes.
- Play the previous II-V-I cadences using chromatic approaches.

EXERCISE:

- Transcribe and notate the voicings from CD track 49.
- Compare your version with the version in the Solution Key.
- Learn these voicings by heart and play them along to the CD.

Track 49 ▸ Progression 27

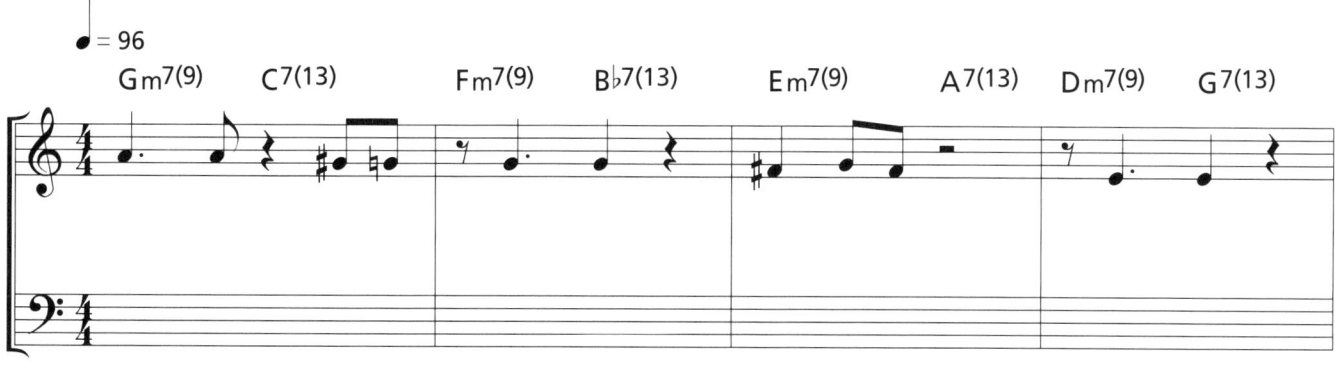

Jazz Piano – Voicing Concepts

EXERCISE:

- Transcribe and notate the voicings from CD track 50.
- Compare your version with the version in the Solution Key.
- Learn these voicings by heart and play them along to the CD.

Track 50 ▸ Progression 28

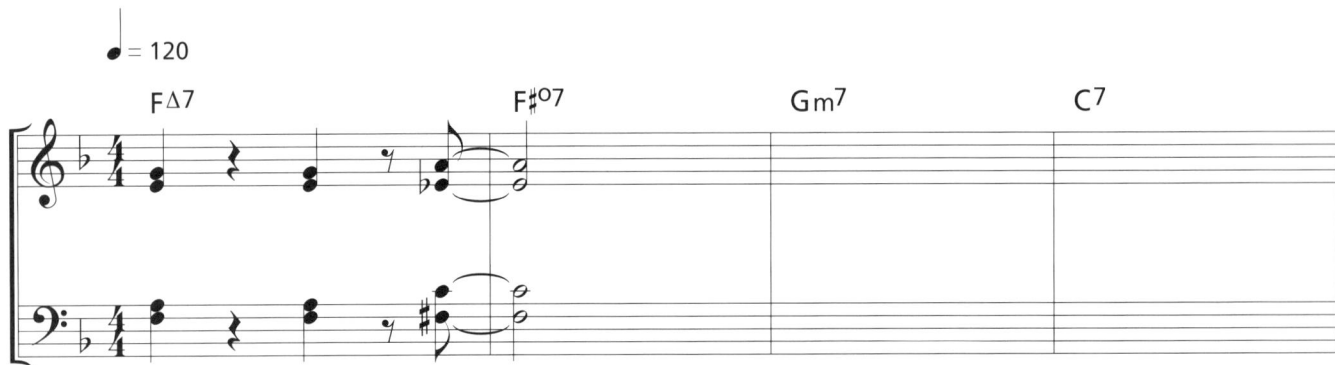

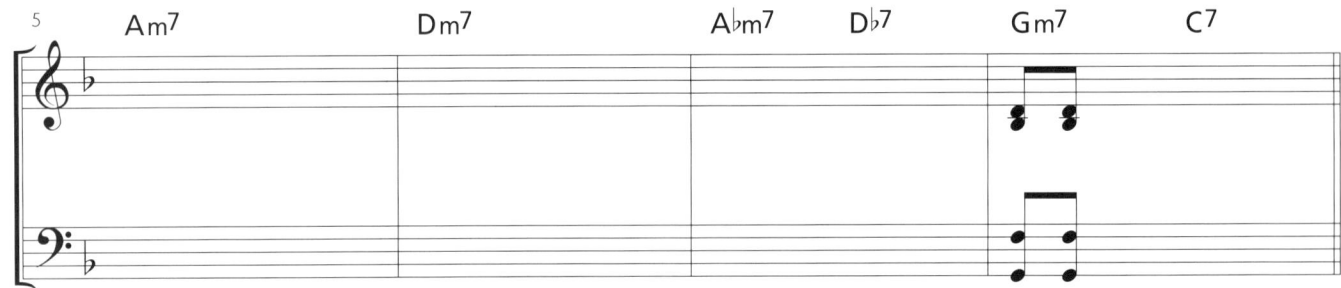

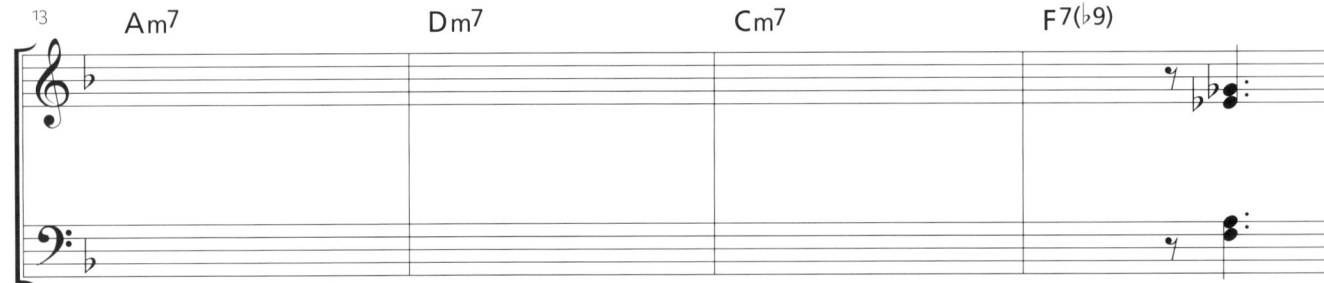

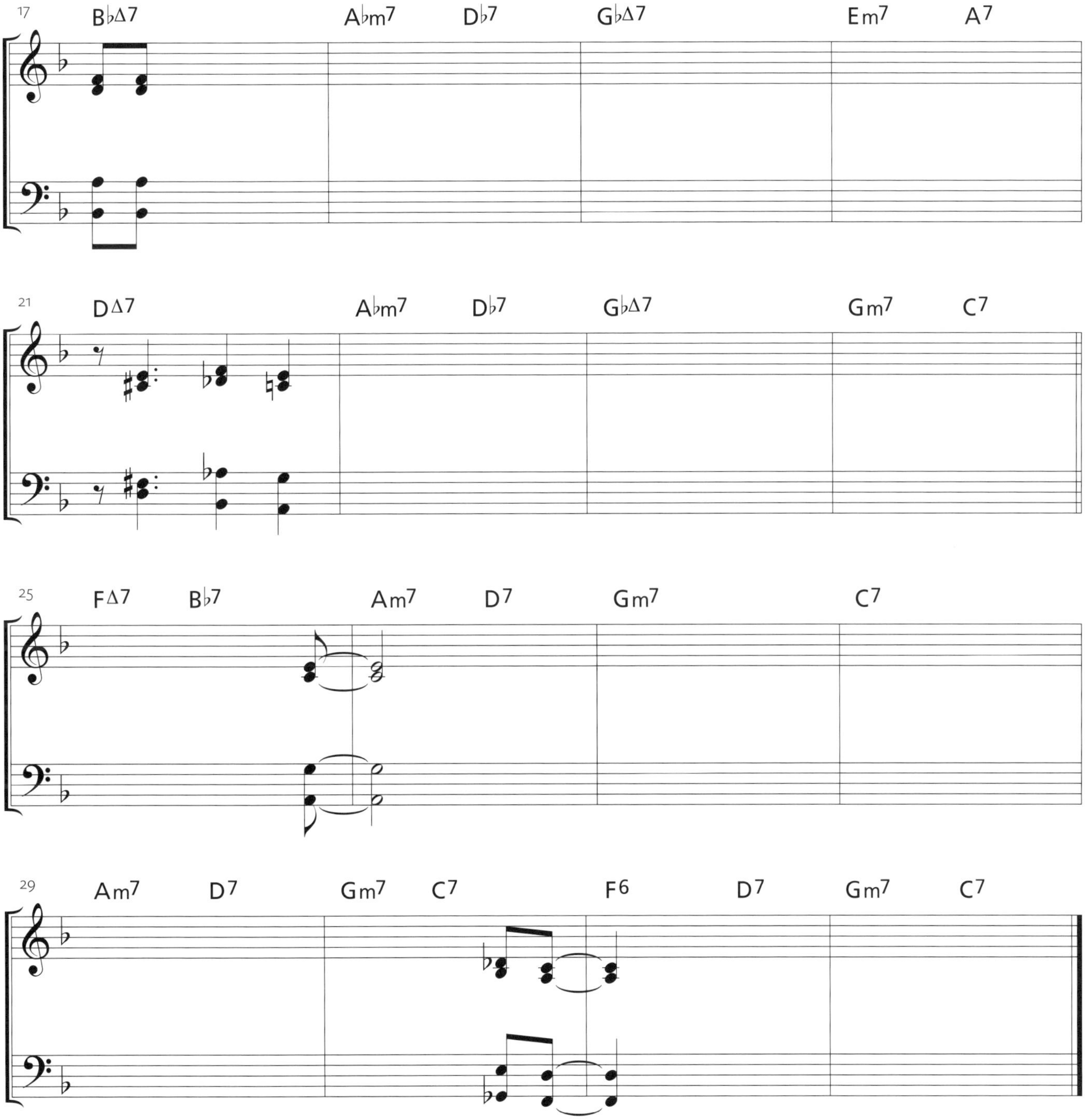
17
B♭Δ7
A♭m7 D♭7
G♭Δ7
Em7 A7
21
DΔ7
A♭m7 D♭7
G♭Δ7
Gm7 C7
25
FΔ7 B♭7
Am7 D7
Gm7
C7
29
Am7 D7
Gm7 C7
F6 D7
Gm7 C7

Jazz Piano – Voicing Concepts

Chord Substitution

Dom7sus4

A simple reharmonization technique is the substitution of a dominant chord by a dom7sus4 chord. This chord replaces the third degree with the fourth. "Sus" is short for "suspension".

II-V-I Original Cadence:

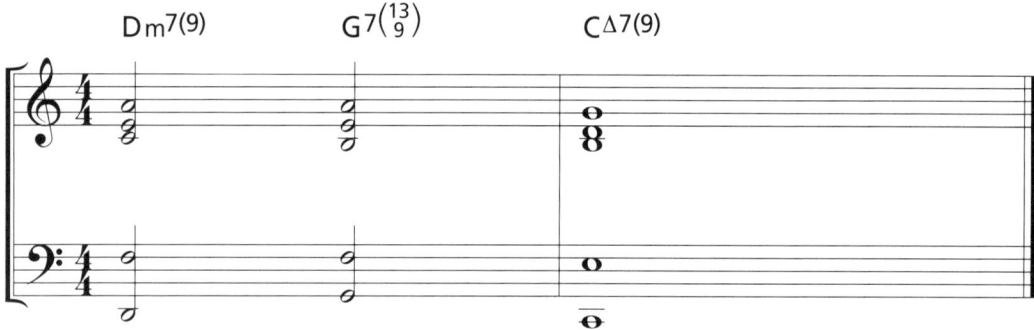

II-V-I Cadence with Dom7sus4:

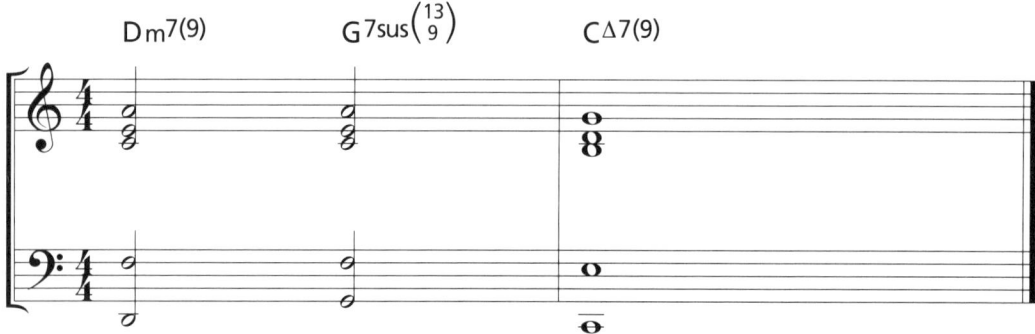

In connection with the known SubV chords, the II-V-I cadence can be played like this:

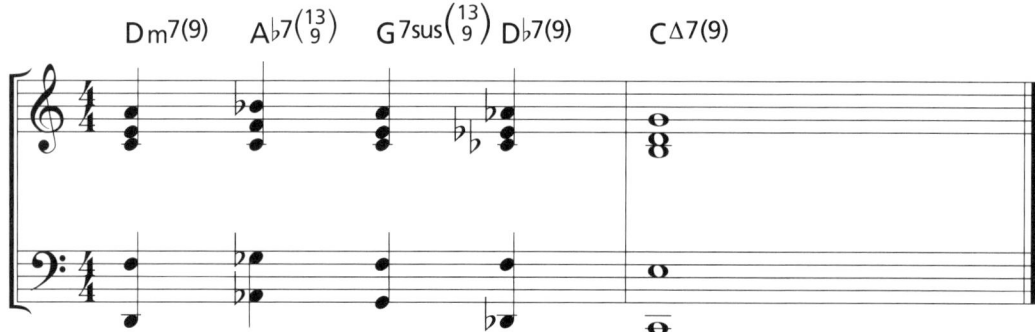

EXERCISE:

- Play this new II-V-I progression in all keys.

Reharmonization

EXERCISE:

- Transpose the following example to G major and A major.
- Try to transpose the example by ear at first.
- If necessary, Notate the example in the new keys.

EXAMPLE

(from *Jazz Piano – Solo Concepts*, "*Jazz Flowers*", p. 64)

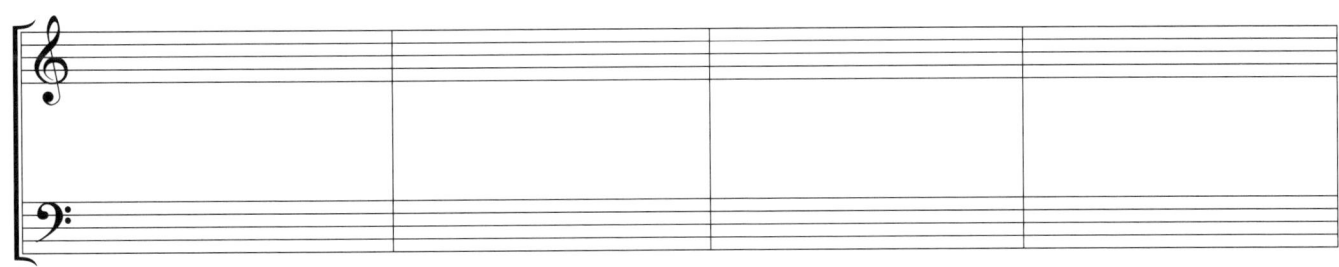

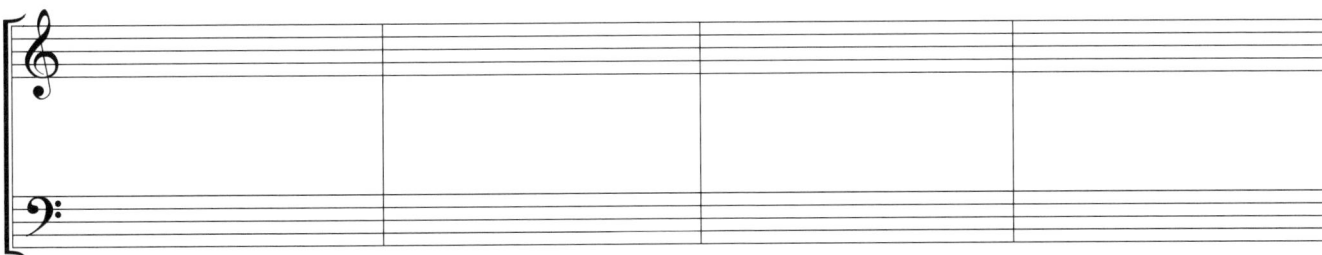

EXERCISE:

- Notate 5 note spread voicings for the given chord progression.
- Compare your version with the version in the Solution Key.
- Learn the progression by heart and play it along to the CD.

TRACK 51 ▸ PROGRESSION 29

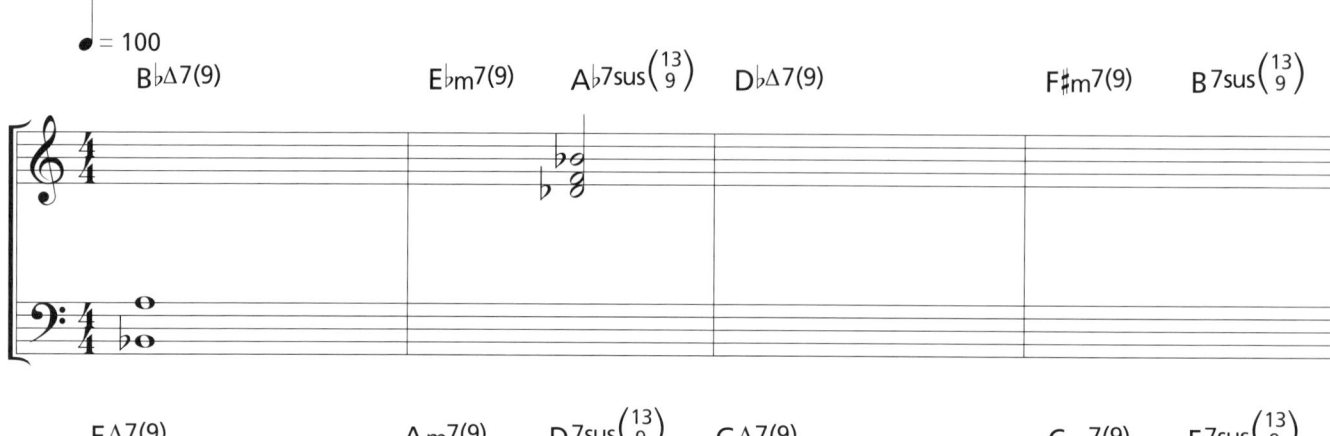

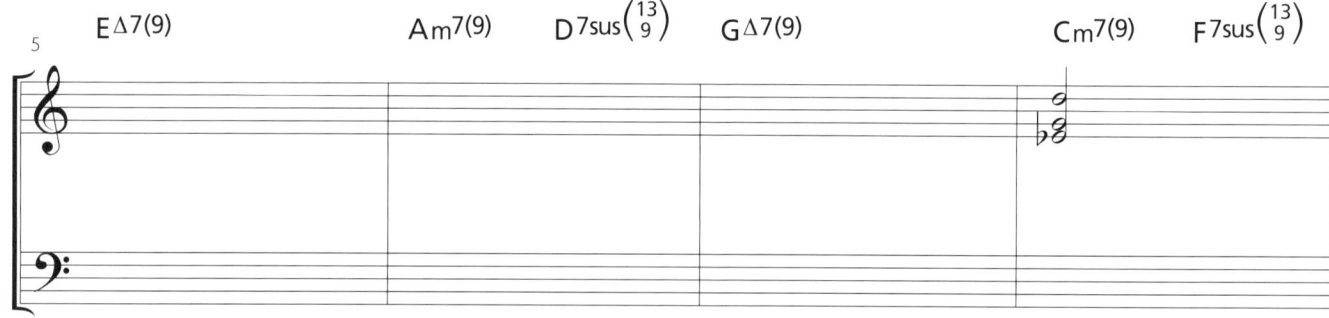

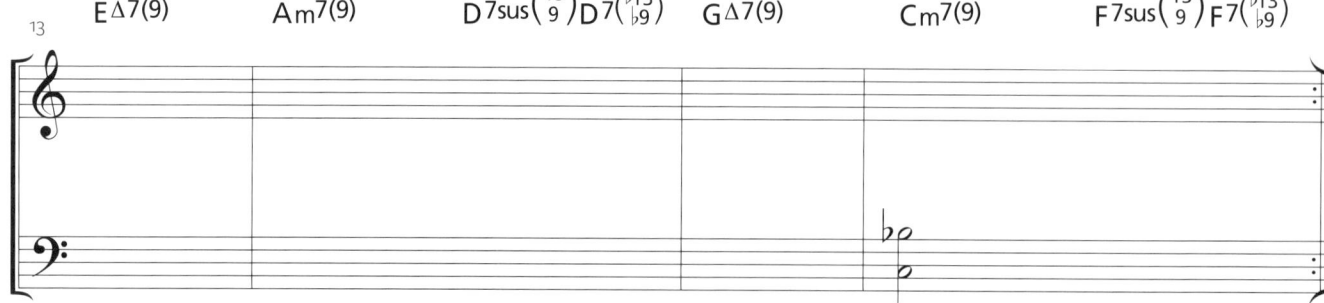

Changing Chord Extensions

The chord extensions (color tones) of existing harmonic progressions can be changed, too.

Chord Progression:

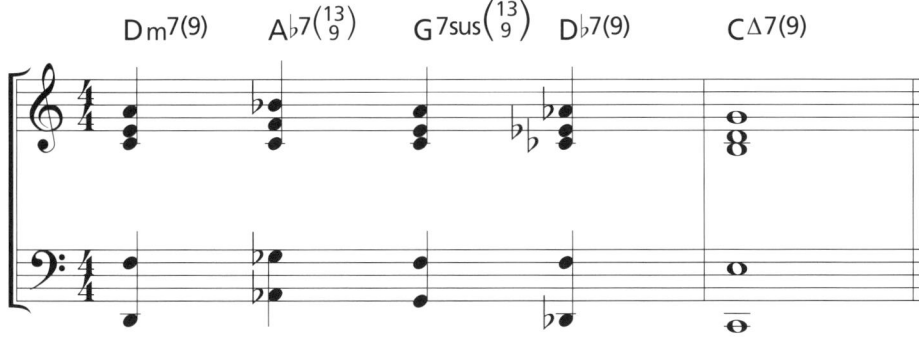

Chord Progression with change of chord color tones:

Changing Chord Type

Even the chord type can be changed.

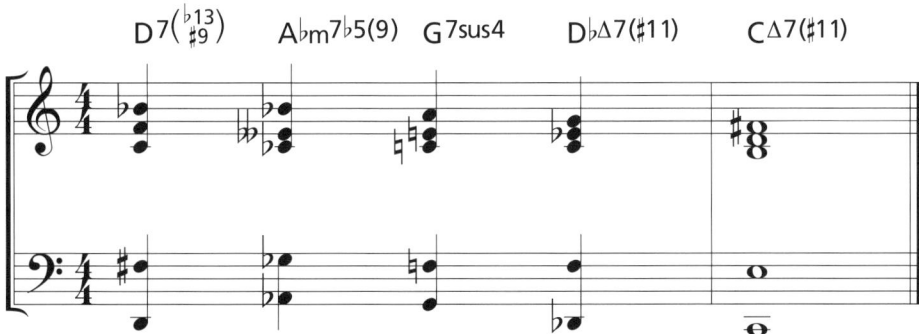

Tip: It takes a lot of practice and experience as well as a well-founded knowledge of harmonic relationships to use the techniques introduced here in a tasteful way. Therefore, start experimenting with these techniques right at the very beginning. Despite all the well-meant rules found in the standard books on harmony, please remember this guiding principle:

What sounds right is right!

Pedal Point

Often a pedal point is used in arrangements: one steady note in either a lower or upper voice. The root note of the key is often very suitable to be used as pedal point. However, almost always the fifth of the key is used (fifth or dominant pedal).

Pedal point in the lower voice (bass pedal):

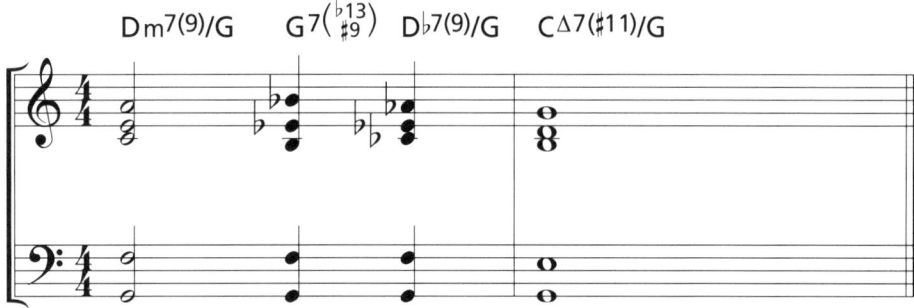

Pedal point in the upper voice (soprano pedal):

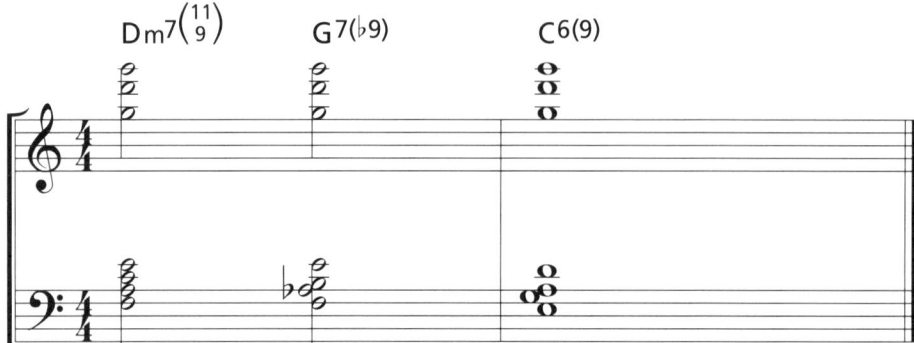

Both pedal points can also be used at the same time:

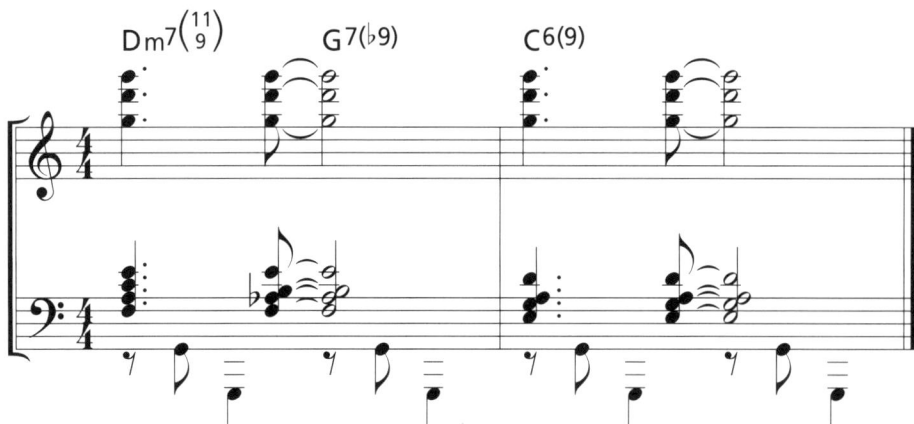

EXERCISE:

- Play this new II-V-I progression in all keys.
- Experiment with pedal points on original arrangements.

Reharmonization

Contrary Motion

In reharmonization you should try to move the bass line in a contrary motion to the melody (counterpoint). If the melody goes up, the bass line should move down and vice versa. This little trick will help your arrangement to sound fuller and more organic. We will demonstrate this technique in the prelude to Duke Ellington's *In a Sentimental Mood*.

First, the original melody:

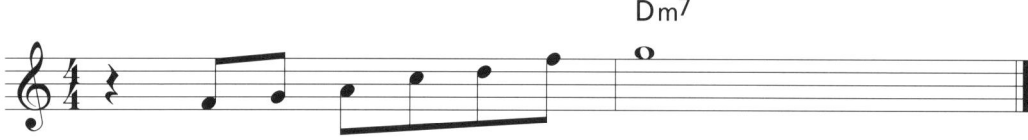

Now a reharmonization using a progression in descending fifths. Note that the harmonic progression was composed **backwards from the ending target note**.

The dominant of Dm7 is A7. The dominant of A7 is E7 etc.

Except for the Ab7, the right hand always plays upper structures (see the chapter *Two Hand Voicings*). As mentioned before, the upper structure (triad or a series of fourths) should be no further than a sixth away from the basic voicing of the left hand. The higher a melody note goes, the more notes that have to be included in the upper structure so that the voicing sounds well-balanced and so that the gap between lower and upper structure does not get too big. The Dm7 chord is an exception to the rule!

In the next example, the bass plays a descending D minor scale. The chords were not chosen according for their functional aspects but rather for the character of their sound (see *Changing Chord Type*, p. 135).

These two examples showed the intent and purpose of reharmonization. Try to apply your already pretty extensive voicing repertoire to jazz standards.

Summary: By now you should have learned the following:

- Dominant Substitution (SubV)
- IIm7 extension
- Chromatic approach
- Chord substitution
- Pedal point
- Contrary motion

Chapter 7: Grooves

Rhythm Patterns for Jazz Accompaniment

Up to this point, most of the examples were chosen so that the voicings would and should be played on the beat. This form of accompaniment is especially liked by vocalists ("Less is more!"). For a rhythmically more interesting accompaniment, some already established rhythm patterns can be used.

One main feature of jazz is syncopated rhythms. In rhythmical jazz accompaniment, chords are often played before or after their notated time.

Common:

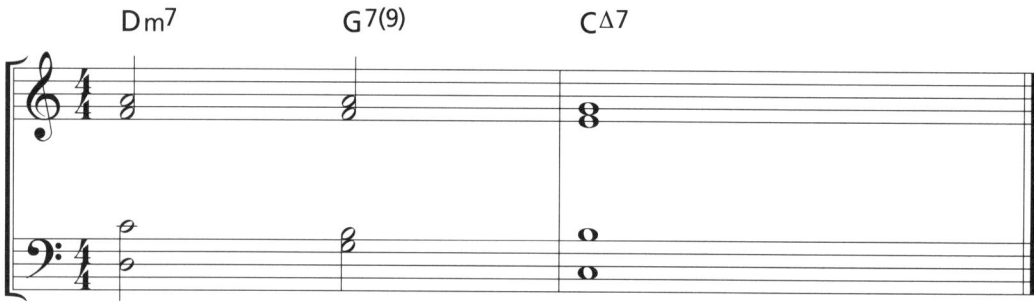

Anticipation:

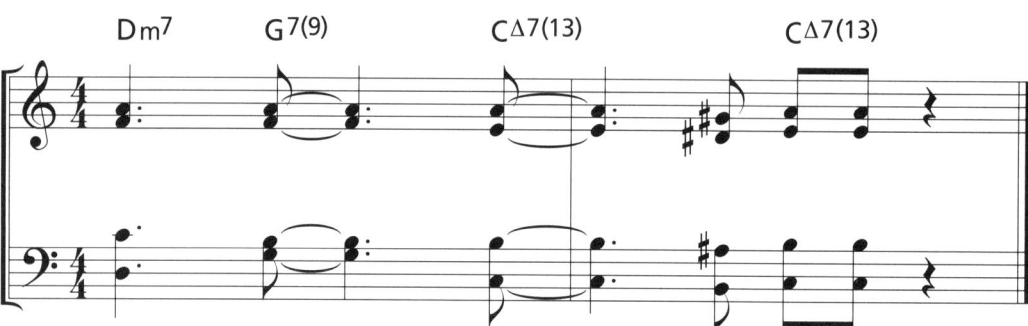

Delay:

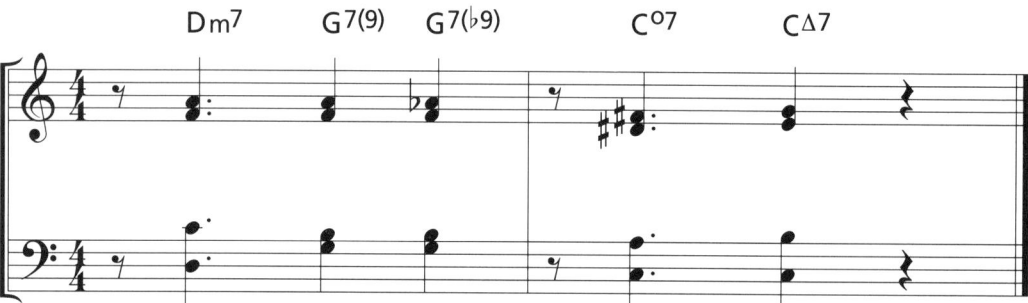

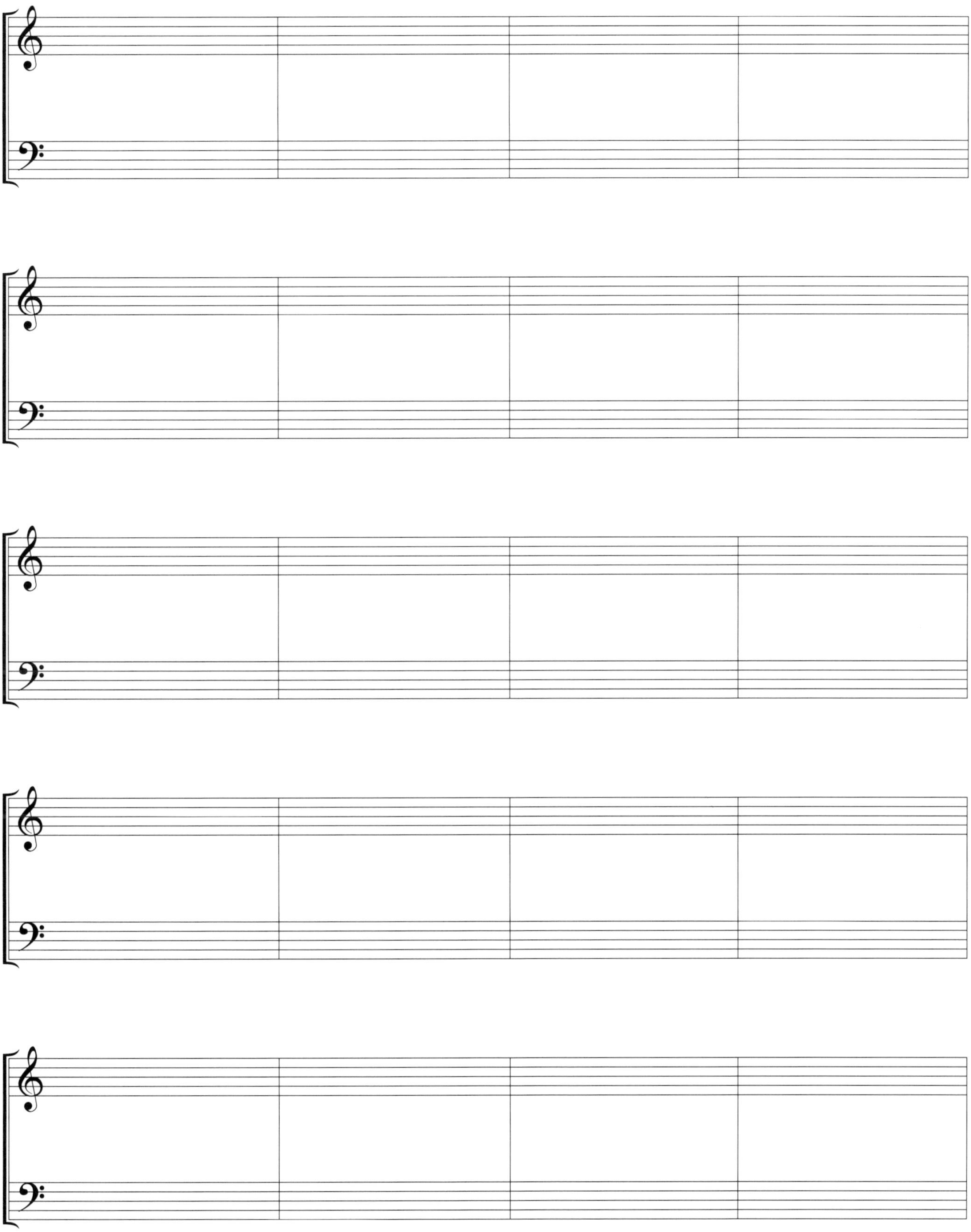

GROOVES

Swing Comping

In the following section you will find some of the most commonly used rhythm patterns for 4/4 straight ahead jazz. The rhythm patterns are notated as simple rhythms and then demonstrated with different voicing techniques.

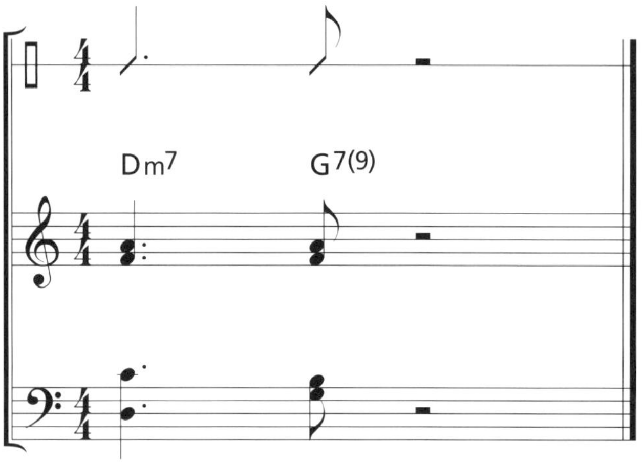

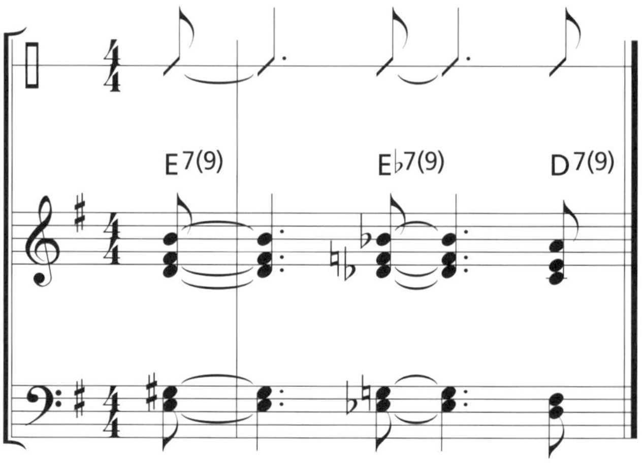

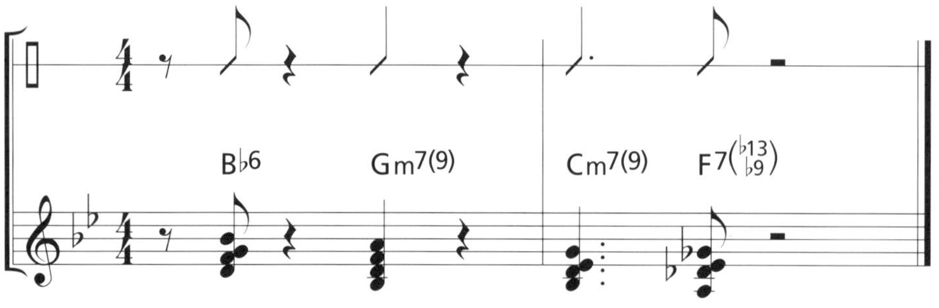

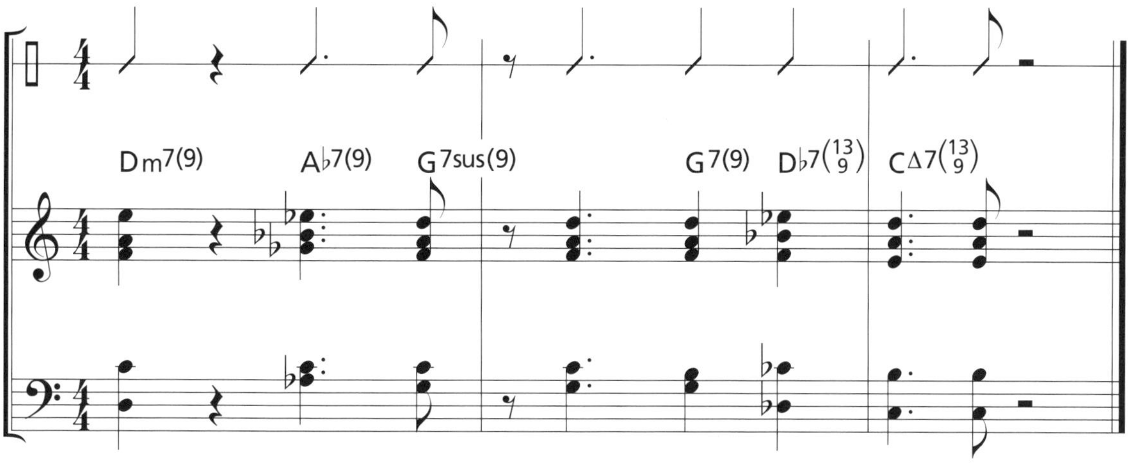

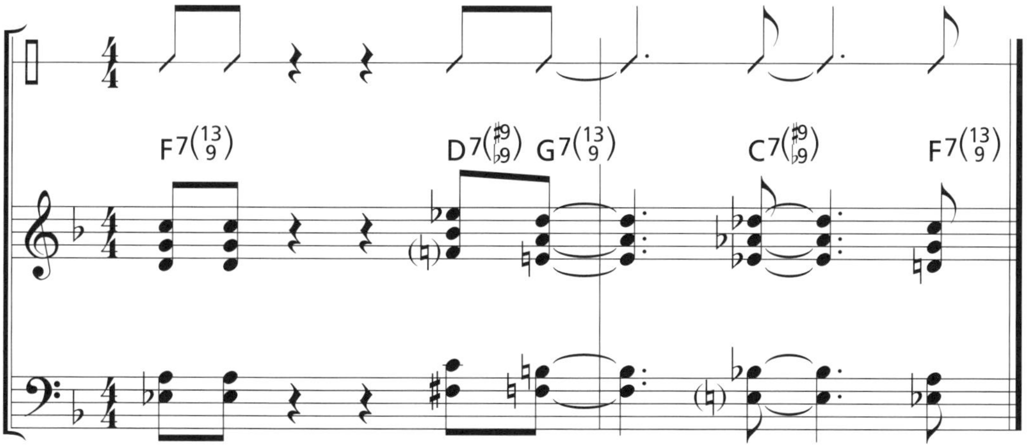

GROOVES

Tip: Trading experiences and talking with bass players and drummers is vital as together, you make up the rhythm section. A good rhythm section can only play strong when each member knows exactly about their function and the function of the other instruments as well. Melody instrumentalists are sadly often not fully aware of the job the rhythm section has to do and accordingly, they cannot use the rhythm section to their fullest advantage.

© 2007 by AMA Musikverlag

Jazz Waltz

At times jazz is played in 3/4. This style is called jazz waltz.

Practice accompanying the jazz waltz by combining different rhythm patterns with both hands. Stay with one rhythm pattern first until you feel comfortable playing it.

Example:

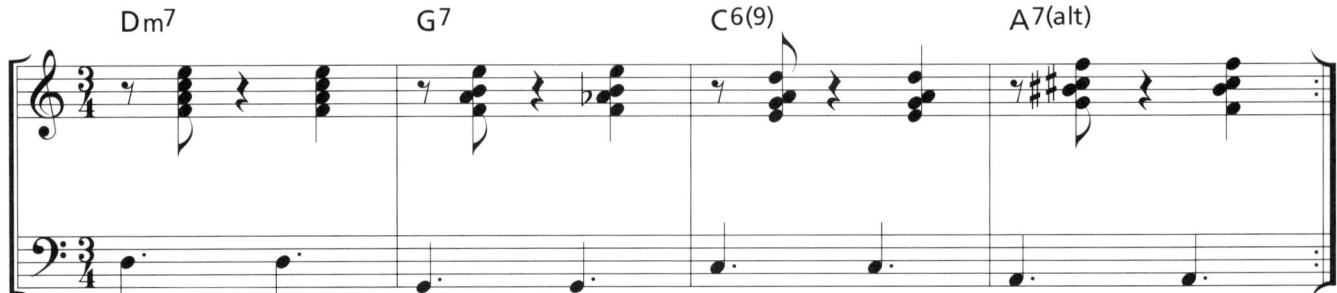

Then play a different pattern with the right hand while the left hand continues the previous pattern.

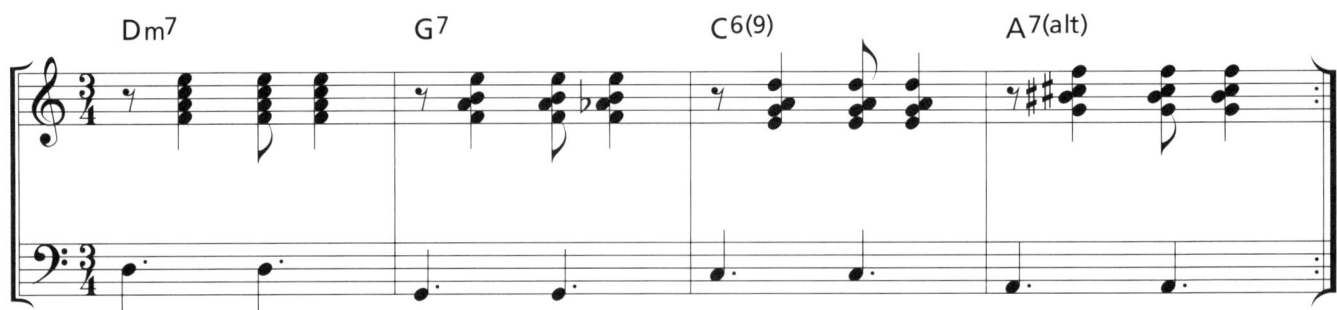

Then change the left hand pattern.

In time you will have combined all the rhythm patterns so that you will be able to mix them spontaneously.

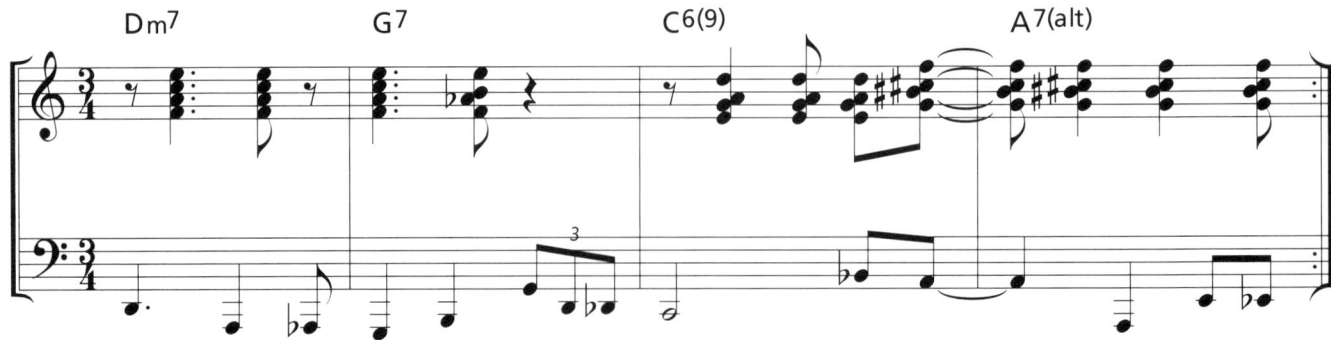

3/4 Rhythm Pattern:

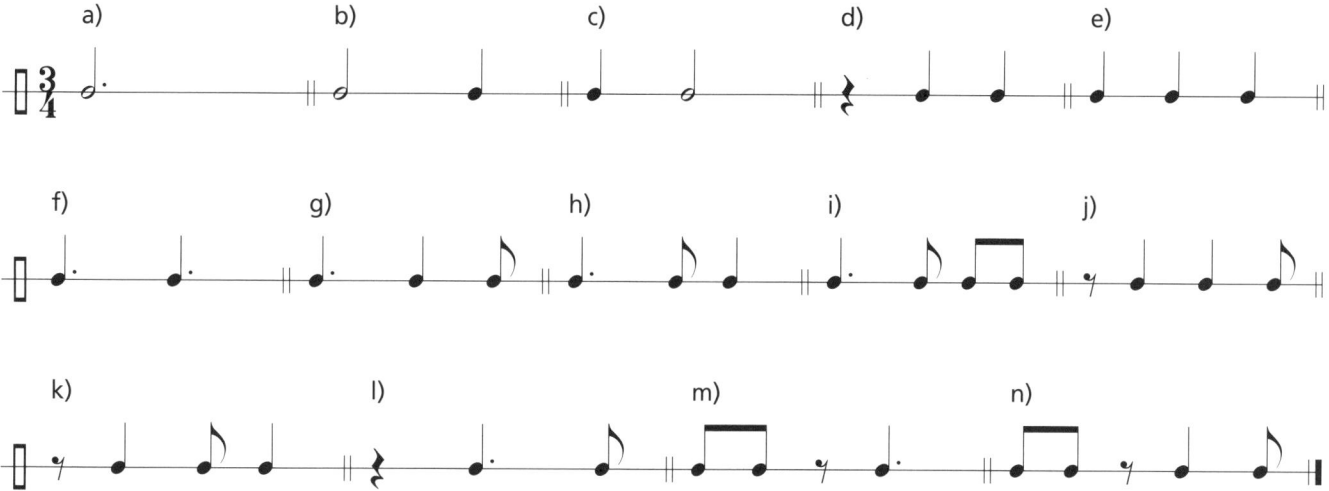

Tommy Flanagan (* March 16, 1930, † November 16, 2001) was an American jazz pianist of extraordinary virtuosity and creativity. His parents were jazz enthusiasts and supported Tommy's musicality already at the age of six with clarinet lessons. At age eleven he switched to the piano. He visited an Art Tatum concert in 1945 (also see *Jazz Piano – Improvisation Concepts*, p. 24) and decided then and there that his dream was to become a jazz pianist. Tommy Flanagan had his first professional appearance that same year at the tender age of 15. He made a successful start in New York in 1956 subbing in for the sick Bud Powell. He made such an impression on Miles Davis that he invited him to his first recording session. The next twenty years were filled with many recordings which are considered classics today. He performed with Dexter Gordon, Coleman Hawkins, Freddie Hubbard, Wes Montgomery, Sonny Rollins and John Coltrane just to name a few. Tommy Flanagan worked as Ella Fitzgerald's pianist during two longer stretches between 1962 and 1965 and from 1968 until 1978. Between those engagements he also worked for Tony Bennett. After a stroke in 1978, he reduced his playing to performing with his own trio.

© 2007 by AMA Musikverlag

Jazz Piano – Voicing Concepts

Easy Stride

An easy technique to learn is the "easy stride" style. It enables you to play a rhythmic accompaniment through all the chords of a standard progression while playing the melody or soloing with the right hand. Use this technique for older compositions from the swing era.

The foundation of the easy stride technique is the 3 note spread voicing (see the chapter Left Hand Voicings). Instead of playing all the notes of the voicing on one beat they are played successively, divided into root note and guide tones.

Beat 1: root note – Beat 2: guide tones – Beat 3: fifth – Beat 4: guide tones

Easy Stride Style

Example

(from *Jazz Piano – Solo Concepts*, "*Swing It!*", p. 10)

EXERCISE:

- Notate an easy stride accompaniment for the given chords.
- Compare your version with the version in the Solution Key.
- Learn the chord progression by heart and play it along to the CD.

TRACK 52 ▸ PROGRESSION 30

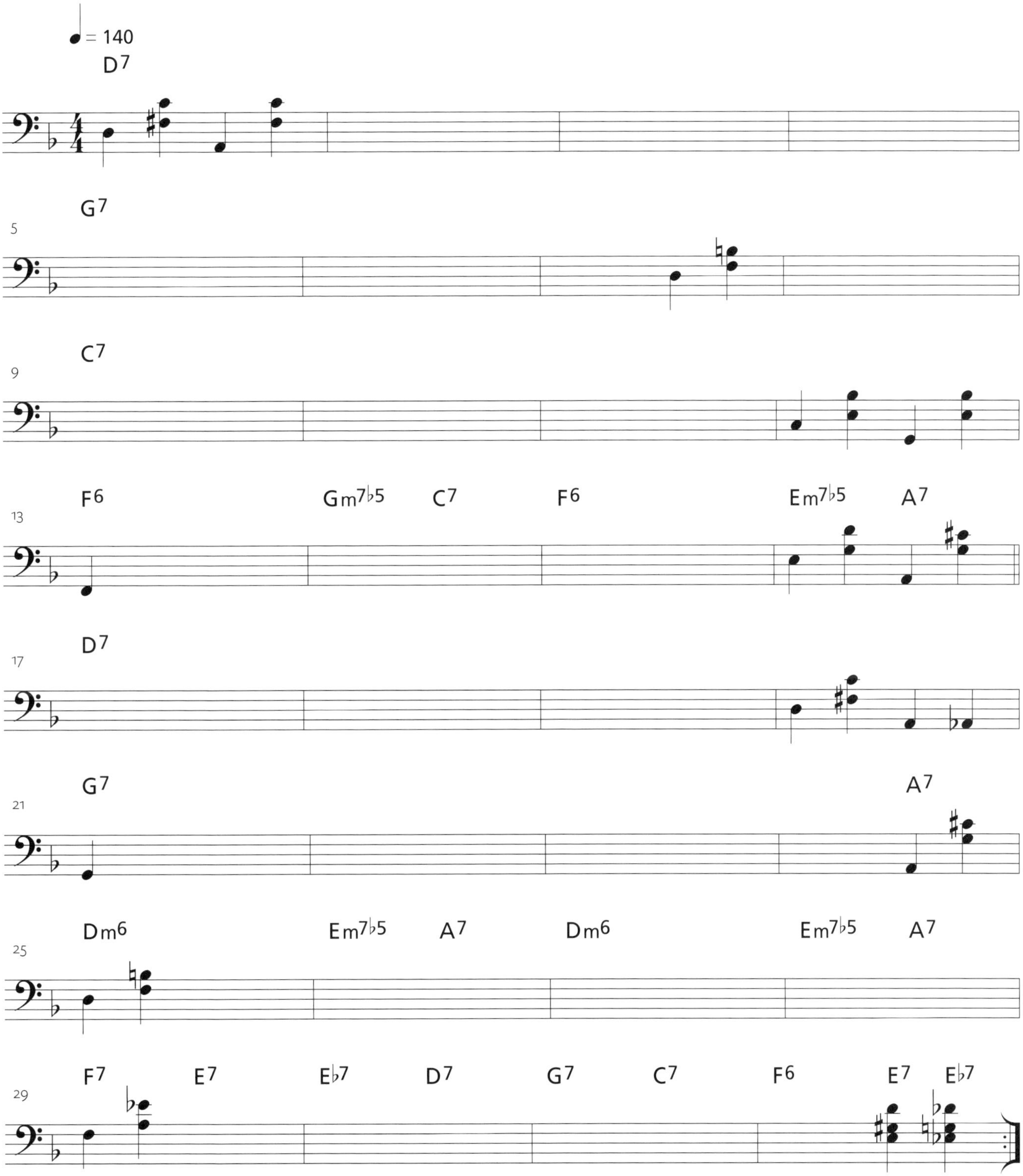

EXERCISE:

- Notate an easy stride accompaniment for the given chords.
- Compare your version with the version in the Solution Key.
- Learn the chord progression by heart and play it along to the CD.

TRACK 53 ▸ PROGRESSION 31

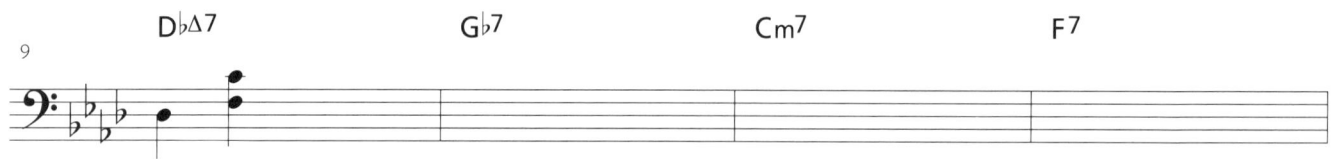

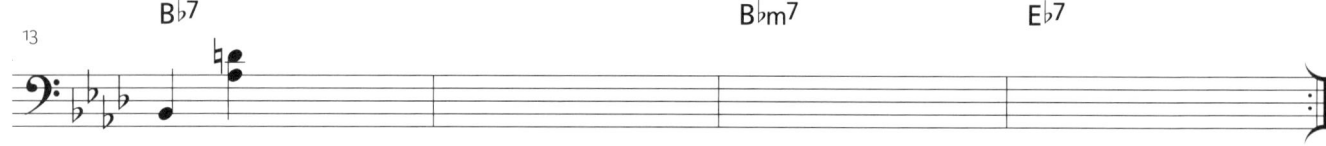

Stride Piano

The original stride piano style went as follows:

or like this:

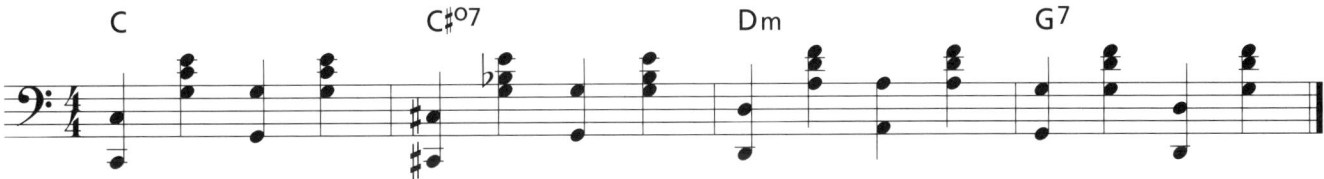

EXERCISE:

- Play the following chords, with the left hand first, through the circle of fifths.
- Pay attention to good voice leading.
- Then, try to improvise along with the right hand.
- Use different licks from *Jazz Piano – Improvisation Concepts*, p. 72.

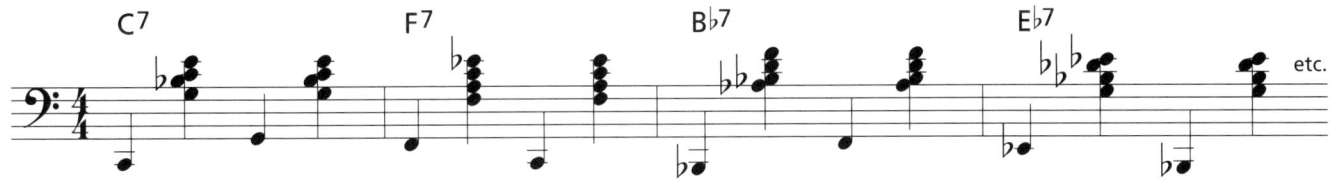

Tip: To learn more about the stride piano style, practice Scott Joplin's famous ragtimes!

© 2007 by AMA Musikverlag

Rolling Tenth

One of the many variations of stride piano is the rolling tenth which is a mixture of stride piano and an extended walking bass:

Option 1:

Option 2:

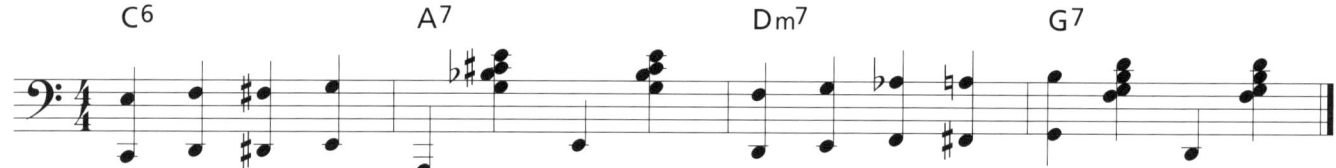

EXERCISE:

- Play the following chords, with the left hand first, through the circle of fifths.
- Then, try to improvise along with the right hand.
- Use different licks from *Jazz Piano – Improvisation Concepts* (S. 72 & S. 60 ff.).

Option 1:

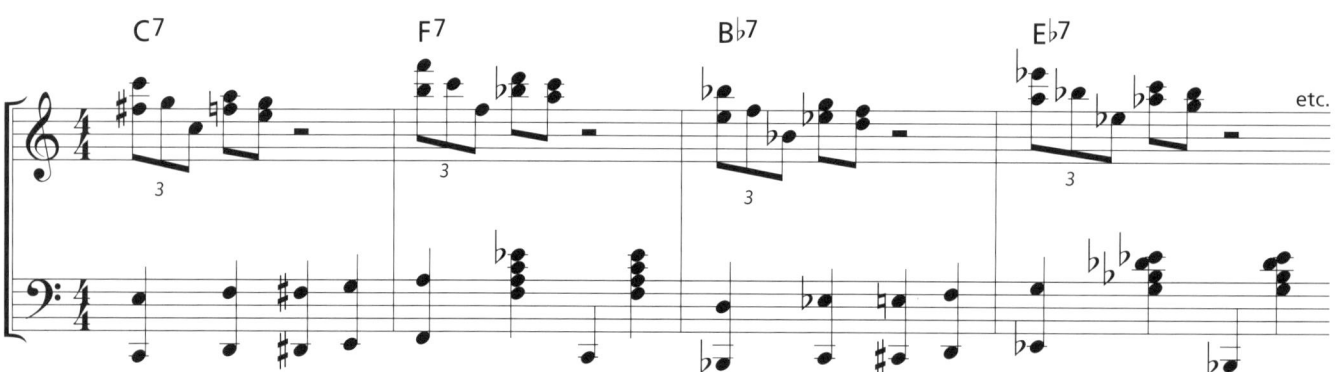

Option 2:

Erroll Garner Style

The famous American jazz pianist Erroll Garner (see *Jazz Piano – Solo Concepts*, p. 13) used the following rhythm for accompaniment with the left hand which is derived from stride piano:

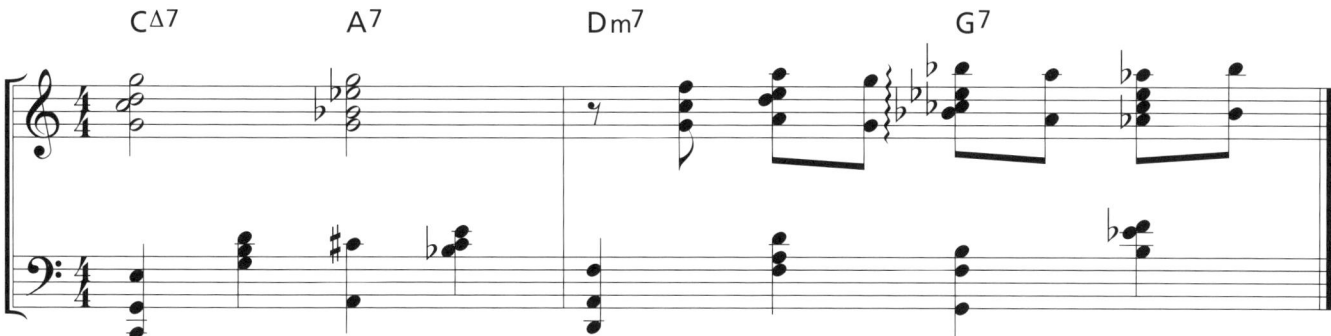

Very effective is also the repetition of the first chord:

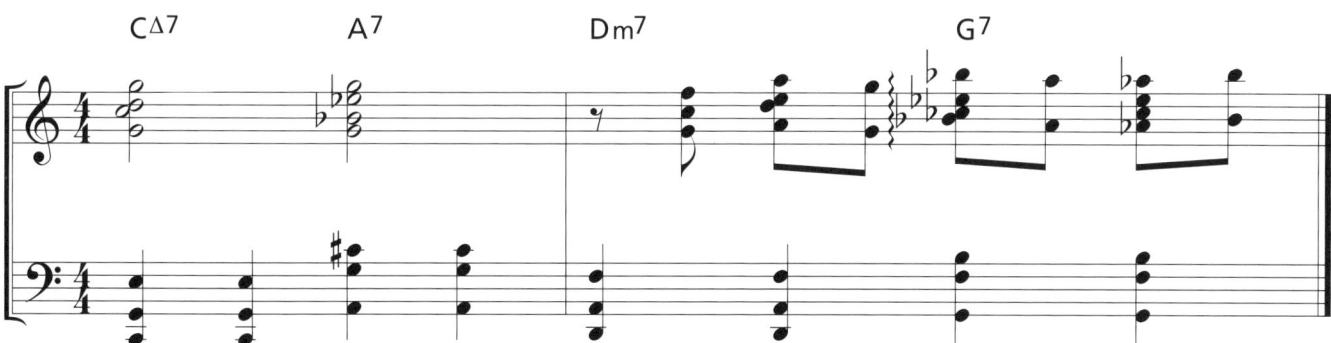

The same progression can also be played with 3 note spread voicings:

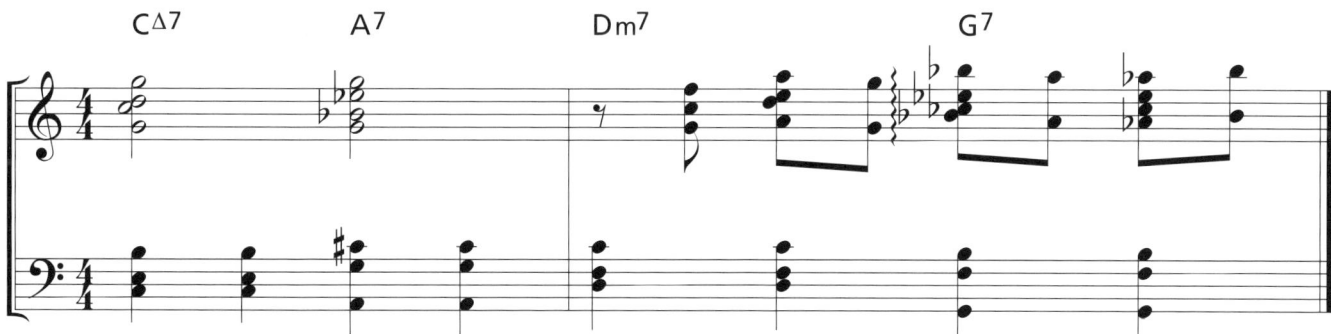

Tip: Find several different recordings of one tune and compare the versions. Never trust anybody else as much as you do your own ears!

Walking Bass

To add more rhythmic interest to an accompaniment, a so-called "walking bass" can be played. It is usually played over a 4/4 rhythm and consists of four quarter notes.

It goes without saying that a walking bass is only played on the piano when no bass player is accompanying you!

The walking bass is usually played an octave lower than notated, marked by the octave sign:

Track 54 ▸ Walking Bass Example

Listen to how a bass player would play these bass lines.
A walking bass line is put together as follows:

The root note is played on beat 1.

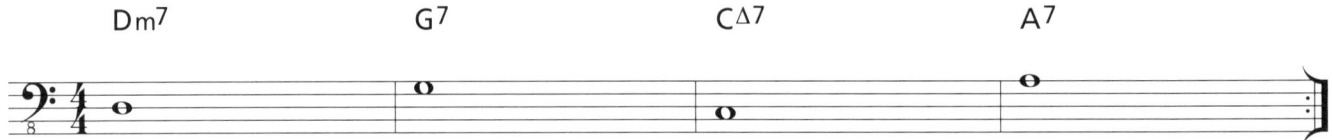

The fifth is played on beat 3.

A chromatic approach note to the following chord from above or below is played on beat 4.

Either the root note an octave higher or the third can be played on beat 2.

Bassists often employ so-called "ghost" notes. Where and when a ghost note is permitted or should be played is up to the individual player.

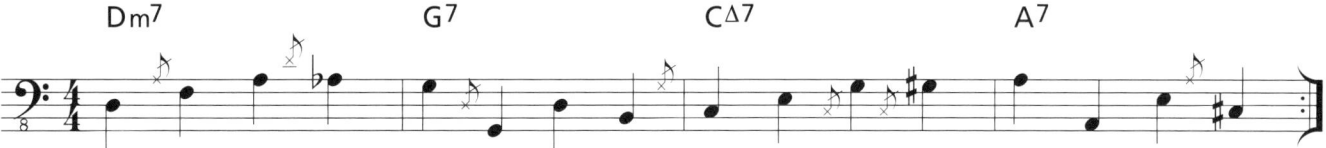

Another stylistic device for walking bass are descending triplet runs, usually consisting of chord notes.

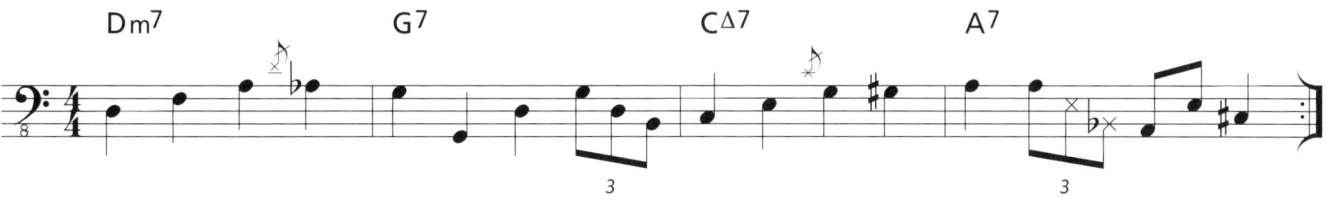

A walking bass can be varied rhythmically.

As soon as the rules have been internalized, playing a more linear walking bass should be the goal.

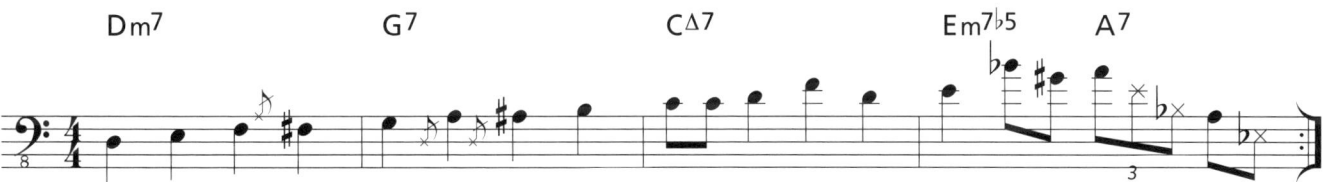

It is recommended to play the root note on the first beat. As an alternative, another chord-note can be played. Precise melodic motion is very important.

Jazz Piano – Voicing Concepts

EXERCISE:

- Transcribe the walking bass from a blues in F.
- Compare your version with the version in the Solution Key.
- Learn this walking bass part by heart.
- Add the right hand only when you can play the walking bass with the left hand fluidly and in time.
- The right hand voicings should eventually employ the rhythms found in *Swing Comping*.
- More accompanying rhythms can be found in *Jazz Piano – Improvisation Concepts*, p. 68.
- Transpose this example to the keys of B♭ und C Major.

Track 55 ▸ Progression 32

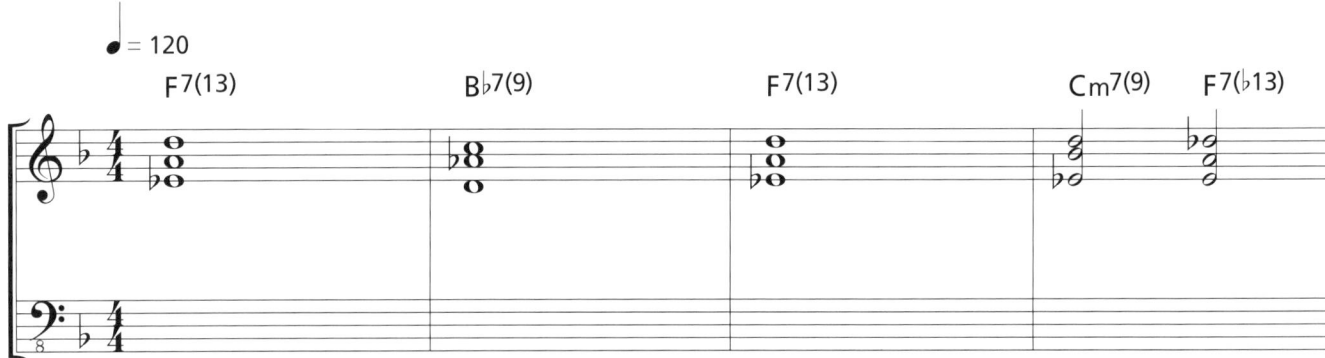

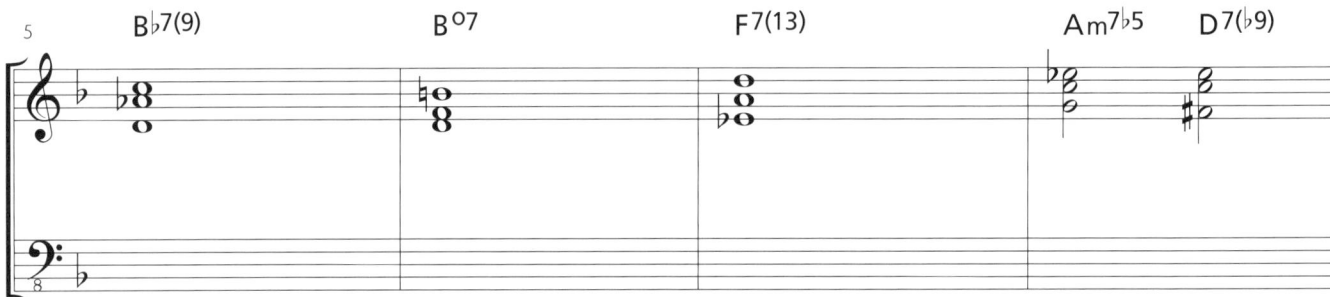

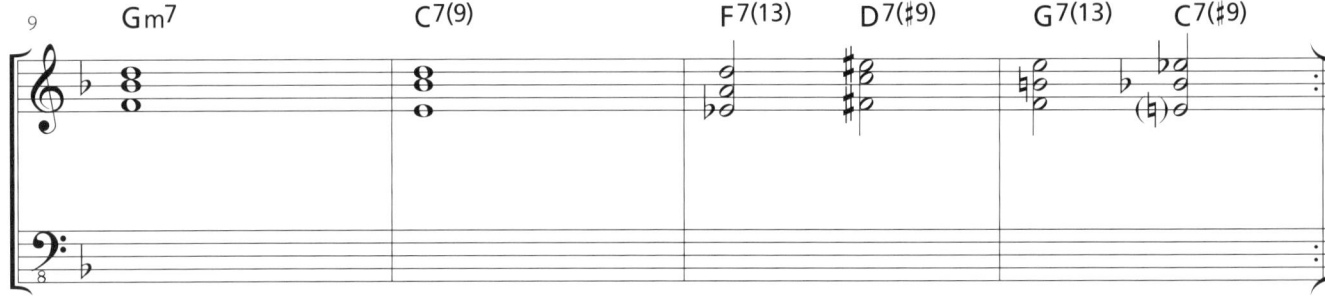

© 2007 by AMA Musikverlag

EXERCISE:

- Create and notate a walking bass for the given chord progression.
- Compare your version with the version in the Solution Key.
- Listen very closely to how the bassist plays the walking bass. The goal of playing a walking bass on the piano is to get as close to the performance of a bassist as possible.

Track 56 ▸ Progression 33

Tip: Play with different (and better) musicians as often as possible even if you consider yourself not experienced enough! This will give you the practice that marks an accomplished and experienced musician.

Example

(from *Jazz Piano – Solo Concepts*, "Biflat", p. 39)

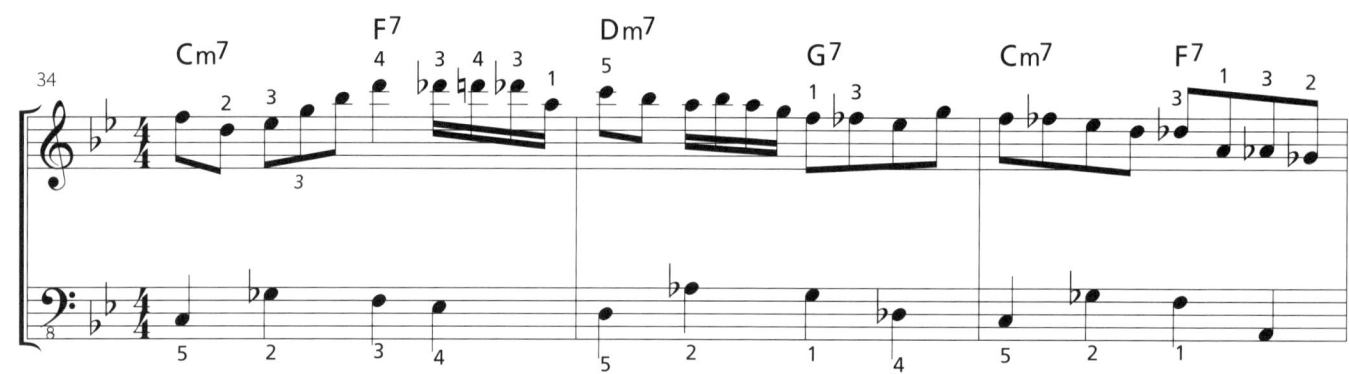
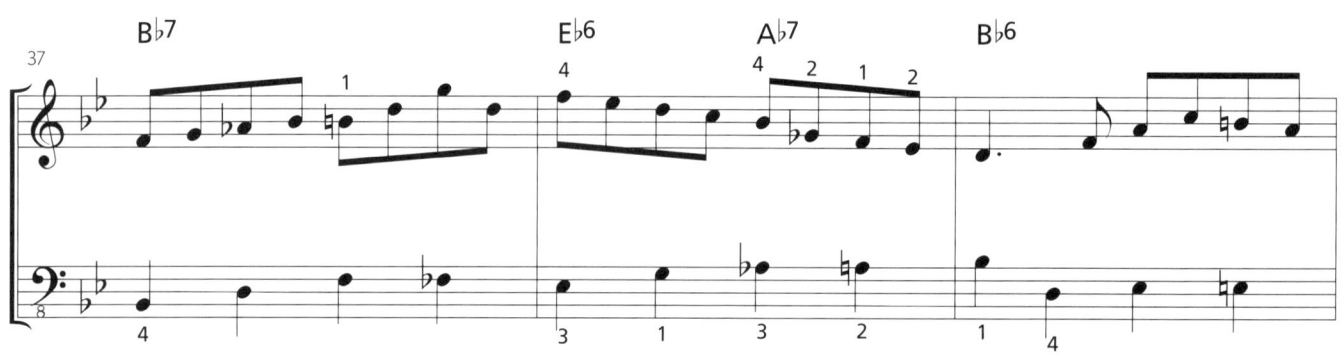
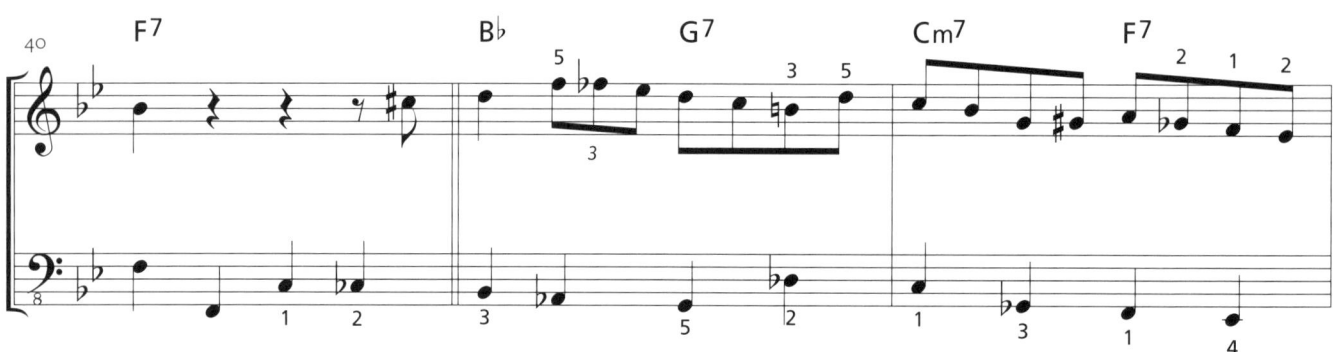

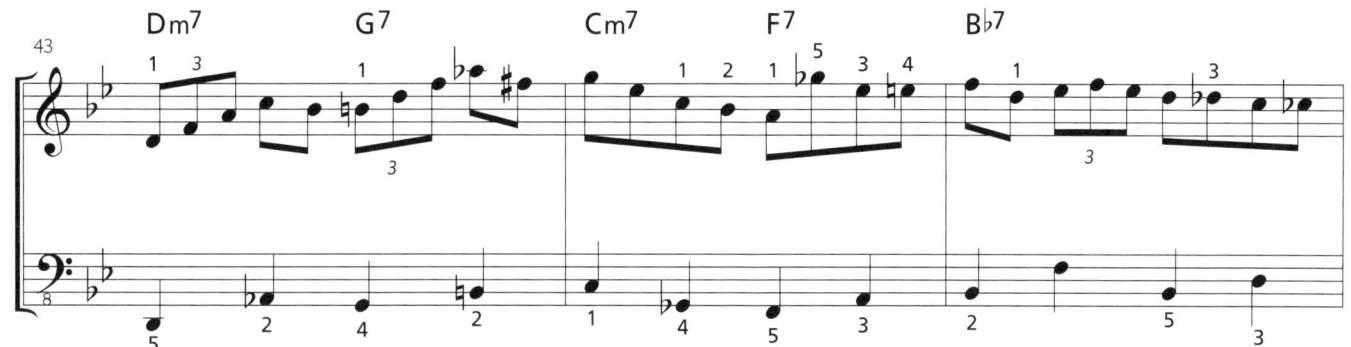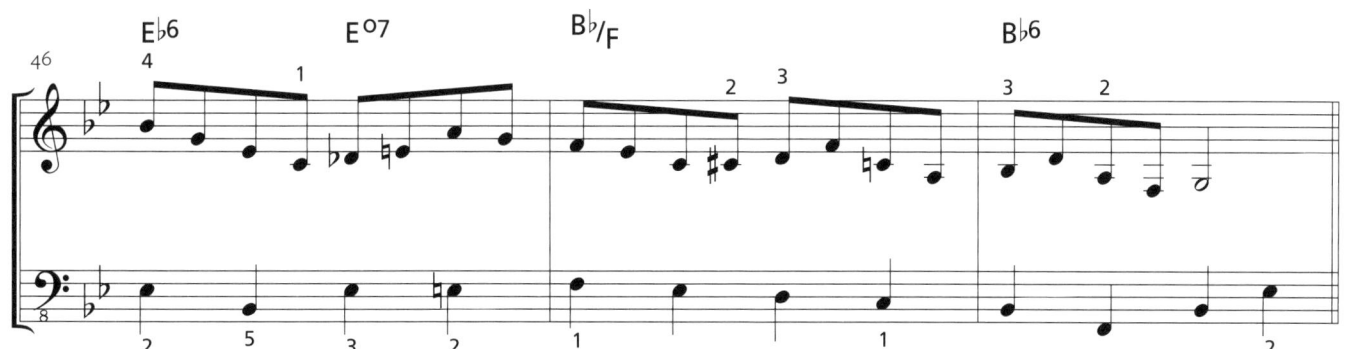

Jazz Piano – Voicing Concepts

Bossa Nova

Many jazz standards have been written in the style of a bossa nova. The basic rhythm of this style comes from Brazil and is very complex. The rhythms for accompaniment that we introduce here can therefore be only an introduction to the bossa nova style. Like with the techniques that were demonstrated before, one can achieve excellent results employing only limited means.

Play the following bass pattern with the left hand. Make sure to play the note on beat 3 lower than the root note as this is a typical feature of this style.

Use the following bossa nova rhythm patterns for the right hand. Make sure you play the anticipation of the chord in the second half of the pattern.

Bossa Nova Pattern 1:

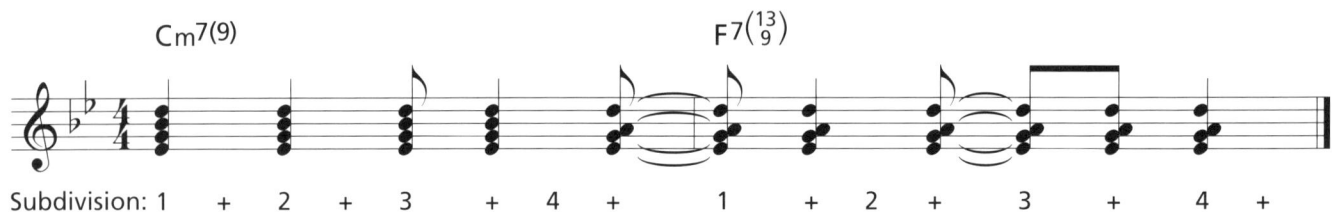

Bossa Nova Pattern 2:

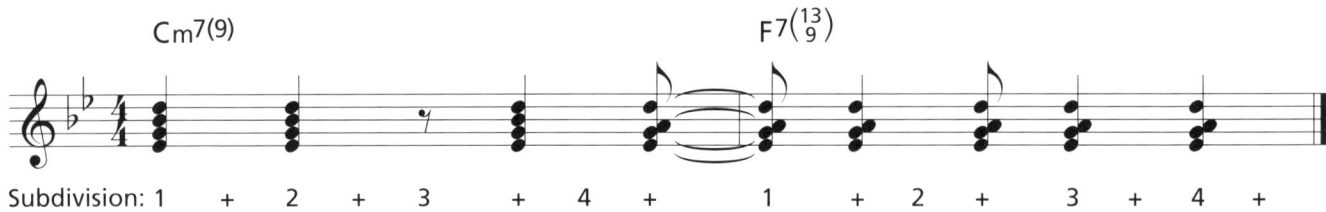

Tip: Take regular breaks from practicing to relax. Sit upright and relaxed at the piano. The wrong posture often leads to cramps. Count the subdivisions if rhythmic coordination problems should occur.

EXERCISE:

- Play the notated bossa nova groove (groove = rhythm pattern) slowly at first and later along to the CD.
- Should you have problems coordinating your hands rhythmically, play the groove very slowly and count the eighth note subdivisions.
- Transpose the example to several different keys.

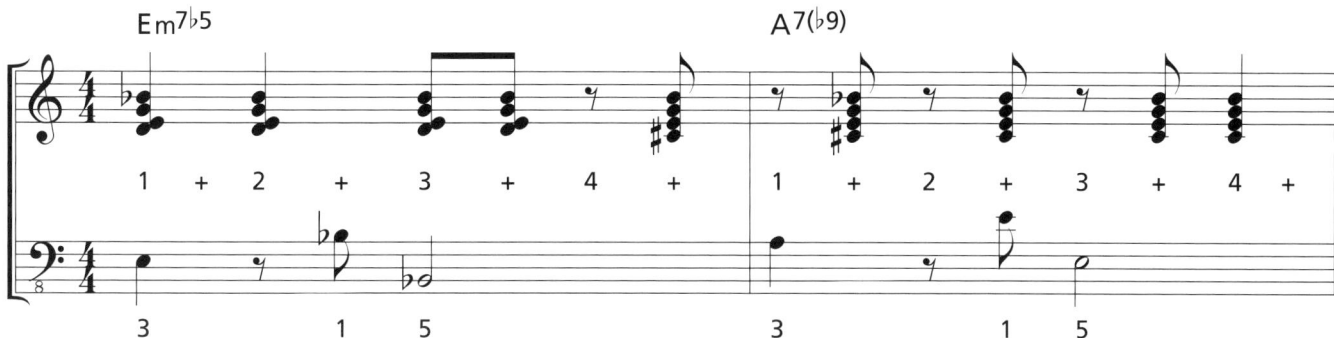

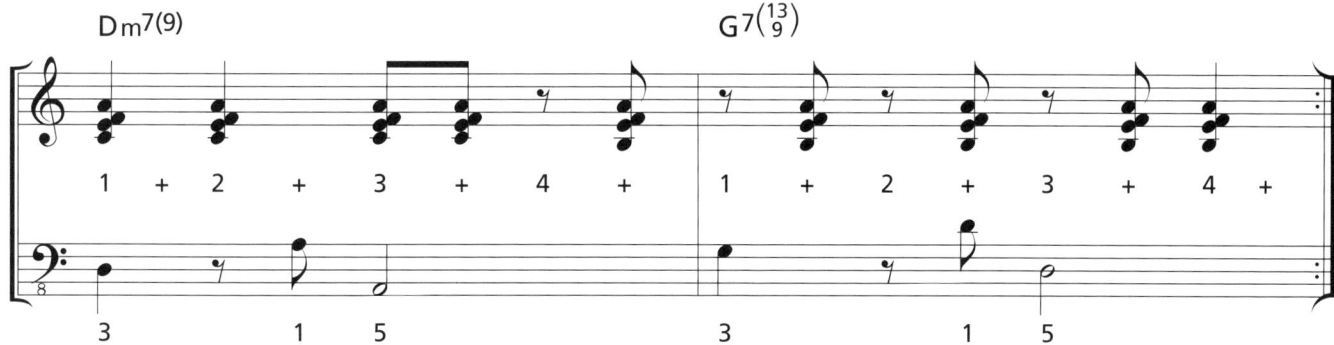

Tip: You can find further grooves in my book *The Groove Piano Book* (*Das Groove Piano Buch*, Advance Music, Rothenburg, Germany).

EXERCISE:

- Notate a bossa nova accompaniment for the given chords.
- Compare your version with the version in the Solution Key.
- Learn the chords by heart and play them along to the CD.

Track 57 ▸ Progression 34

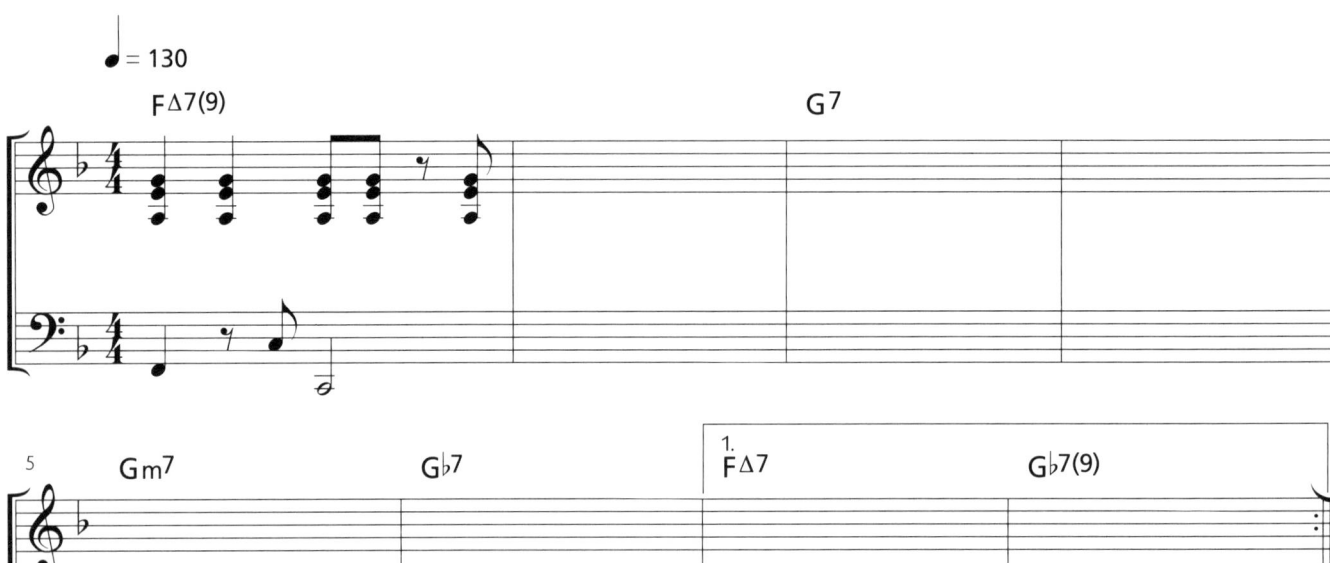

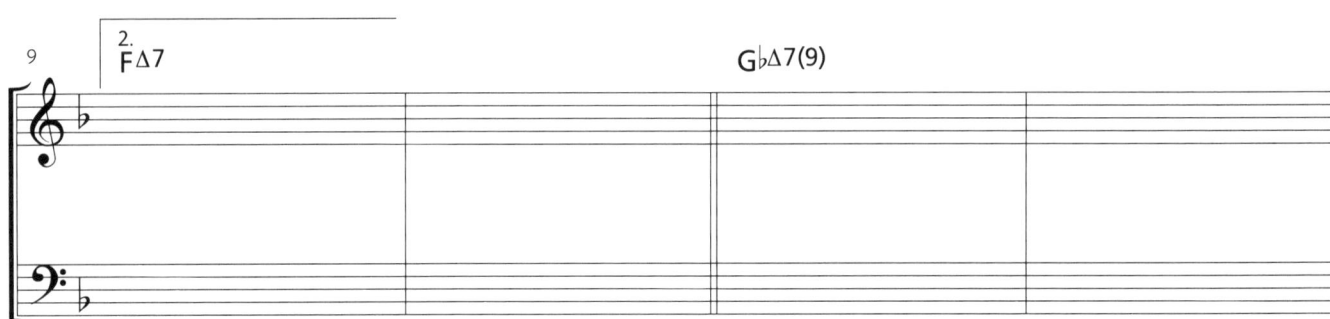

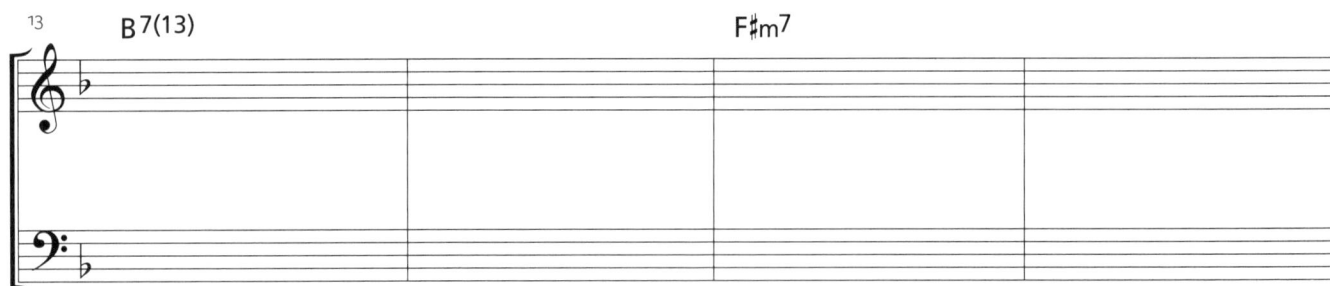

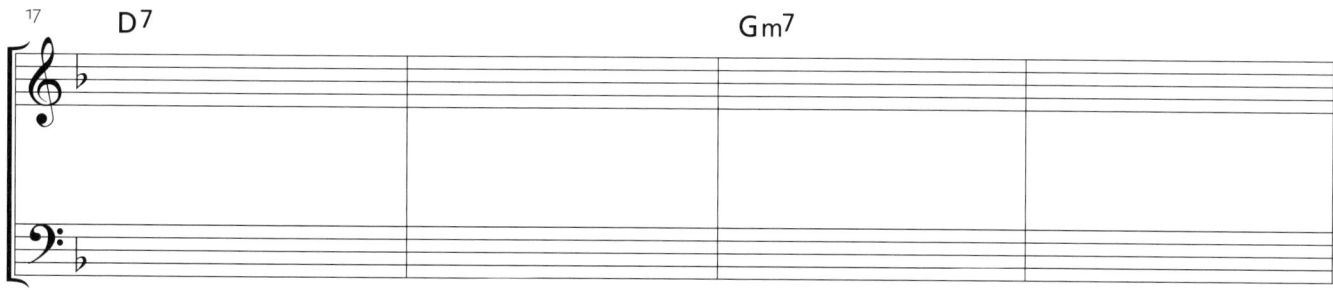

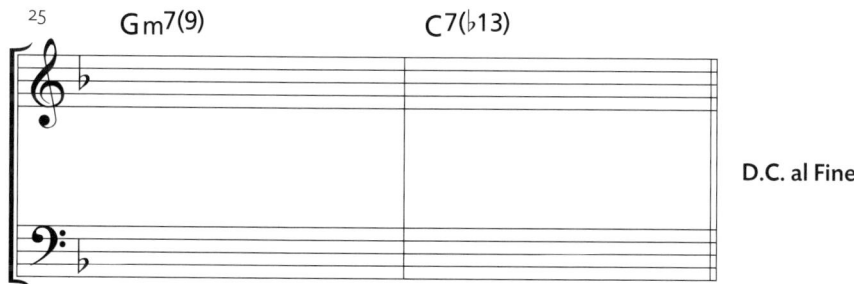

Example

(from *Jazz Piano – Solo Concepts*, "Brazilian Mood", p. 18)

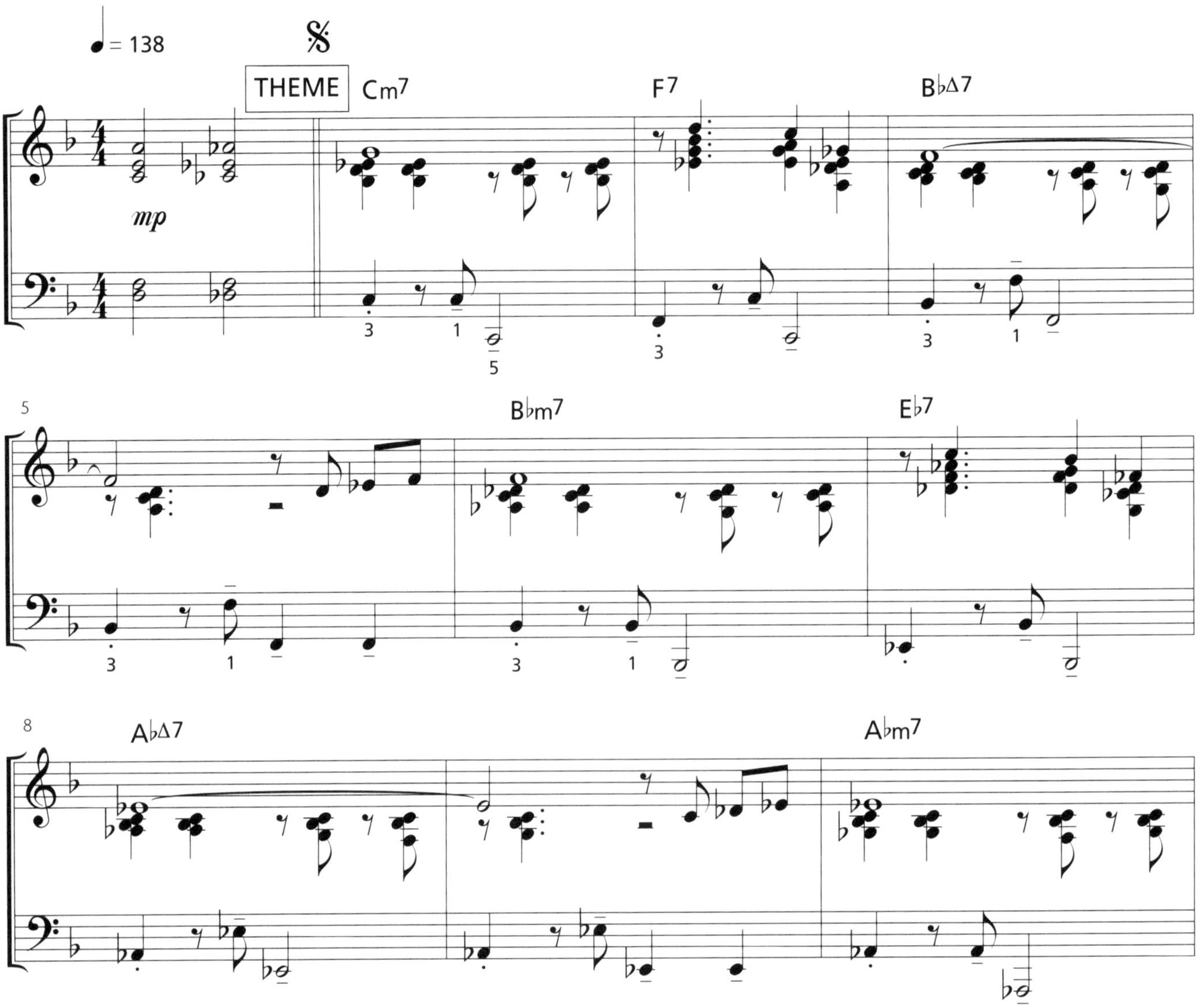

Summary: By now you should have learned the following:

- Easy Stride
- Stride Piano
- Erroll Garner Style
- Walking Bass
- Bossa Nova

GROOVES

Chapter 8: Arrangement

Spread Voicings with Melody

Tunes with only little melodic movement, for example ballads, are very well suited for harmonization with spread voicings. Here the voicings lie directly under the melody. The highest note of the individual voicing must always be identical to the respective melody note.

When arranging, the following system should be used:

Melody – Bass – Guide Tones – Chord Extensions – Rhythm

Here is an arrangement of the first four bars of the jazz standard *Someday My Prince Will Come*.

1. The **melody note** is given:

2. The **bass note** is added:

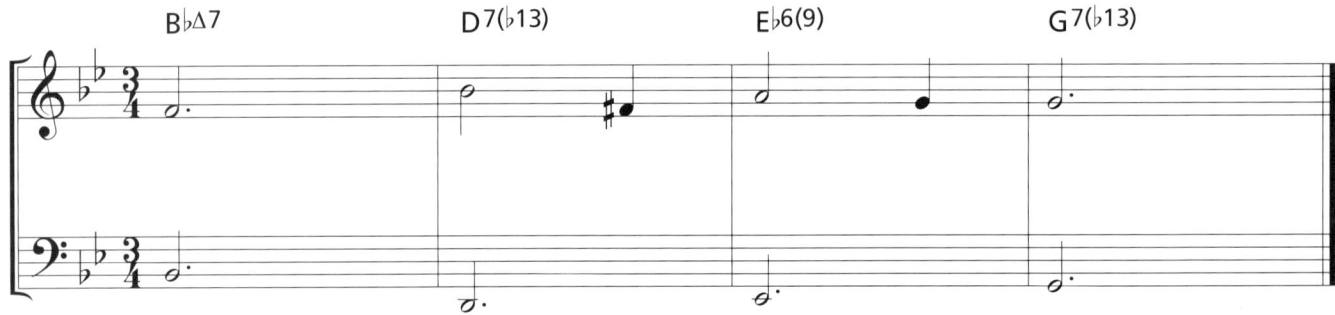

3. The **guide tones** are added:

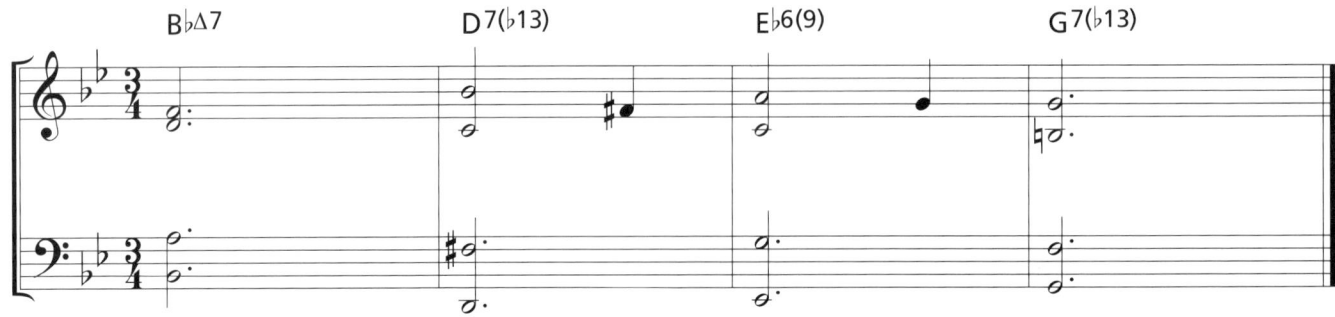

4. **Chord extensions** are added:

5. **Rhythmic variations** can be used:

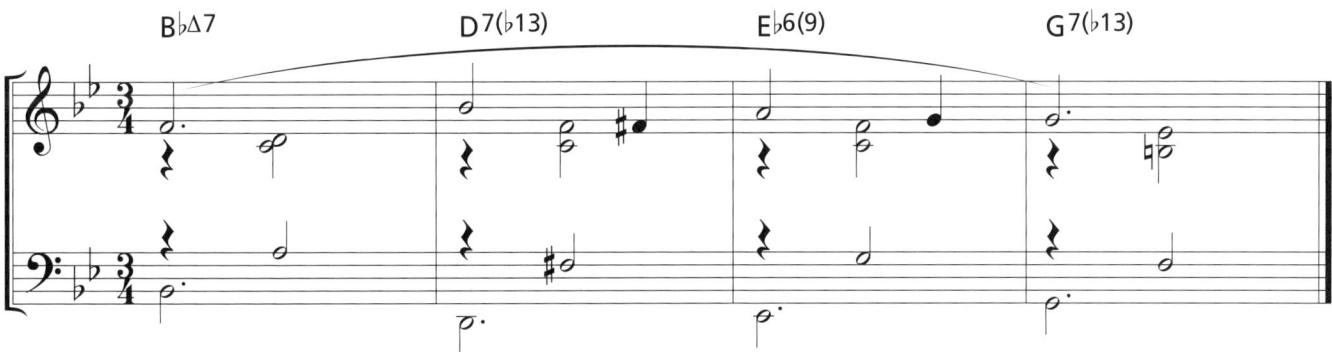

EXAMPLE

(from *Jazz Piano – Solo Concepts*, *"Waltz For Dario"*, p. 32)

Jazz Piano – Voicing Concepts

Another example using the first two bars of the jazz standard *Darn That Dream*.

1. The **melody note** is given:

2. The **bass note** is added:

3. The **guide tones** are added:

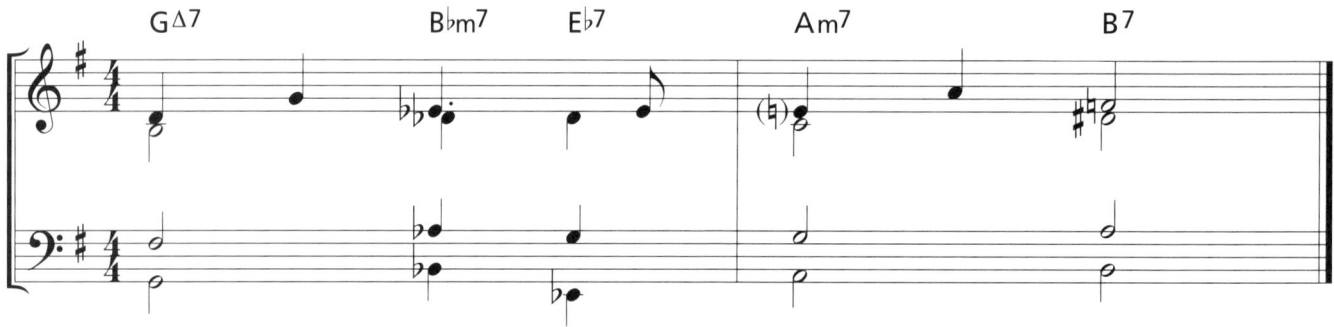

4. **Chord extensions** are added:

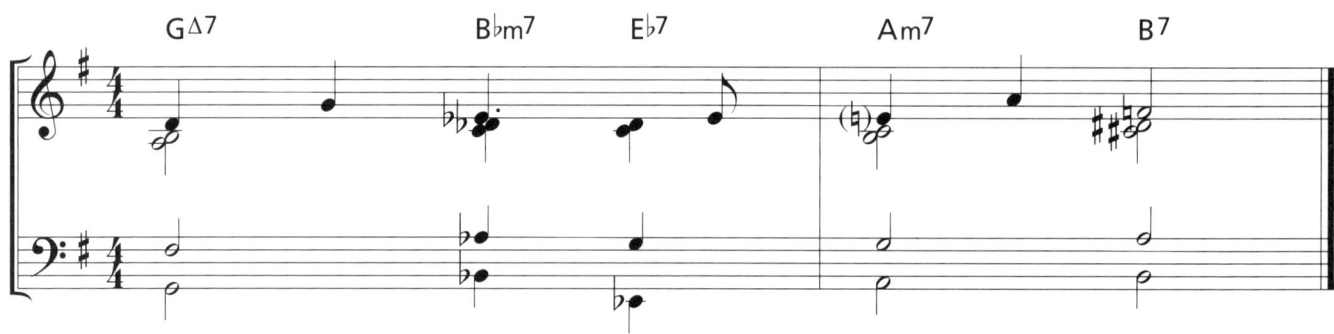

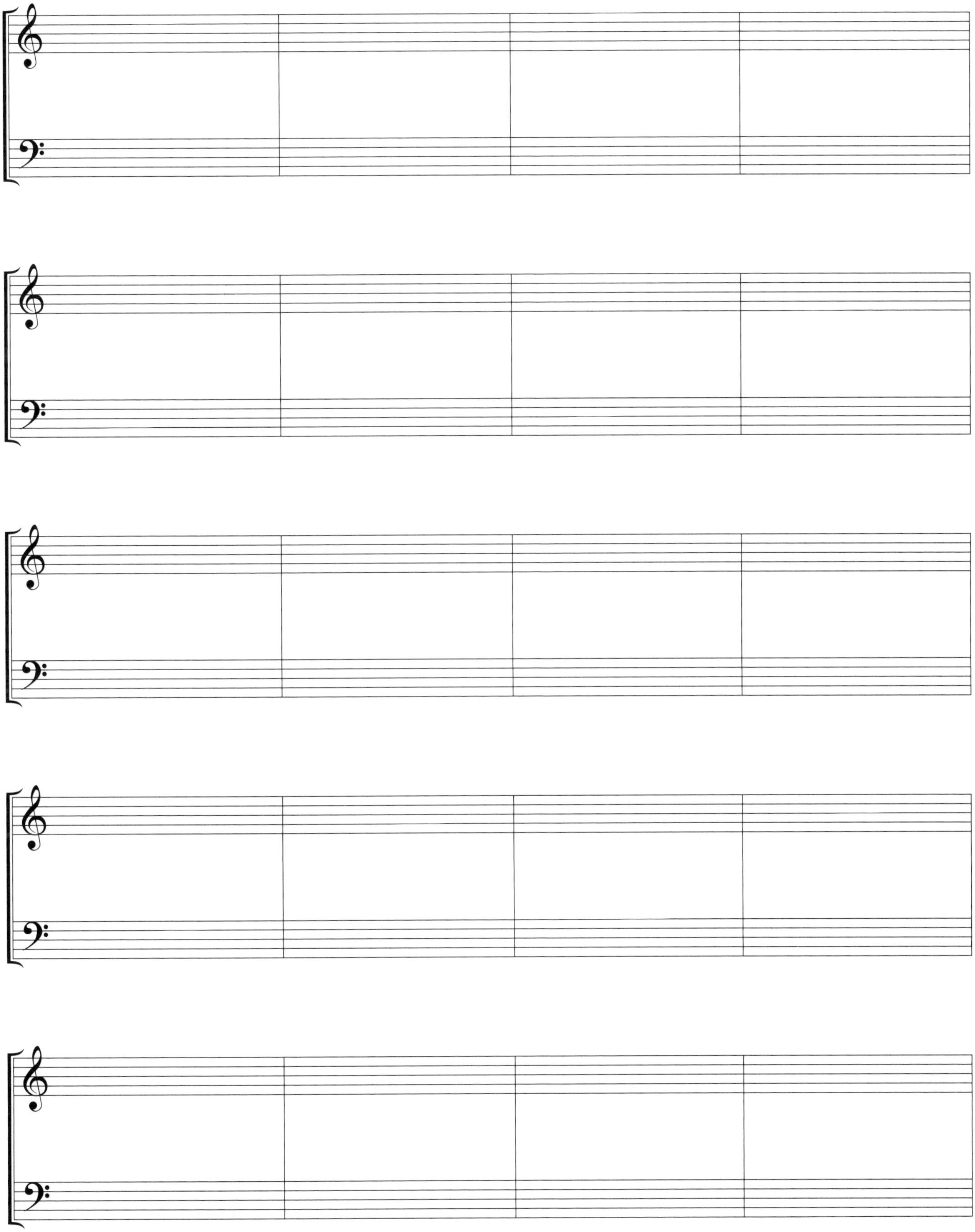

Arrangement

EXERCISE:

- Arrange a 5 note accompaniment for following melodies.
- Compare your version with the version in the Solution Key.

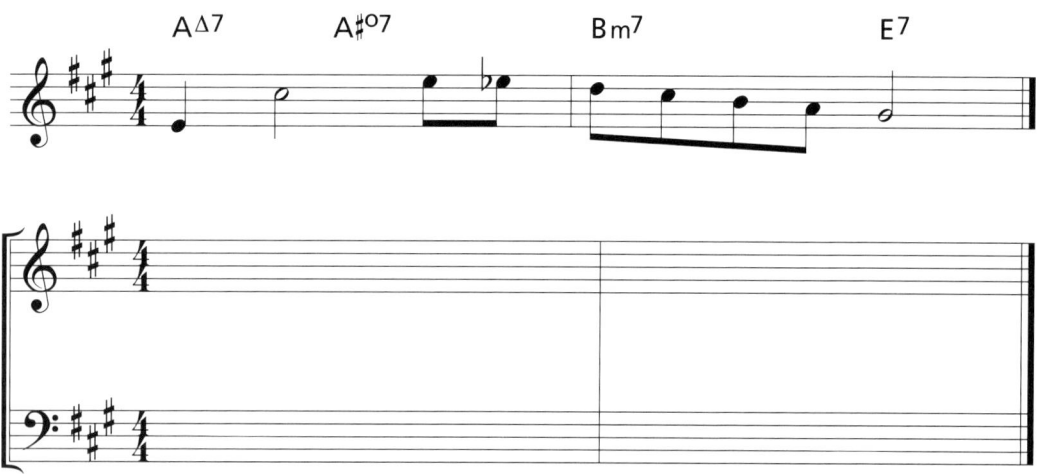

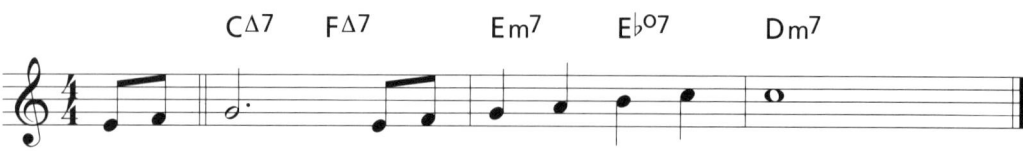

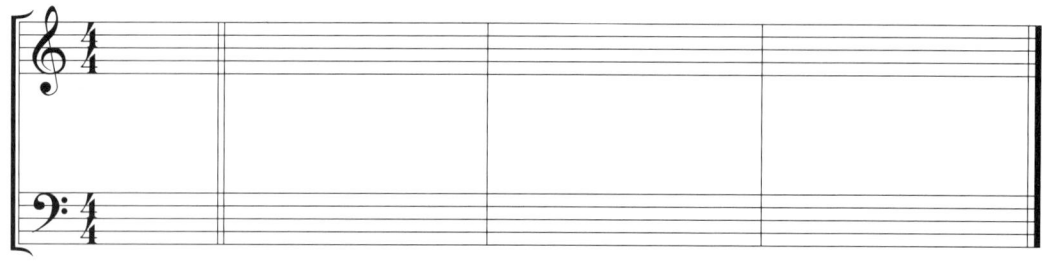

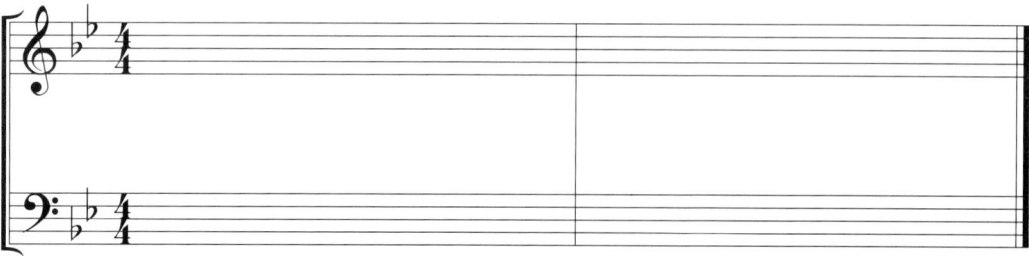

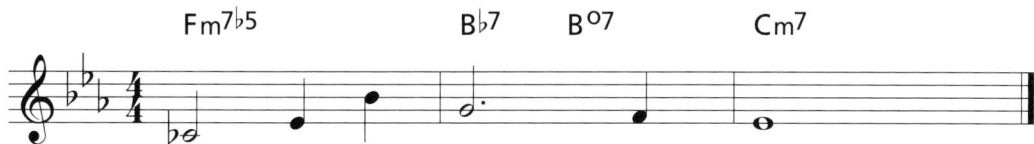

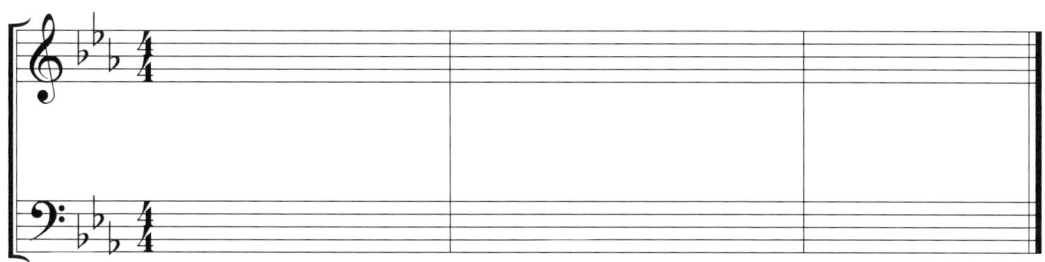

Summary: By now you should have learned the following:

- Construction of 5 note spread voicings for a given melody.

Congratulations!

If you worked through this book up to this point you should now have a working knowledge of the basics of jazz harmony and jazz piano playing. Use your (well-earned!) knowledge to creatively practice and perform jazz standards and most importantly, try to find new pathways in music to walk down.

Good Luck!

Appendix

CD Track List

CD Track	Topic / Subject – Tempo (BPM)
1	Voicings: Maj7 - Dom7 – 120
2	Voicings: Maj7 - Dom7 – 130
3	Voicings: Dom7 - Minor7 – 115
4	Voicings: Dom7 - Minor7 – 125
5	Voicings: Minor7b5 - Dim7 – 105
6	Voicings: Minor7b5 - Dim7 – 115
7	Voicings: Maj7 – 120
8	Voicings: Dom7 – 120
9	Voicings: Minor7 – 120
10	Voicings: Minor7b5 – 120
11	Voicings: Dim7 – 120
12	II-V-I in Major: Circle of Fifths – 120
13	II-V-I in Major: Circle of Fifths – 90
14	II-V-I in Major: Whole Tone Descending – 90
15	II-V-I in Major: Chromatically Descending – 100
16	II-V-I in Major: Chromatically Ascending – 100
17	Progression 1 – II-V-I in Major – 100
18	Progression 2 – II-V-I in Major – 126
19	Progression 3 – II-V-I in Major – 130
20	Progression 4 – II-V-I in Major – 108
21	Progression 5 – II-V-I in Major – 100
22	Progression 6 – II-V-I in Major – 120
23	II-V-I in Minor: Circle of Fifths – 130
24	II-V-I in Minor: Circle of Fifths – 100
25	II-V-I in Minor: Whole Tone Descending 1 – 90
26	II-V-I in Minor: Whole Tone Descending 2 – 90
27	II-V-I in Minor: Chromatically Descending – 108
28	II-V-I in Minor: Chromatically Ascending – 98
29	Progression 7 – II-V-I in Minor – 100
30	Progression 8 – II-V-I in Minor – 115
31	Progression 9 – II-V-I in Minor – 160
32	Progression 10 – II-V-I in Minor – 130
33	Progression 11 – II-V-I in Minor – 125
34	Progression 12 – II-V-I in Minor – 70
35	Progression 13 – Bud Powell Voicings – 260
36	Progression 14 – Bud Powell Voicings – 160
37	Progression 15 – 3 Note Spread Voicings – 90
38	Progression 16 – 3 Note Spread Voicings – 100
39	Progression 17 – Guide Tone Voicings – 130
40	Progression 18 – Guide Tone Voicings – 160

41	Progression 19 – 3 Note Voicings – 126
42	Progression 20 – 3 Note Voicings – 140
43	Progression 21 – 4 Note Voicings – 140
44	Progression 22 – 4 Note Voicings – 92
45	Progression 23 – Drop 2 – 130
46	Progression 24 – Drop 2 – 110
47	Progression 25 – Upper Structure Voicings – 90
48	Progression 26 – Upper Structure Voicings – 60
49	Progression 27 – Chromatic Approach – 96
50	Progression 28 – Chromatic Approach – 120
51	Progression 29 – Dom7sus4 – 100
52	Progression 30 – Easy Stride – 140
53	Progression 31 – Easy Stride – 124
54	Walking Bass Example – 120
55	Progression 32 – Walking Bass – 120
56	Progression 33 – Walking Bass – 108
57	Progression 34 – Bossa Nova – 130

Credits:

Philipp Moehrke: Piano
Eric Karle: Drums
Jörgen Welander: Bass
Matthias Füchsle: Drums (CD Tracks: 22, 29, 30, 46, 47)
Roland Pfeiffer: Guitar
Matthias Anton: Alto Sax
Claudia Moehrke: Announcements

Tuning: A = 440 Hz

Recording, Mixing and Mastering: Philipp Moehrke – Biflat Studio © 1996–2006
Bass Programming: Steinberg "Virtual Bassist"
Piano Sound: Steinberg "The Grand 2"
All other sounds: Steinberg "Hypersonic"

Philipp Moehrke would like to thank Apple Computers, Logic Pro, Sibelius Notationssoftware, Steinberg Plug-Ins, Yamaha Keyboards.
Matthias Füchsle would like to thank MEINL Cymbals, AGNER SwissDrumsticks, SONOR Drums.
Matthias Anton would like to thank Selmer Saxophones, Rico Reeds, Apple Computers.

Voicings, Voicings, Voicings

Here is a loose collection of different voicings and chord progressions. Play all the voicings on the piano first. Transpose the voicings you like best to different keys. Use these in your own compositions and for your arrangements of jazz standards.

Same Voicing – Different Chords!

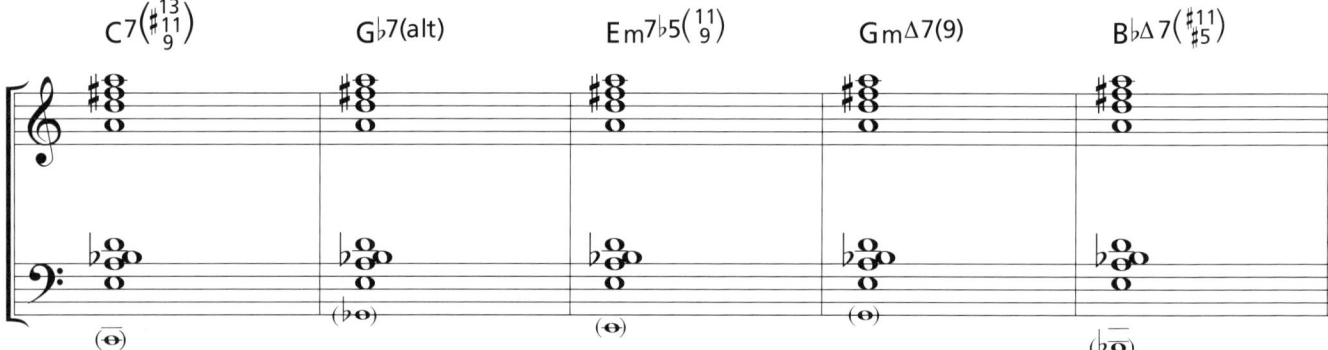

II-V Progression

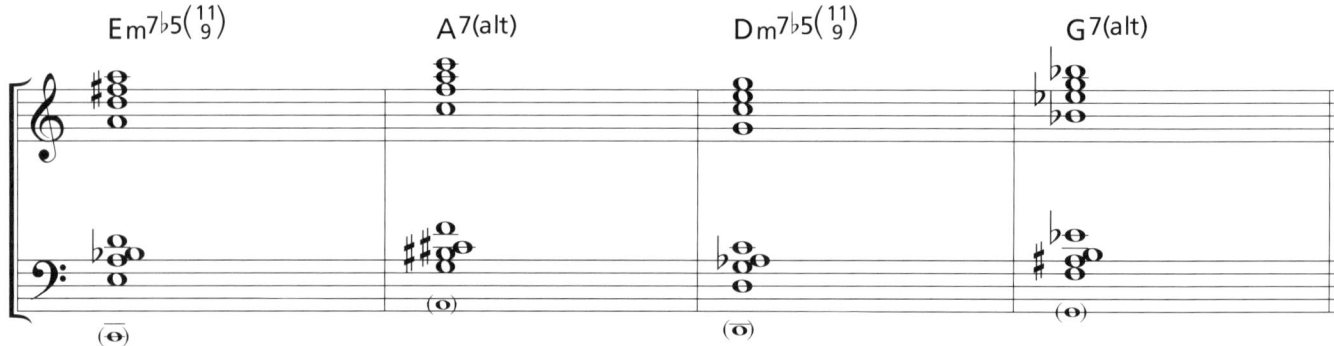

Fifth Voicing

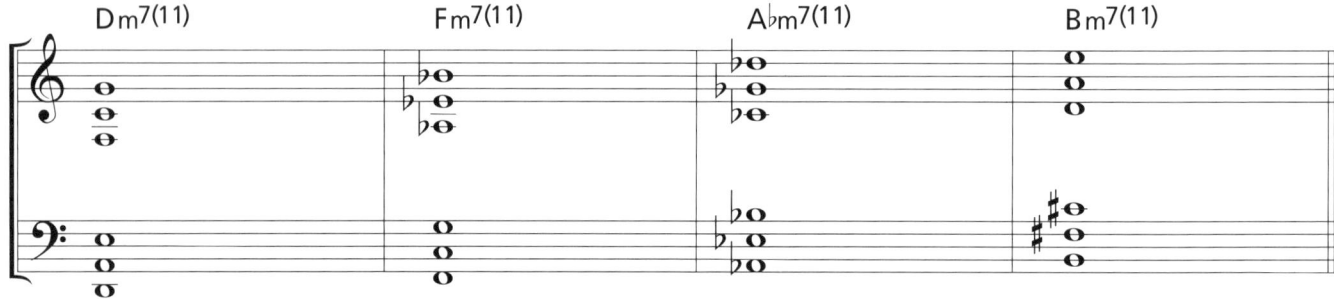

Half-Tone-Whole-Tone (HTWT) Voicings

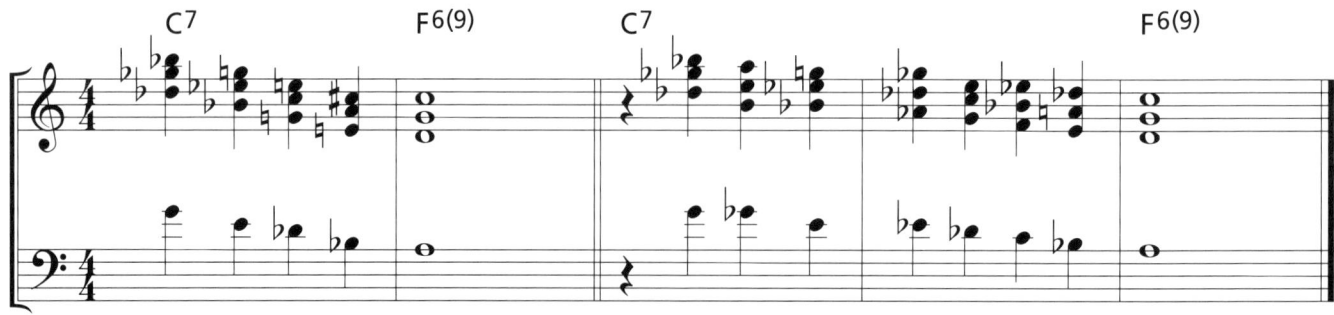

Appendix

Giant Steps

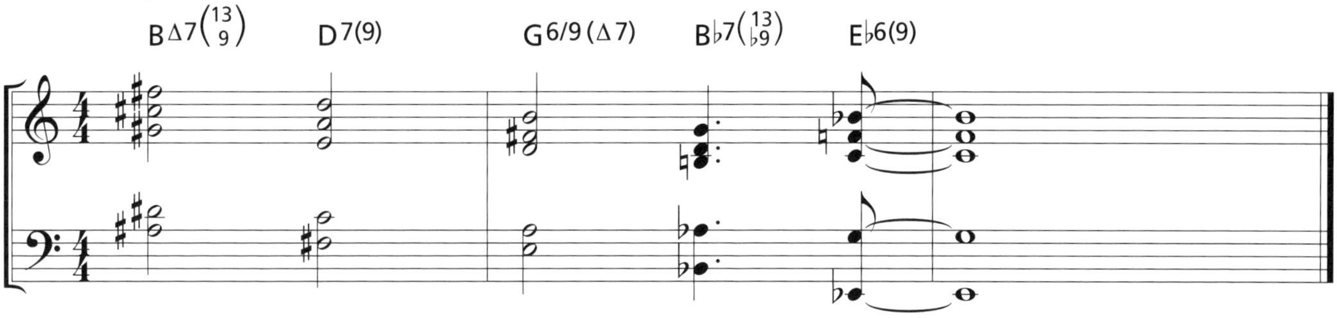

Modal Voicings

Sounds great!

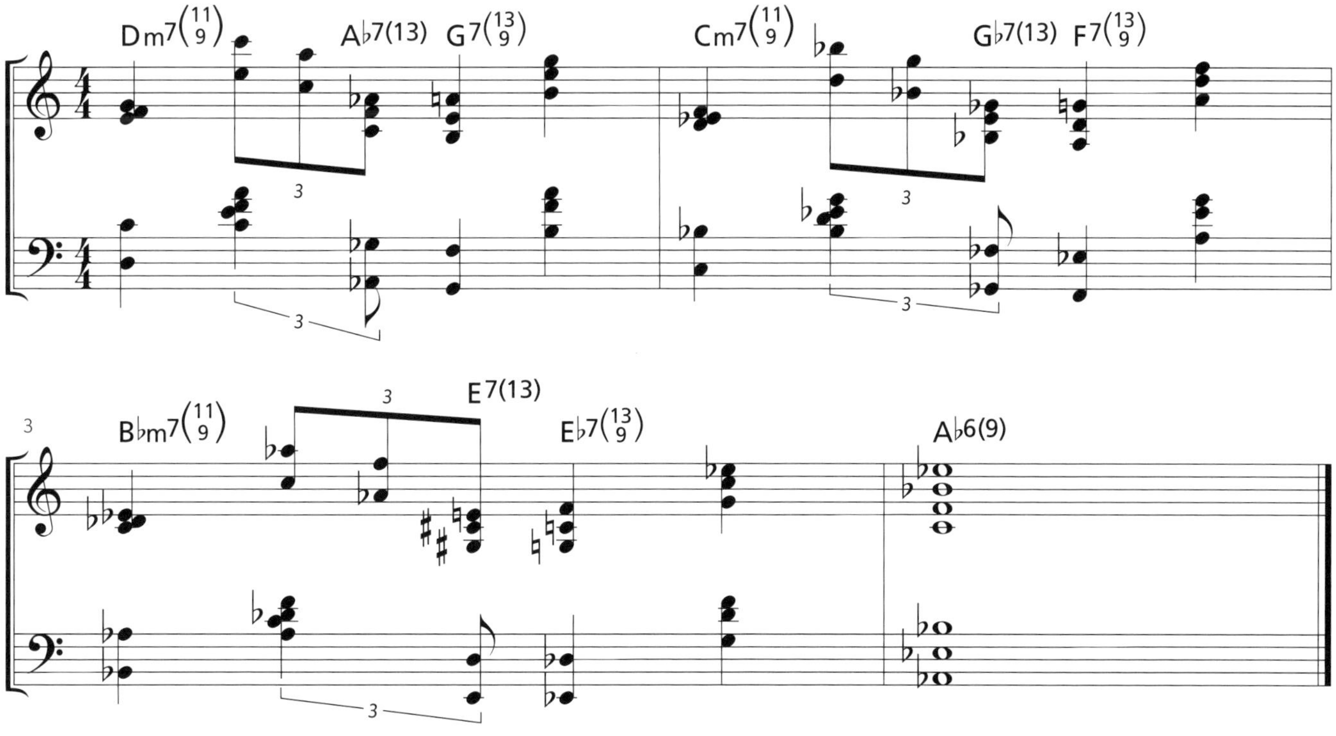

II-V-I Circle of Fifths

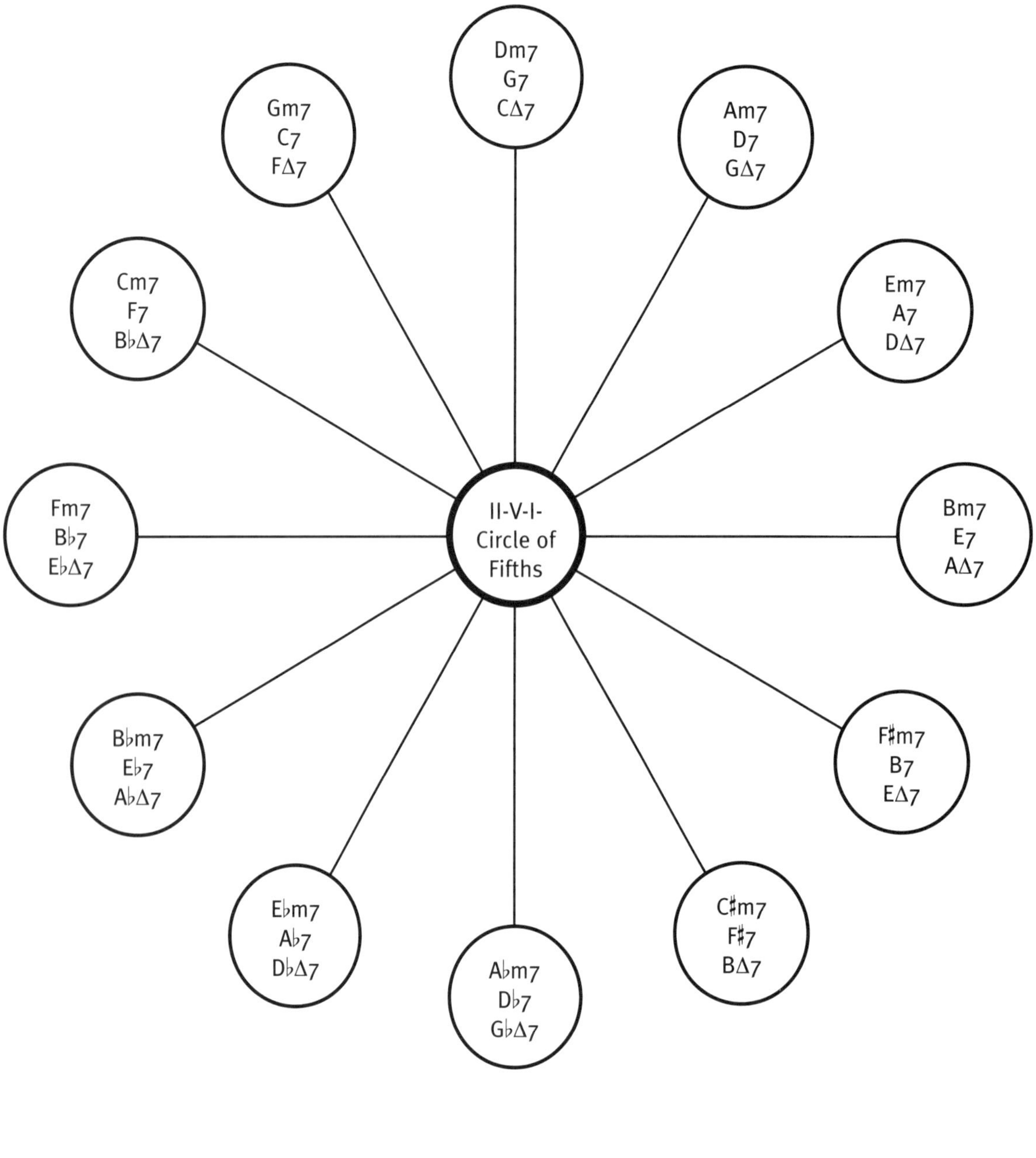

- Dm7 / G7 / CΔ7
- Am7 / D7 / GΔ7
- Em7 / A7 / DΔ7
- Bm7 / E7 / AΔ7
- F#m7 / B7 / EΔ7
- C#m7 / F#7 / BΔ7
- Abm7 / Db7 / GbΔ7
- Ebm7 / Ab7 / DbΔ7
- Bbm7 / Eb7 / AbΔ7
- Fm7 / Bb7 / EbΔ7
- Cm7 / F7 / BbΔ7
- Gm7 / C7 / FΔ7

APPENDIX

Repertoire Checklist (Master Copy)

Keep track of your progress working on jazz standards using this table.

Theme / Standard											
Melody and progression internalized?											
3 Note Spread											
4 Note Spread											
5 Note Spread											
Guide Tones											
3 Note Left Hand											
4 Note Left Hand											
Drop 2											
Upper Structure Voicings											
Chromatic Approach											
Reharmonization											
Stride Piano											
Walking Bass											
Bossa Nova											
Solo Piano Arrangement											

© 2007 by AMA Musikverlag

Reference Books

Hofmann, Bernhard: Arrangement & Orchestration. Alfred Verlag, Neustadt/Wied.
Levine, Mark: Das Jazz Piano Buch. Advance Music, Rottenburg.
Levine, Mark: Das Jazz Theorie Buch. Advance Music, Rottenburg.
Moehrke, Philipp: Jazz Piano – Improvisations Concepts. AMA Verlag, Brühl.
Moehrke, Philipp: Jazz Piano – Solo Concepts. AMA Verlag, Brühl.
Moehrke, Philipp: Das Groove Piano Buch. Advance Music, Rottenburg.
Moehrke, Philipp: Morgen, Kinder, wird's was geben. Bärenreiter, Kassel.

I am grateful for any suggestions for this book.
Please visit me at:

www.biflat.de